MOLLY B'DAMN

The Silver Dove of the Coeur d'Alenes

A. JAYDEE

ISBN 978-1-63630-115-0 (Paperback)
ISBN 978-1-63630-116-7 (Digital)

Covenant Books, Inc.
11661 Hwy 707
Murrells Inlet, SC 29576
www.covenantbooks.com

Introduction

Years ago, we lived in the panhandle region of northern Idaho, a region full of history, amazing tales of ore discoveries, labor union wars, and legendary tales of settlers of the Old West. One story in particular caught my interest and held it for years while this story played out in my mind. Some people, I believe, earn the right never to be forgotten. Molly B'Damn was one of those people, and this story is written for her.

Molly's story is that of a colorful, larger-than-life woman who was dealt a hand not of her own choosing but who accepted her lot in life by living each day on her own terms. In her lifetime, she was loved, betrayed, compromised, and disillusioned; yet she kept her eyes to the future and helped hundreds along the way.

Each August, in Molly's memory, the ghost town of Murray lives again when hundreds of visitors flock there to celebrate Molly B'Damn Days.

Chapter 1

Late April 1873

"COME ON, MAGGIE GIRL," NICHOLAS taunted her. "Fight like a man!"

"I'm not a man, y' ornery snake. And ye ought to be treatin' me kinder," the girl snarled back.

For the past several weeks, Maggie's tall, fiery-haired cousin Nicholas had been teaching her how to box like a man—an Irishman, to be specific, and with only her bare hands as weapons. There was motive and intent in what they were doing so Nicholas went about the task with both skill and determination. At first, he went easy on her, instructing her in the art of self-defense, but as she grew more competent, he took to purposely antagonizing her with taunts and jabs to the ribs just to get her to respond more aggressively. To Maggie, what had started out as a novel activity had become increasingly stressful and annoying. To Nicholas, it was not only important but also necessary.

"Up on yer toes, Girl. Be quick and light on yer feet if ye want t' have the advantage," he insisted. Using charges and feigned lunges, he danced around her, poking and prodding, grabbing her arms, yanking on her curls, tripping, and anticipating every move.

"Ye need to catch yer adversary off guard, not stand there like a puny little girl." Sweat dripped from his brow and trickled into his eyes.

She swung at him with her fists, losing her footing when she tripped, but before she could regain her balance, he had her around the neck, her arms pinned to her sides with his other arm. He held her tightly, his heavy breathing right in her ear.

"Let go of me, ye worthless scoundrel," she yelled, yanking her arms free then clawing at him like a mad cat. His laughter was annoying her more and more every minute. She faced him head on, her chest heaving as she gasped for air. Perspiration had drenched her shirt and was running in rivulets beneath it, all down her back and chest. Her face was covered in sweat-dampened dirt. Her temper was near a boiling point. This game was no longer fun. Truth be told, it was becoming torturous.

"Ye are a ruthless taskmaster," she muttered. Her knuckles were so sore and bruised she could hardly force them into a fist. Lashing out, she caught him on the corner of his chin.

"Ow," he yelped. "There's no need to be mean."

He backed off, rubbing his chin, then had a proud grin spread across his face. "Ah, I think ye finally are getting to it, Maggie Girl."

Pleased to hear that, Maggie bent over and rested her hands on her knees, panting heavily. Then she began a wary, slow creeping in a circle around Nicholas. Still acting exhausted and vulnerable, she faked him into making another move on her. When he leaped at her, she spun around so he would grab her from the back. Then she fell limp and heavy in his arms. Startled, Nicholas stepped backward, relaxing his grip just long enough for her to straighten up and stomp down hard on his instep. He bellowed in pain but Maggie wasn't yet done. She snapped her leg around his ankle and yanked forward causing both of them to fall backward onto the ground.

Nicholas scrambled to regain the upper hand but Maggie had already squirmed around on her knees to face him. Leaping on top of him, she pinned his arms beneath her knees then pressed an elbow into the hollow of his neck. With her full weight, she held him there until his face turned crimson and he gasped for air. With her sodden curls hanging down around them like a curtain of gold, she taunted him.

"Say Uncle," she demanded, beads of sweat dripping off her face onto his.

"Never," he croaked, bucking up and down in an effort to toss her aside.

She dug her bare toes into the thick, green grass and held on.

"Say it, ye loser," she grinned. "Ye know ye're pinned."

"Aye, uncle it is," he groaned at last, gasping for breath as she released the weight from his windpipe. "Let me up. It's humiliating to be pinned by a girl. I think we've practiced enough fer today. I don't want ye to get hurt."

"Ah yes, now the girl wins so ye want to quit and run away," she snorted, rabbit punching him in the gut as she rolled to the side and allowed him to stand.

Back on her feet, she spit onto the ground just like the boys did when showing off then wiped the sweat from her brow onto her shirtsleeve. She pushed her wild curls back behind her ears.

"Do ye think I kin defend myself now?" she asked sweetly.

"Aye, ye have learned well," he admitted, brushing the dried grass off his trousers. "Just don't be telling the boys about this. They'll think me soft and will try t' test yer skills fer themselves. I tell ye this, I pity the fellow what weds ye 'cus ye're a mean little wench. And God help the poor fellow if he ever turns a rough hand to ye."

"I don't intend to wed, ye know that already," she giggled, her hands planted firmly on her hips. "No man's gonna claim m' affections, not 'til I say so. I got no time fer romance anyhow, much less a passel of young 'uns followin' me around, hangin' on m' legs."

"I've seen ye with children, Maggie," Nicholas chuckled. "Ye're a soft little pussycat when they're around. And about a lover, someday a fellow will catch yer eye when ye're least expectin' it, and when he does, yer heart will float away like a feather in the wind. 'Til then at least ye can defend yerself. M' thinks ye kin fend off any scoundrel that threatens ye, except maybe a tomahawk-wielding heathen in America who's determined to chop off yer golden curls."

He bent to lift his sweater off the rock wall near where they were standing.

"Now why did ye go and say that?" she asked. "What do ye know of America anyhow?" Nicholas had piqued Maggie's curiosity.

"Not much," he replied, unaware of Maggie's sudden interest. "Them rebel patriots of Boston did a fine job routing the British so now all eyes are on settling the uncivilized lands where the redskin heathens live. From what I've heard, America is huge and the west is still wild and needin' tamed. Them Americans seem to thrive on adversity. The cities like New York and Boston are full of refinement, even fine universities, I hear tell, but them what are longin' fer adventure don't care at all about that. They're lookin' to go huntin' gold in the unsettled west. Ah, t' would be a fine adventure to go there someday, wouldn't it?" He looked at Maggie and saw her staring, mouth agape.

"Let's go there, Nick," she giggled, clapping her hands together and bouncing on her tiptoes. "Let's go right now, not later."

"What? Are ye daft? I was talkin', that's all. I wasn't serious." Nicholas felt like a rock had fallen from the sky and hit him right in the gut.

"Ye said it would be exciting, did ye not? Things in Ireland ain't so bright, ye know. Every day there's more fightin' 'n killin' 'cuz of hunger 'n desperation. 'T won't be long before it finds us and ye and the boys are dragged into the fightin'. Let's get away while we can."

"It's bad, I know, but our parents would never abide our goin'. Not now. We're too young. And yer parents won't let ye go anyhow. Ye're a girl. Young girls don't wander off to strange countries."

"Why not? Do ye think girls can't want adventure and excitement in place of killin' and brutality in the streets?" She reached for Nick's arm and gripped it tightly. "Nick, let's go. We're old enough. If our parents say yes, will ye go?"

Nicholas yanked his arm away. His throat was powder dry and he desperately needed to get out of this situation before it worsened. She was right about the fighting between the British, Irish Catholics and Protestants, and he was already being pressured to join the resistance but he dared not tell that to Maggie.

"We'll talk later. Da is waiting for me."

"Nicholas, don't leave me standin' now ye got me to dreamin'. I think we should go. I'm gonna go, do ye hear me? I'll go with or without ye, ye know I will!" she yelled as he quickly walked away.

Nick cursed his own stupidity. Somehow, he was gonna be held to blame for opening up this new Pandora's box with her. Just one careless sentence and Maggie was off on another daydream and once her mind was set nobody would be able to sway her. He knew that better than anyone.

Chapter 2

Late April 1873

"Maggie," her father told her when she was still a child, "ye think it's all right to do anything ye've a mind to where yer ol' Da is concerned but I'm here to tell ye there's rules in life and ye best learn to abide by 'em. First off, ye take responsibility fer yer actions—do what yer mother and I expect of ye, such as being thrifty and being kind to the less fortunate, then learn all ye can in school, and last of all, love the Lord God without condition. Ye're a child of two worlds, Protestant English and Irish Catholic, so ye need always t' be tolerant of both. Plus, ye must learn basic skills so ye can provide fer yer own self. That means learnin' how to cook like yer mum does. Pay attention and step up to help when she calls to ye. If ye can do those things, ye'll be a fine young lady and the world will pay attention to ye."

Maggie took his words to heart as she always did. She adored the man and he returned the adoration. By the time she reached her teen years, she had become well educated far and above her friends and was learned in the arts and sciences as well as being fluent in several languages. She loved poetry nearly as much as she loved playing the fiddle. Her mother, Margaret, a lovely, soft-spoken woman who took deep pride in being a homemaker, taught her to bake wonderful breads and pastries and to cook hearty cottage foods so delicious they were renowned throughout Kingstown County. When berries were ripening in the bogs and forests, the two of them would seek them out to use as delicious fresh preserves. As her father insisted, Maggie became learned in the art of homemaking—except when it came to stitchery. She hated sewing.

"Nay, Mum, I do not want to sit like a kitten in front of the fire stitching fancy things fer m' hope chest. Stitchin's fer giggling girls wantin' to snare foppish husbands and ye know that's not fer me. I'd rather die than be a prissy little stay-home mama. Please don't make me stitch."

"Maggie, young girls need to prepare fer the day when they wed," Margaret argued. "There's things ye'll need."

"I'll do anything ye ask, Mum, ye know I will, but please don't ask me to be a seamstress."

Margaret finally gave up. At least Maggie took to the other homemaking skills.

Secretly, Maggie's rebellious nature pleased her father. He enjoyed her high-spirited personality. She was far more gregarious than a son could ever have been. Besides, she was a quick study at everything and was every bit as industrious as were the sons of his friends. She could chop wood, plow a garden, ride her uncle's horses bareback, and harvest more apples from the trees than anyone else in town. His great delight was watching her out compete her male friends, reaching the top of a tree first, or racing barefoot down the hill to the beach, daring the boys to beat her to the cliffs above the emerald waters of the sea. He remembered hearing a young lad challenge the others to climb the oak tree in the center of town. Before the words were out of his mouth, Maggie had spit on the ground, kicked off her shoes, hiked her skirts clear to her waist and was already scrambling to the top. Once there, she taunted the others, climbing from limb to limb like a natural-born monkey. The boy should have remembered not to challenge her unless he wanted all the boys to get beaten by a girl.

"Ye cheated, ye conniving little wench," Nicholas called up to her. "We didn't get a fair start."

Her spontaneous laughter always vaporized the sting of their losing but even Nicholas wondered if he would ever learn not to challenge her, even in jest.

All of Maggie's friends were boys. She had no tolerance for the fluttery little girls always flirting with her friends. Any boy choosing to hang out with a girl other than herself ran the risk of being ostracized from her group, and none of the boys were willing to take that chance since where Maggie was, that's where the adventures were.

Maggie's parents didn't realize she had developed a deep fondness for Irish whiskey early on. By age fourteen, she could drink it straight from the bottle and seldom showed the effects of it for quite some time. With Nicholas around, it was controlled drinking and he hung around like a guardian angel.

"Hey, Maggie, we're goin' fer crabs at the bay," he told her one evening some weeks before their boxing lessons began. "Ye coming?"

Maggie leapt off the kitchen stool and dashed to the door, shoving Nicholas to the side as she snatched up her fiddle and a blanket to lay on the sand. Over her shoulder she yelled to her mother where they were headed and that they would most likely be gone all night.

"Here, Nick, take these," Margaret insisted, holding out two freshly baked loaves of bread and a brick of goat's cheese. "Ye'll be wantin' more than just crabs."

Nick grabbed Margaret in a big bear hug, causing her to giggle like a schoolgirl, then kissed her on the cheek before heading out the door. Margaret trusted him to watch over Maggie as he always did. Once outside, he retrieved a keg of Maggie's favorite whiskey from beneath a bramble bush.

The beach was less than a mile from the town of Dublin so they sprinted across the open meadows, their bare feet flying down the well-worn path leading to the plateau beneath the granite cliffs above the beach. A small, arched bridge spanned one of the inlets flowing into the icy cold waters.

"Hey, ye losers, wait fer us!" Maggie yelled to the boys who were already staking out sleeping spots in the sand near the blazing campfire. Piles of driftwood were stacked close by, ready to be fed into the fire beneath the cauldron of boiling water.

As soon as Nicholas and Maggie arrived, they, like the others, peeled off their outer clothing and raced toward the cliffs guarding the pools of the lagoon where the crabs were most abundant. A challenge was called out to only take the biggest crabs.

In less than an hour, three wooden pails were filled with snapping crustaceans about to be surrendered to the cauldron. The warm afternoon sun had dropped below the horizon and the night was beginning to chill. The youngsters huddled around the fire, rubbing themselves for warmth. Using a forked stick, Nicholas dropped the crabs one by one into the boiling water, listening for the sizzles and watching the shells turn bright pink. Once cooked, the crabs were flung from the water onto the sand where the boys scrambled to retrieve them. Sturdy rocks were used to crack open the claws to expose the inner meats.

"Ah, crabs must be God's manna," Nicholas exclaimed as he dipped a long morsel of crabmeat into a crockery vat full of freshly-melted butter. Tilting back his head, he dropped the meat into his mouth and swallowed it whole, oblivious to the butter dripping down his chin.

"Aye, manna soaked in hot butter with plenty of rum to wash it down," another boy quipped.

"Maggie's mum makes good bread too," another added, eliciting a cheer from the crowd.

Twilight darkened the heavens touched up with brilliant oranges, pinks and purples from the setting sun. With tummies full and bodies warm from the fire, the group grew quiet, enjoying the satisfaction of the moment. They lay on their blankets staring into the hypnotizing embers of the fire—and watching Maggie.

Maggie picked up her fiddle and began to play melancholy tunes then livelier tunes that brought everyone back to their feet to dance. Like a woodland nymph, Maggie also danced, fiddling all the while. Nick's rich tenor voice brought a thrill to her soul since he sang in that deep, strong voice much like her father's.

> "At Boolavogue as the sun was setting o'er the
> bright May meadows of Shelmalier, a rebel hand
> set the heather blazing and brought the neigh-
> bors from far and near. Then Father Murphy

from Old Kilcormac spurred up the rock with a
warning cry, 'Arm, arm' he cried 'for I've come to
lead you, for Ireland's freedom we'll fight or die.'"

After a while, the fire dimmed and the revelers grew weary.
Nicholas moved in to bank the fire but noticed how the boys were
staring at Maggie who stood beside him, her hands turned to the
flames. He stepped back to see what they were watching then gasped
in surprise. Her shadowed silhouette revealed that Maggie was no
longer a young girl. She was maturing into a woman.

"Put on m' shirt," Nick insisted, dropping it over her shoulders.

"Nay, tis not cold," she replied, shrugging the shirt off into the
sand.

"'Tis cold enough," he repeated, picking it up again. "Put it on."
His voice was stern.

Maggie glared at him. "I'm not cold, Nick!"

Nick scowled, again insisting she put it on.

Visibly annoyed, Maggie left it on but noticed Nick had turned
to watch the boys. When they saw him watching, they turned away
and pretended to fall asleep.

Nick began to pace. *What should he do?* he wondered. Then he
made a decision.

"Git yer things, we're goin' home," he told her.

"What? I told Mum we'd be out all night."

"Things changed," he insisted, roughly grabbing onto her arm.

"What's wrong with ye?" she demanded, pulling away. "I'm
staying."

"No, ye're not. Look at yerself, Maggie," he whispered. "Ye're
nearly naked in the firelight and all the boys are noticin'. Ye're not a
little girl anymore." He gestured toward her scantily clad body.

Maggie looked down then gasped when she saw how transparent her undergarments were.

"Fine!" she exclaimed, only slightly embarrassed. "I'll go but
I'll not be givin' up all m' fun just 'cuz I'm growin' up. It's not fair,
Nick—and it's not m' fault."

Tears welled up in her eyes as she snatched up her blanket, fiddle, and clothes, kicked sand at Nicholas, then stomped back to the cottage. She slammed the door in Nick's face and went straight to her room.

In the days following, Maggie refused to talk to Nicholas, blaming him for somehow causing the situation. Still, try as she may, she couldn't deny the changes taking place in her body even though she wasn't ready to come to terms with them either. This could only mean the end of her fun times, she reasoned. It would mean no more horseback rides through the glens and along the white-sanded beaches, no more crab fests, no foot races, no swimming together.

"Why must things always change, Mum?" she asked. Margaret just smiled.

"In time, ye will find yer own answers to that question. Maybe a visit to the priest will help if ye're troubled, little one."

At St. Andrew's, she sought advice that might help her understand.

"Father, I don't want to grow up if it means givin' up the fun times with m' friends. On the other hand, I find m'self longin' to go and see the world. I'm torn both ways. I'm not wantin' to hurt m' parents but the fightin' and poverty here frighten me. M' friends will be dragged into the killin', sure as kin be, and they'll be torn from their families. Surely there are better places, places where people aren't at war with each other. M' parents will say no to m' leavin', I know that, but m' heart tugs at me to go away from here."

"And where are ye wantin' to go, Maggie?" the priest asked.

"I don't know. France or Germany?"

"Ah, Lassie, ye have foolish, childish ideas. Fergit them and make a life fer yerself here, close to parents what love ye. The fightin' cain't go on forever, now can it?"

"But, Father, m' heart says I should go."

"Maggie, why do ye question God's counsel if ye really don't want it? Ye balk at everythin' God tells ye, ye balk at yer parents. Ye even push away other girls just because they're dreamin' of marryin' and settlin' down. Girls are supposed to marry and have children. 'Tis God's plan. Yer mum is happy in that role, is she not?"

"But, Father…"

"The advice I give t' ye is to marry a nice boy, have a passel of children, and make a life fer yerself here in Dublin."

"But I'm not like m' mum, and I don't want to be like other girls," she argued.

"Are ye gonna keep questioning God's counsel, Lassie?" he asked impatiently.

"No, Father," she sighed heavily. "'Tis just that I dream of other places, other adventures. Forgive me."

Her heart was heavy when she walked slowly out of the church. Why, she wondered, did God create such a wonderful world then let only the men enjoy it? If she were a boy, the elders of town would proudly pat her on the back and encourage her to find her way in the world since boys were expected to follow their dreams no matter where they led. It didn't seem fair. Why couldn't boys be the ones sitting in front of the fires rocking their babies and stitching up doilies for the tables. The vision of Nick sitting by the fire sewing doilies made her giggle. Maybe she would suggest that to him.

"Something's ailing Maggie," Margaret and Thomas agreed when their daughter returned home, her eyes sad and her lips drooping. She refused to talk to them and even skipped supper.

In desperation, they sent for Nick. It was a rain-filled afternoon with clouds hanging low over the bay when he stopped by. His cap was pulled down over his red hair, his jacket collar turned up around his ears.

"Maggie hasn't talked to me in a week, not since the crab boil," he explained, telling them what had happened. He shook the rain off his cap and hung it on a hook alongside his coat near the front door.

"Ah," Thomas replied. "That's why she ain't talkin' to us either."

"'Tis her loss of childhood that's most upsetting," Nicholas stated frankly as he knocked on her bedroom door.

"I am not in a mood to talk with ye, Nick," Maggie told him bluntly. "I need time to m'self now since I'm growing up, ye know." Her voice dripped with ice.

After much coaxing, she allowed Nick to enter but refused to look at him. He sat down on the cot.

"Look at yerself, Maggie, pining like a puppy o'er somethin' ye got no control over. Ye knew yer childhood would pass by the way-side someday. All children grow up. That's the way of it. Look at me, twenty years old now, old enough to marry and father children. How do ye think that makes me feel, knowin' m' own childhood days are endin'? I'm taller, m' muscles are thicker, there's hair growin' on m' upper lip so thick it looks like a bird's nest."

Maggie sneaked a look at him then giggled in spite of herself.

"I have to shave twice a day," he grinned.

Suddenly Maggie laughed aloud. She hadn't done that in a while and it felt good.

"It's natural to grow up, Goldilocks," Nick continued, using his pet name for her. "More importantly, it's God's plan. There's no sin in it unless ye plan to go against Him and act like a child yer entire life. Ye don't want to be doin' that now, do ye?"

"Easy for ye to say, Nick. Boys slide out of childhood and into manhood with hardly a notice. Ye grow tall, yer voices get husky, and yer muscles pop out of yer shirts. 'Tis not so easy fer girls. When our bodies change, so do our lives. And things never go back to what they were. That breaks m' heart, Nick, it truly does. Must I give up being around m' friends now lest they decide to molest me because I'm a woman? Is that God's plan, too, fer me to be heartsick like this?"

"No, He wants ye to be happy. That's what we all want. Ye're the sunshine of our lives, that sparklin', adventuresome spirit who never sees shadows 'cuz she's always lookin' fer the sun. Ye never walk when ye can run. Ye never cry when ye can laugh, ye never give up when ye know ye can win. Yer smile lights our darkest days and turns 'em into kaleidoscopes of color. Ye control our happiness, don't ye know that? This time in yer life should be seen as a new challenge—and ye know how ye love challenges!

"Maybe I kin help ye through this time. Let me teach ye how to protect yerself. That way ye can still be with us fellows but if anyone gets too personal, ye can deal him a personal blow to teach him some manners. Want to try?" Nicholas waited for an answer.

"When do we start?" she laughed, leaping up and hugging him tightly. "Oh, Nick, what would I ever do without ye?"

"Let's start now by not doin' that huggin' anymore. Ye're too soft and cuddly to be huggin' us boys anymore."

Two days later, after the clouds cleared away, the boxing lessons began. Unfortunately for Nicholas, it led right to the day when he pronounced her competent in her defensive skills and inadvertently mentioned America. That was the day when Maggie's dreams took off again.

Chapter 3

Early May 1873

"THERE'S A HORSE RACE SATURDAY," Nicholas told Maggie one morning. "I signed us up. Uncle Portie says ye can ride his gray mare Lizzie."

"He's letting me ride Lizzie?" she gasped. The little black mare was her favorite, small but fleet.

"In truth, he thinks 'tis me will be riding the mare," Nick laughed. "What say ye?"

Maggie was delighted. He was daring her to race with the men.

"I'm in!" she squealed, ready to hug Nick but remembering his admonition of no more hugging.

Race day dawned bright and clear. Crowds gathered early to set up stools and lay blankets on the grass where they could watch the children play. Beneath the blossoming trees, tables were spread with fruits, crackers, pastries, breads, cheeses, and various kinds of ale while the men haggled over wagers on who would win and by how far. The first race would cover just over two miles down along a dirt road leading out of town, over the heather meadows, past the bogs, along the beach, then back into town. Other races would follow.

As planned, Maggie arrived on jittery little Lizzie. To everyone's surprise, she came wearing leather breeches fashioned for a boy, a silken shirt billowing loosely beneath her long, loose curls, and a red scarf barely tied around her neck. Her lips were painted red to match the rouge on her cheeks.

All the women gasped then dropped their eyes, giggling in amusement when Maggie paraded around astraddle Lizzie right in front of the judges' table.

The judges were very uncomfortable since girls seldom rode in horse races despite there being no set rules barring them from doing so. It simply wasn't deemed proper yet here was Maggie, ready to ride. The judges huddled together trying to decide what, if anything, should be done about this.

Maggie's plan was to astonish everyone and she relished the attention, all except where her parents were concerned. She avoided looking at them, deciding instead to dig her heels into Lizzie's sides while yanking back on the reins. Lizzie reared up and pawed the air with her hooves. The other horses went into a frenzy of excitement and confusion. Then Maggie kicked Lizzie again and set off in a short burst of galloping that sent women screaming and children dashing for cover, the dogs barking. Maggie yanked a yellow scarf from her pocket, waved it around and around in the air as Lizzie spun around in circles. The other riders cursed both of them.

"Is it time to race?" she asked sweetly as she smiled at the sputtering judges.

Before they could find their voices, Nicholas rode up. He had witnessed Maggie's performance.

"Maggie, what are ye doing" he demanded, grabbing onto her reins. "Have ye lost yer mind?"

"I'm ready to race, cain't ye see?" she replied arrogantly. "Don't ye approve?"

"Yer behavior is irresponsible!" he shouted, glaring at her.

"Can I do nothin' right in yer eyes these days, Nicholas?" she spat, her eyes flashing as she yanked the reins free. "Either I be child or woman. Which am I today?" Her smirk was both defiant and challenging.

"Ye can't ever make anything easy, can ye?" he scolded, grabbing the reins again and leading her away from the course. "Would it be so difficult to simply make the transition out of childhood with grace and dignity like yer parents expect? Do ye have to defy everyone? Must ye always test the limits?"

"'Perhaps 'tis m' nature, Nick. M' dreams are dyin' here but no one seems to care. Here ye are, thinkin' ye know me better than anyone, but ye don't know me at all, do ye, cousin."

The judges disqualified her for improper behavior but she was certain it was because she was a girl. Had she been a boy, everyone would have chuckled at a young fellow's feeling of his oats. For a brief moment she considered protesting the judgment but then decided to simply walk away. After all, it was just another game. When she left, no one followed, not even Nicholas.

That evening, Maggie poked at her meal, inwardly sorry for embarrassing her parents but lacking any real remorse for her behavior. She excused herself from the table and curled up on a couch near the hearth in front of a crackling fire. Margaret went to bed but Thomas came to talk to her.

"'Tis time to talk to me, Lassie. This has gone on long enough. If somethin's eatin' at ye, tell me." He rested a gentle hand on hers.

"'Twas not m' intent to embarrass ye, Da, and I'm sorry fer that. It's just that m' heart and mind are in turmoil. I kin tell ye what's troublin' me but the words will only hurt ye, and I'm not wantin' that."

"I need to see yer smile again so tell me."

Tears welled up in Maggie's eyes. He was such a good father, so loving and so kind. How could she say the words that would only cause him pain? A long silence followed as she stared at her hands and struggled to find the words.

"I want to go to America," she whispered.

"America?" he repeated. As the words sunk in, his eyes grew wide. He exploded in anger. "America? Are ye daft, Girl? Ye can't go off to America!"

Maggie had expected a strong reaction but nothing like this. Her father stormed around the room, cursing, yelling, slamming his fist on the table, and kicking the table legs. He hit the stonewall with his hand then sent things flying off shelves onto the floor. Finally, when he began to calm down, he rested his head against the wall.

"Nay, ye cannot go to America," he said quietly, not ready to face her. "I forbid it. Ye are a stubborn, willful child, always wanting to break the rules, always thinkin' ye know what's in yer own best interest. Now ye think ye can just run off to a godless, unsettled country all by yerself without anyone to help ye, without anyone who loves ye being close at hand."

"Da, I'm not helpless," she sputtered. "Please, just hear m' words." She fidgeted with her hands, wondering how to get through to him.

"No, no, no! Ye cannot go! Don't even try talkin' to me about this." Suddenly, he whirled around to face her. "Ye've already decided, have ye not?"

She nodded.

"As I suspected. Are there no words I can say that will affect yer decision?"

"No, Da."

"I see." He released a heavy sigh then walked slowly back to her side. "Well then kin ye tell me how ye plan to survive? Ye'll need shelter and food and a job. Oh, I know, I know. Ye think yer're invincible, what with yer fine schoolin' and yer flighty notions that nothin' kin ever git in yer way. But tell me, Lassie, who will ye go to when ye need help?" He pointed his finger directly into her face. "No one—no one will be there fer ye. Not me, not yer mum, not even Nicholas. No one will care if ye're cold and alone or if ye have food fer yer stomach or a place to lay yer head. No one will even let yer poor father know if anything terrible happens to ye. We'll be here, an ocean away, too far to come fer yer rescue. Please, Lassie, do not do this. Ye're our only young'un and I cannot bear to think of lettin' ye go." A cry escaped his mouth causing him to turn away as he began to cry, his big body shaking as he gasped for air.

It broke Maggie's heart. She rushed to his side and wrapped her arms around him. "I'll work as a nanny or maybe in a bakery. I kin clerk in a mercantile shop or maybe be a teacher. Ye know I'm not lazy."

"Why not go to France or England or somewhere near?" he asked, wiping away his tears.

"I love ye, Da. I'll miss ye terribly but m' heart is set on America. It's pullin' at me to go."

"Why must ye put an ocean between us?" he asked again. "We'll not see ye ever again and that's what pains me most. How can ye ask that of us?"

"Wanderlust is a curse, Da, but I'm driven and my mind tells me m' destiny lies in America."

Thomas knew his words would not affect her decision. She had made up her mind and he was helpless to change it. Then, as little girls have done since time began, his daughter slipped into his embrace and smiled up at him through tear-sparkled eyes. He held her close to his chest, nestling his chin against her forehead as he stroked her silken hair just as he had done countless times over the years.

"Yer mother will be heartbroken. How do I tell her?" he asked at last.

"Tell her I'm followin' m' heart, Da. She'll understand I'm escaping the fightin' and violence and lookin' fer a better life. If things don't work out, I'll come home again, I promise ye."

Thomas pushed her away. "Very well, I'll pay yer way if ye go to Boston where a friend of mine lives. He will help ye, I know he will. Ye kin carry a letter to him askin' fer help. Will ye do that fer me?"

"Aye, Da. I will," she beamed.

"Ye know this is a waste of a fine education," he chastised her. "How will ye use yer schooling in that heathen land?"

"Da, I've studied about America and talked to people who say America's made much progress since the revolution. There's culture there and fine universities and cathedrals, even opera houses."

"What about the rebels?"

"Oh, Da, the insurgency is long over. Some dissenters may still live around Boston but mostly America is progressing. It's a land of opportunity. Everyone says that."

"Is 'everyone' named Nicholas?"

"Aye, Nicholas has told me much about America," she admitted. "I want him to go with me but he's being stubborn."

The father and the daughter talked long into the night, sharing poignant memories while adding this night to them to look back upon once an enormous ocean separated them. This night would be a snapshot in time, a binding moment to carry them through long dark days of loneliness for one another.

When silence settled over the room, Maggie hopped up and grabbed her fiddle. "Sing fer me, Da," she said as she put the bow to the strings and started one of her father's favorite tunes. He immediately began to sing.

> When once I rose at morning, the summer sun was shining, I heard the horn awinding and the bird's merry songs; there were badger and weasel, woodcock and plover, and echo repeating the music of the guns. The hunted fox was flagging, the horsemen followed shouting; counting her geese on the highway some woman's heart was sore; but now the woods are falling, we must go over the water. Sean O'Dwyer of the Valley; your pleasure is no more.

Setting aside the fiddle, Maggie took her father's hand and pulled him into a lively jig, whirling and dancing all around the room, their laughter bouncing off the ceiling. Finally they dropped exhausted onto the sofa gasping for air.

After a brief rest, Thomas went to the mantel where he picked up a small wooden box. "This was meant fer yer birthday but now 'tis a going-away gift, I suppose. Something to remember us by."

He opened the lid to expose a beautifully crafted pure gold ring shaped like a serpent with eyes of sapphires. The color matched Maggie's own eyes.

"Da, it's a treasure," she whispered, her eyes filling with tears. "I'll wear it always." A week later, Maggie was on a ship to America.[1]

[1.] Maggie Hall actually emigrated to New York City rather than Boston.

Chapter 4

Middle May 1873

14 May 1873

Dearest Parents,

The ship is packed with immigrants, all with dreams as grand as mine. The seas are calm, the sky is blue, and I am anxious to reach land. I will send word when I am settled and have made contact with your friend Charlie.

Your adoring daughter,
Maggie

STARING TOWARD THE HORIZON, MAGGIE Hall willed land to appear. It had been nearly two weeks since the ship left Ireland and she was growing impatient to reach America. The nausea of those first days had long since passed so she was able to stay on the upper deck as long as she wanted which was usually from dawn until late at night. She enjoyed the feel of the invigorating salt air and watching gray clouds vaporizing when the sun came out.

The trip had been without incident so the days were pleasant but boring. Below deck were more than two hundred other passengers, most traveling steerage. They were packed tightly together making the air stifling to breathe. There were also crates of chickens, ducks, geese and goats; huge barrels of molasses, salt, corn and sowing seeds; bales of fabric; and other merchandise in the hold, all destined for the free world. Compounding the stench of the livestock and fowl was the smell of human sweat and vomit from those still plagued with seasickness. Maggie wished she could sleep outside in one of the long boats lashed to the ship's rails rather than down in the stifling hold, but that wasn't allowed.

By anyone's standards, Maggie was an exceptionally pretty girl. She was tall, slender, and had a face that glowed with an obvious love of life. She knew she was attractive but appearances mattered little to her. Personalities accounted for more. Nicholas sometimes mentioned how pretty she was which caused her to chastise him for saying such things. He argued it was probably because of her smile or her soft golden hair. That always made her smile since it was probably her father who had started such rumors. From as far back as she could remember, he had been telling people her bouncy yellow curls were spun from the gold he found in a leprechaun's pot at the farthest end of a rainbow. The most startling thing, however, was how her blue eyes could change to black if someone riled her. Her father blamed that on a distant grandfather whose temper was like a thunderstorm, always loud and threatening.

"Do ye need anything, miss?" a square-faced young sailor asked shyly, breaking her out of her reminiscing. He was holding two cumbersome, water-logged wooden pails destined for captain's quarters up front. Maggie smiled sweetly but shook her head. She winked playfully at him, causing a bright pink blush to light up his face. It brightened his morning and put a bounce in his step as he hurried on with his duties.

Passengers were emerging from the hold down below, pushing toward the bow of the boat, eager for fresh air. Everyone was anxious to reach America.

Maggie stepped away from the ship's railing, taking a seat on a coil of hemp rope. From her perch she could watch the other immigrants and wonder where they were from and where they were going. Were people waiting for them or were they traveling alone as she was? Most, she suspected, had sold what few possessions they owned just to buy passage since the effects of Ireland's great potato famine was still affecting thousands of people. Maggie considered herself well off, by comparison. After all, she was highly educated, bright, articulate, and in the hems of her petticoats were sewn over fifty dollars in gold coins to see her through until she found employment.

The rhythmic rocking of the ship and the slap, slap, slapping of the waves made her drowsy so she leaned back, closed her eyes and tried to remember the faces of her parents standing on the dock waving goodbye. Margaret had wept nonstop for two days before Maggie's departure so the day she left was no different. Despite promising to be brave, Margaret couldn't hold back her tears. Thomas, on the other hand, kept his eyes glued on Maggie at all times. He was stoic and stern, hardly daring to blink. It was a show of bravery on his part but his resolve dissolved when the ship's horn announced time to weigh anchor. As the heavy chains clanked and groaned, he broke down, too, and both parents wept openly. That made Maggie cry too. First Margaret buried her head in Thomas' shoulder, hiding her eyes, but then she had to watch again, waving at Maggie with a white handkerchief as she mouthed the words "We love you, we love you." Maggie couldn't hear the words but she could read them on her mother's lips.

Nicholas was there but he had stayed far to the side refusing even to wave. He was still angry that she was going to America without him. Maggie blew him a kiss as she tried to elicit a smile but he wouldn't respond. Ah well, she told herself, if he had wanted to come he could have made arrangements. It wasn't her fault he was so stubborn.

"Girl, can't ye wait a bit?" he had argued over and over again, his fingers nervously combing through his tawny red hair. "Ye are so damned determined. Why do ye behave this way?"

"I've a mind to go now, Nick," she had told him. "Not next year nor the year after. There is naught to stop ye from coming with me, naught except yer own bullheadedness."

"That's not fair, Maggie. Da needs m' help to work at the shop. He's still lame from the fall and his bruises are slow to heal. He can't even stand yet. How can ye ask me to abandon him?"

"I'll send ye m' address," she chirped, not at all uncomfortable with how her words hurt him. "Come when ye can." No wonder he wouldn't say goodbye.

She wished she hadn't said those words, at least not in that way. At the time, it sounded glib and cute but now it only made her feel bad for being so inconsiderate of Nick's feelings. He had always taken care of her and kept her safe but all he got in repayment were sassy words that only hurt him. She resolved to write him a long letter of apology once she was settled in Boston.

"Land ho, land ho!" a sailor cried out from the birds' nest. Everyone jumped to their feet and pushed forward to the ship's railings. An hour later, the ship's horn released haunting bellows as the behemoth vessel slowly moved to line up with Long Wharf where it would dock

By the time it docked, Maggie had pushed her way to where the gangplank would drop, determined to be among the first to set foot on American soil. When the wooden gangplank crashed heavily onto the dock, shaking even the buildings, waves rocked the ship back and forth. The captain beamed proudly at having accomplished such a successful trip across the ocean.

Maggie's heart was pounding as she hurried down the gangplank feeling almost giddy as she watched people's expressions. Could they see how excited she was? With baggage in hand, she hurried to a spot where she could watch everything.

Boston Harbor, Maggie had learned on ship, was one of America's busiest and most popular ports. Goods arriving included livestock, foods, pickled foods, crates of tea, vats of oil, cartons of salt pork, and luxury items meant to furnish wealthy homes in Boston and all across the country. Besides being the most-heavily traveled destination, Boston was also the most prosperous. Lined up along the dock as far as the eye could see were countless horse-drawn wagons waiting to be loaded up with the wares businessmen were waiting for. Some of the horses stood patiently, tails flicking to dislodge pesky flies, while others stamped their feet and shook their harnesses, anxious to be on their way.

The docksters worked with determination, unloading cargo and stacking it where the businessmen could find it. Some were checking off the bills of lading and whistling to businessmen they recognized who were anxiously waiting for their merchandise.

The heady scent of water-sodden timbers mingled with that of salt water and fish permeated the air. Street urchins were everywhere begging for coins, their little eyes large but wary. She hated seeing children begging for food and wished she could help them but all she had were a few stale biscuits still in her pocket. She might need them.

Dozens of businessmen were milling about, mostly in groups, some puffing on expensive cigars, some cussing the perceived-as-incompetent deck hands.

"The price of shipping freight is getting out of control," one man complained. He was standing with two other men ignoring the beggars and homeless waifs begging for a coin or two.

An evil-looking wharf rat scurried out of the shadows and ran right across her boot. She stifled a scream, not from fear but from surprise. He was the biggest rat she had ever seen! It stopped, rose up on its hind legs and bared its teeth viciously at a mongrel dog standing too close to a morsel of food they both wanted. Maggie shuddered. She hated rats.

She began to walk down the dock but hadn't walked far before she saw the hungry dog again, this time dashing for a crust of bread that had fallen from a child's hand. Barely had he reached the bread when a portly gentlemen puffing on a cigar kicked the dog squarely in the face. It yelped in pain, dashing into the shadows with its tail between its legs.

"That was mean, ye pompous ass," Maggie snapped, dropping her bags onto the boardwalk as she stormed up to the man, glaring right into his face.

"Who are you?" the man asked, unamused at being called a pompous ass. He was a small-eyed fellow, double-chinned and barely taller than Maggie. Due to his excessive girth, he leaned heavily to one side leaning on a stout cane that helped support his weight.

"Do ye find pleasure in tormenting starving animals?" she asked. "If so, perhaps I should ask if ye hit yer wife and little ones, too?" She was annoyed, and it showed.

The man took an awkward step backward.

"I think God should strike down greedy old men who are deliberately cruel. And the rest of ye, why are ye party to such poor behavior? Why do none of ye step up and stop such bad behavior?"

The men grew somber as the spunky little immigrant chastised them and their friend.

Shaking her head in disgust, Maggie elbowed between them, bent down and retrieved the bread from the ground. Crouching low, she crooned to the dog in a soft, gentle voice, coaxing him to come toward her but he backed away, still hurting. She tossed it to him anyway before taking one of her own biscuits from her bag and tossing it to him also. The dog gulped the morsels down with one bite. From somewhere behind, she heard the men laugh.

"The wench is a good Samaritan," one chortled.

"Something funny, is it?" she asked, standing up straight and slowly turning to face them. "What makes ye believe ye have God's permission to hurt innocents? Or perhaps ye wanted the morsel for yerself, ye fat swine," she told the portly man. "'Tis obvious gluttony is a big part of yer life." She brazenly patted the fat man's belly. "Do ye want the rest of m' bread so ye don't starve?"

"You can't talk to me that way," the man sputtered, snatching a cigar from between his teeth and tossing it to the ground. He attempted to stomp it out but couldn't for fear of losing his balance.

"Ye are grown men behaving like snakes. I detest snakes," Molly scolded.

The rotund fellow grabbed her shoulder.

"Look here, you little tart. You're in America now, not Ireland. You need to learn manners." He looked to his friends for moral support but was suddenly floundering as Maggie's foot caught his and upset his balance, dropping him backward onto the dock with a sickening thud. Maggie stood over him, clicking her tongue as he groaned in pain.

'Tis not me that needs manners, sir," she assured him, pleased that Nicholas's training had paid off. "And do not call me a tart."

Maggie stepped past them, picked up her baggage and took off down the boardwalk. She wasn't sure where she should be headed but she knew she didn't want to stay here. When she looked back, she saw the dog following her, happy to have found a benefactor.

"Miss, wait up" someone called out. She turned to see one of the men running toward her. "Please, let me apologize," he exclaimed, tipping his hat. "You were right to call us ill-mannered. The dog did us no harm." He glanced down at the dog that was now growling at him.

Maggie eyed the man suspiciously. He was a handsome fellow, perhaps a foot taller than she, with brown hair and a neatly trimmed moustache. His expensive tweed suit was immaculate, and he wore it well.

"If ye feed the wee beast, perhaps I'll believe ye are remorseful. Starvation's not pleasant—no matter if ye be man or beast, of that I'm certain."

"You just arrived on the ship?" he asked, avoiding the subject of the starving dog.

"Ah, so quickly the little beast is forgotten," she scowled, turning away. "As I expected."

"Can I walk you somewhere?" he asked, hurrying to keep up with her.

"I'd prefer to walk alone. Ye are annoying me."

"You're a spunky one," he grinned.

"Do not think I care what ye say t' me," she answered, unoffended by his words. "Direct me if ye will to The Iron Ram tavern."

"You're headed for a tavern? For whiskey or work?"

"Both. M' father's friend owns the tavern and might have work fer me. And why do ye keep offending me?" She glanced back at him.

His smile faded. Pointing to the west, he suggested the tavern might be in that direction. Again he offered to escort her.

"No, thank ye," she insisted, walking off and leaving him standing alone. "And do not follow me lest I sic this dog on ye," she called back over her shoulder.

"I'm David Burdan," he yelled.

"I care not who ye are," she replied.

At the end of the wharf, perfectly aligned cobblestone streets fanned out in every direction. Street signs gave the streets their names. Along her way, Maggie passed a bakery bustling with customers, the delectable scent of freshly baked breads causing her stomach to growl. She stepped inside, asked for directions to The Iron Ram, then bought a lemon-filled pastry drizzled with cream frosting and a hot-cross bun for the dog. The dog wolfed the biscuit down in a few bites then looked to her for more. She laughed, explaining the pastry was for her, not him.

They walked past tobacco shops, cheese and wine stores, barbershops, boarding houses, and dozens of taverns, some small, others large and rambling with rentable rooms on the upper floors. Most of the boarding houses catered to the lower income folks, she suspected, while others must be for those of higher income. On one of the smaller porches sat a few scantily clad harlots who smiled wickedly and beckoned Maggie to stop and chat.

"Hey, darlin', looking for work? Let's talk."

Maggie cringed, shook her head, and walked faster toward Water Street. Once there, she turned east along Charles River Avenue to where she thought The Iron Ram was located.

The tavern names she saw were famous in history. Inside their walls secret meetings had been held by infamous colonial rebels plotting the overthrow of Britain. Trumbull's Inn, Lamb's Tavern, and the Franklin House were all places she'd read about where the Sons of Liberty met to plot the riling up of the colonists to give up all they owned, including their lives, to fight Britain's dominance and tyranny. It seemed ironic that America, like Ireland, had battled with the same oppressive rule yet the Americans won their war. Perhaps Ireland would be as lucky someday.

Just beyond Franklin House, squeezed in between two rather imposing stone buildings, stood a small, slate-gray building labeled by a swinging wrought-iron sign with the name The Iron Ram. The sign's caricature, carved into dark wood and surrounded by straps of steel, was that of a powerful Celtic ram, its head lowered as if ready to charge. Beneath it was the oversized wooden plank door.

Pleased to have arrived, Maggie set her bags down, rested a moment, and summoned up the courage to meet the man she and her father had staked her future on. Putting her shoulder to the door, she pushed it open then peered inside, trying to see beyond the darkness. She stepped inside then waited for her eyes to adjust.

The tavern was larger than it appeared from the outside. A dozen tables occupied the center of a room flanked on one side by a long marble counter above which hung a gold, over-sized mirror reflecting rows of mugs on the shelves below. Wooden kegs weeping with moisture from the beer and ale within were stacked on the floor. On the opposite side of the room was a fireplace crackling with a low-burning fire.

"Hello?" she called out. "Anyone here?"

"Not open!" a gruff voice replied from somewhere in the darkness.

"Are ye Charlie McTavish? If so, I bring a message from Ireland."

"What do ye want with Charlie?" a grizzle-faced middle-aged man asked as he stepped into a patch of light. He looked at Maggie as though she were a troublesome tyke up to no good.

Maggie grinned brightly, dropped her bags to the floor, and rushed to grab Charlie's hands with hers.

"I be Maggie Hall, daughter of yer dear friend Thomas Hall."

"Thomas Hall?" Charlie exclaimed, snatching a stubby cigar from between his teeth. A robust laugh rumbled up from his gut, exploding from his mouth like the bellowing of a bull as he swept Maggie into his arms like a rag doll and whirled her around in a circle.

"What a surprise! Saints preserve m' Irish bones, I imagined yer Da to be dead and gone by now. Lord knows I ain't heard naught from him in years. Let me look at ye!"

Pushing her an arm's length away, he looked her over, smiled, and then exclaimed she was every bit as beautiful as was her mum.

"Ye have her face, that's fer certain," he exclaimed. "She was a beauty, that she was, clamored after by every boy in town. I wanted her fer myself, ye know, but she only had eyes fer that scoundrel Thomas. Tell me quick, how are yer parents?"

"Good," she replied, delighted at his welcoming words. "They send best wishes to ye. M' orders were to come directly to ye so ye can help me settle here in America. I'll be needin' work and a place to lay m' weary head."

"Ye came here without a chaperone?"

Without hesitation, Maggie launched into a lengthy, animated dialogue of all her wishes and dreams, most of which centered on experiencing America. She made slight mention of the mayhem still gripping Ireland but focused instead on Boston. Her speech was so electric that Charlie couldn't help but laugh causing Maggie to suddenly launch herself into his arms, hugging him around the neck.

"I am so excited to be here! 'Tis m' dream come true," she giggled, bouncing up and down on tiptoes.

Charlie hugged her back. With him she had found safe haven.

"Well then, we'd best find ye a place to live," he declared, taking her by the hand and leading her out into the daylight. After bolting the door behind them, they strolled down the street, Charlie pausing now and again to point out landmarks.

"It's a good place to start anew, Boston is," he stated simply. "Never regretted comin' here, leastwise not until I lost m' darlin' wife. I still miss her terribly but life keeps goin'. And who does the mutt belong to?" He looked back at the dog walking on their heels.

"I shared a morsel so he's adopted me, it seems."

Charlie grunted and kept walking.

Within the hour, a sleeping room was secured in a reputable boarding house not far from The Iron Ram. It was sparsely furnished with only a bed, a worn sofa, one small table holding a washing bowl, and a single wooden chair.

"It's a fine place," she told Mabel Forrest, the owner.

Mabel, a comely-looking widow of middle age with silver braids coiled perfectly on top of her head like a silver halo, smiled but kept her gray eyes focused on Charlie. She found him to be a very handsome man. She fussed with her heavily starched apron while explaining the rules regarding linens, towels and dishes. Fresh water would be provided each morning for washing, and the shared commode was located at the end of the hallway.

"Fer an extra coin, meals are possible at sunup and sunset. Hot porridge, fresh biscuits, bread, fresh milk, sometimes fresh fruit," the madam explained.

"She'll take meals with me most days," Charlie replied. "Her workdays begin at mid-day and end late so she'll need not to be disturbed when she's sleepin'. Do ye maintain order and quiet times?" He winked at the madam then smiled when a pink flush crept up her neck and onto her cheeks. He did have a way with the women.

"Aye, that I do. She's welcome to take a meal here whenever she wants. Ye can join us if ye'd like," Mabel smiled coyly. "Perhaps I kin even bake ye up a pastry now and again."

Charlie paid the rent then left Maggie's satchels locked inside the room when they left.

"Can ye cook?" Charlie asked Maggie as they walked back toward the tavern. "Yer mum was a glorious cook if I remember correctly. Did she happen t' teach ye? If so, it would be a fine thing if ye could cook a surprise fer our patrons now and again. Any chance of that?"

"Mum taught me well," she admitted, "so I'll not disappoint."

"Kin ye bake pies?" he asked hopefully.

"Aye, I kin bake most anything. Now, do I call ye Charlie, uncle, friend, or cousin?"

"Ye kin call me Uncle," Charlie insisted.

It had been years since Charlie and his adored wife Martha had set aside their hopes of ever having children of their own. Martha's health was bad so she was warned not to bear a child but, for the love of Charlie, she ignored the doctor's warnings. Months later, she and the tiny baby girl both died in childbirth. Charlie, overcome by grief, went into seclusion, even pondering the taking of his own life. In the end he dared not challenge God in such a way so left their home and moved into the back room of his tavern. Now, like a miracle from heaven, his life was changing. Maggie Hall would be like the daughter he had never known.

As twilight signaled an end to Maggie's first day in America, they walked slowly as Charlie told colorful stories of his early days in Boston. Maggie reported all the news of Ireland, including the social unrest. At the Franklin House, they stopped for an evening meal.

"What of your tavern's hours?" she asked, thoroughly enjoying a hearty meal of bangers and mash, sharing morsels under the table with the dog. "Shouldn't yer doors be open now?"

"The place opens when I choose. At this moment, ye are more important."

Charlie walked her back to the boarding house and gave her directions to the tavern. He instructed Maggie to sleep well but to show up at midday to begin her waitressing lessons.

After he left, Maggie sat down on the stairs and called to the dog, coaxing it to come closer. When it was finally close enough to pet, she felt pleased to have found such a devoted friend. "I think I'll call ye Nicky," she decided. "Nicholas was m' guardian in Ireland so ye will be m' American protector. I'll most likely have to smuggle ye into m' room, though."

The dog wagged its tail then was scooped up into Maggie's arms and hurriedly carried up the stairs.

Chapter 5

End of May 1873

31 May 1873

Dearest family,

    As expected, Charlie was delighted to meet me and to hear the news of you and Ireland. He helped me find lodging and has given me work in his tavern. A little dog adopted me. I call him Nicky. Boston is as I dreamed it would be, alive and exciting. I imagined hoards of people but Charlie says they live only in the cities. Beyond are thousands of miles of unsettled lands.

Your daughter,
Maggie

CHARLIE'S LESSONS BEGAN WITH THE basics—drafting beer without spilling, being pleasant to customers, checking kegs, keeping customers' tankards full at all times, and managing inebriated patrons. She was warned against encouraging the attentions of lonely sailors wanting affection. Most, he assured her, had wives and sweethearts in other ports.

When the door opened for business that first day, Maggie was anxious but ready. By midnight, however, she was exhausted. Every part of her body was aching from carrying so many trays of beer. Her clothes were damp from spilled ale, her hair hung in her eyes, limp and lifeless, and all she could think of was finding her way home to bed.

"Here are extra coins," she told Charlie, holding out what had been left behind on the tables.

"Those are yers, darlin'," he beamed, "fer a job well done."

Maggie was delighted. With those coins she could buy more practical working clothes. Shorter dresses, perhaps, so the hems would not get wet from the spilled brews on the floor. She had seen the serving wenches at Franklin House wearing shorter dresses so if she bought two, she could trade them off from day to day. She decided to speak to Madame Forrest about where to find such dresses.

Maggie turned out to be a natural serving girl, able to do everything and anything Charlie needed her to do, and more. She kept the fire burning, the glassware polished, the customers happy, and the mugs full. She even began planning what types of foods she would prepare in the days to come. Charlie, pleased with her work, soon decided to make her his legal ward and beneficiary. He had no other family so she was the obvious choice. When he told her his plans, she laughed.

"Ah, Charlie, ye know I've no long term vision. Cain't see beyond tomorrow. Just let me be yer friend and worker and I'll repay yer kindness in m' own way. I don't deserve more than ye've already given me. Havin' a chance at a life in a new world means more t' me than gold." She kissed him on the cheek then bounced away, eager to keep up on her tasks. Charlie, nevertheless, moved ahead. Maggie would be his heir.

To the customers, Maggie was introduced as Charlie's niece. His grim warning to the regulars was that she be respected or barred from the tavern forevermore. To make the point, he repeated the threat often but, as her popularity grew, the patrons enjoyed flirting and teasing with her in spite of it all, and she encouraged it. A well-timed wink or a tweak on the cheek brought higher tips and made the men adore her all the more. The regulars became like brothers or uncles and she came to know them all by name. Sometimes downhearted dockworkers would stumble with their inabilities to speak good English so she would often speak to them in their own native languages. It made them feel more at ease. Other times, when business was slow, she pulled out her fiddle and added lively tunes to the atmosphere within the tavern. Even Charlie got caught up in those.

"Charlie, the place is busy," she told him one night. "Ye always send me home at midnight. Let me stay tonight and help ye."

"Nay, 'tis too dangerous for ye to walk home so late at night. I kin handle things m'self. Been doin' it fer years. Now git on yer way and don't forget the dog." Charlie had no intention of allowing Maggie to stay. Too many unsavories wandered the late night streets.

Turning his back to her, he assumed the matter was closed but Maggie stubbornly decided not to leave when they were so busy. The men were getting a bit rowdy, too. When Charlie tried to catch her eye, motioning for her to leave, she stubbornly shook her head and kept working. Finally he cornered her and insisted she leave.

"No, Uncle, I'm stayin'," she argued. "Ye need m' help and I'm givin' it."

He kept insisting but she refused, causing him to mumble under his breath about stubborn children. Reluctantly he gave up and allowed her to stay longer.

The night was unusually ominous so she crept into the back room while Charlie was closing, pulled a blanket off Charlie's cot and made herself a bed on the floor. When Charlie went looking for her, there she was curled up with Nicky, sound asleep. Chuckling softly, he shook his head and let her sleep.

Days later, she again refused to leave early. This time Charlie got angry. He insisted she head for home. It was just past midnight when she left the tavern. The streets were deserted but a thick mist from the harbor hung heavy in the dark night air. Maggie walked quickly, keeping to the shadows. Anytime she heard a voice in the distance, she slipped into the shelter of a doorway to wait until the person passed by. She was almost to the boarding house when she heard a muffled cough behind her. Her heart skipped a beat. She tuned but saw no one and heard nothing more so walked on, her heart pounding.

"Need company?" said a deep, coarse voice. Maggie whirled around.

"Ye frightened me," she snapped. "No, I don't need a companion." Despite her bravado, her voice trembled. She tried to remember everything Nicholas had taught her about self-defense.

Nicky was suddenly between her and the stranger in the dark, his fangs bared and his throat emitting a deep, ominous growl. He took a step toward the stranger, ready to defend Maggie.

"Whoa, Maggie, call off the mutt," the man laughed. "It's me, Simon—yer friend from the tavern."

"Simon? Oh, Simon, ye frightened me half to death," she gasped, her hands covering her heart. "Nicky, it's okay." She clicked her fingers bringing the dog to her side.

"It was worrisome t' me knowin' ye were walkin' alone so I followed along. 'Course, I forgot ye had the mongrel dog watchin' over ye. Guess there was no need to worry." He laughed robustly.

"Well, since ye came this far, walk with me," Maggie replied, extending her hand to Simon. He was a big old fellow, grizzled and frightening in appearance but gentle as a kitten. He was one of Charlie's dearest friends, too, so Maggie felt completely safe with him.

At the apartment, she hugged him warmly then sent him on his way. "Tell Charlie not t' worry so much," she laughed as she hurried up the stairs. She knew Charlie had sent Simon to watch over her.

Simon chuckled. "Aye, I'll give the scoundrel yer message."

Once inside the apartment, Maggie coaxed Nicky onto the bed alongside her and watched as he ate a piece of sausage and some dried bread from the day before. It had been another good day.

"Ye certainly are m' champion, little one," she told the dog, scratching him behind the ears.

Maggie arrived early at the tavern the following day. Charlie was still sleeping so she went about the tasks of stoking up the fire, straightening the tables, and washing up the glasses and mugs. When finished, she swung a large kettle of water over the flames alongside the pot used for coffee. Into the kettle she dropped the fixings for a mutton stew, complete with potatoes, onions, carrots, and chunks of cabbage purchased from street vendors. Madame Forrest had kindly agreed to buy a chunk of mutton at the market for her for this occasion. Into the water she dropped a handful of her mother's favorite seasoning then covered the pot with a lid to allow the soup to simmer. She mixed up bread dough and fashioned it into cottage loaves that would hold the soup when it was done. Once the bread had risen, she baked it over the fire. By then, the soup was ready. She dipped in a spoon and took a taste.

"Ah, Mum would be proud," she beamed.

Charlie was roused from sleep by the tantalizing scents of freshly-baked bread. He stumbled blurry-eyed from his room, his thick, gray hair askew and his shirttails hanging nearly to his knees. He blinked hard, trying to clear his sleepy senses.

"What are ye doin' here so early, Girl? And what do I smell cookin'?" His voice was raspy.

Maggie grabbed a fresh-baked bread bowl off the counter, slit off the top and scooped out its insides before lading some of the thick, steaming soup into the center. With spoon in hand, she held it out to Charlie, nodding for him to eat. "Ye are m' first customer," she grinned.

First Charlie inhaled the scents wafting up from the soup, then he dipped in the spoon. As the first taste passed over his lips, a moan rose up from somewhere in his gut and his eyes rolled back in his head. He was like a thirsty man taking a long-overdue drink. In minutes he had gobbled up everything in the soup bowl and was excitedly gesturing for a refill. He ate the second serving more slowly, dipping small pieces of bread into the liquid. Then he ate the bowl itself.

"Where did ye learn to cook like this? From yer mum?" he asked, his mouth still full.

"Aye, I promised I could cook. Do ye like it?"

Charlie wiped droplets of food from his beard before answering. "The Lord God Himself has blessed me," he muttered, his eyes rolling toward the heavens. "The food is like manna from the heavens."

"Uncle Charlie, yer language!" she gasped, crossing herself.

Charlie wiped his mouth on his nightshirt then reached out to accept the glass of milk Maggie was offering.

"Do I like it, ye ask? Aye, I love it!" he laughed, after draining the glass and setting it down. He grabbed her up in a rough bear hug.

41

"Ye sure do know how to make an old fellow happy, that's the truth of it."

Maggie was delighted. She owed this gruff old fellow everything and now she knew exactly how to show him how much she adored him. Tomorrow she would bake him a pie.

Charlie ladled a small amount of soup into a bowl and set it on the floor for Nicky.

"Fer yer protector," was all he said.

Maggie laughed. She knew then that Simon had told him about the night before. Most importantly, she had learned. A man's greatest happiness comes from having a full belly.

Chapter 6

Late August 1874

25 August 1874

Dearest Cousin Maggie,

I regret not having written sooner. I am not
angry with you any longer but I still wish you
had waited for me. I know now the Lord had
other plans for me. Father has not recovered as
expected despite our hiring a nurse named Emily
to care for him. Emily is a fine woman, skilled
and kind. She and I have fallen in love and will
marry in September. I wish you could know her.
She has your spirit. Be happy for me, Goldilocks.

Your cousin,
Nicholas

August 28, 1874

Dearest Nicholas,

I am happy for you but I miss you every day
and know how you would have loved America.
Here there is always talk of freedom, opportunity, and expansion into the vast western lands.
Freedom to Americans is like sweet candy on the
tongue. They can't get enough of it. Be happy,

dear one, and tell Emily she is a very lucky girl. Perhaps you can name your firstborn daughter after me—Goldilocks.

Lovingly,
Maggie

THE DAY BEGAN AS A dreary, overcast day, humid and full of bursts of rain and lightning. It had been more than a year since Maggie arrived in Boston and she still had seen nothing beyond the workings of the inner city. Nick's letter made her melancholy and she longed to see her parents. She missed them terribly.

At the window, rivulets of water trickled down the glass then onto the rain-puddled streets. Frequent flashes of lightning lit the skies while smaller spearheads of electricity danced between the clouds, charging up the heavens with light games. Storms didn't usually bother Maggie. She rather enjoyed them. Before coming to America, she and her friends would often dash from building to building hiding from the storms and witnessing their awesome power. As she grew older, she would ride Lizzie bareback through the rain down across the thick tangles of the bogs and over the meadows leading toward the beaches. The races were always just to stay ahead of the thunder and lightning. It was dangerous but intoxicating and she loved the thrill of it. Nicholas often begged her to seek shelter but she always refused. Back then, he had been her protector but now he was an old friend who had taken himself a bride. It seemed so long ago that she and Nicholas had been nearly inseparable. Now their lives were distinctly different and even more distant. Maggie felt a pang of jealousy that Nicholas had found himself a companion. It was sad knowing she would no longer hold a special place in his life.

She was haunted by memories of her mother humming in the kitchen while her father bent over his desk working on a fine piece of jewelry.

Trying to shake off the melancholy, Maggie thought about life in the west. She had heard tales of wild Indians still being on the run from the military and gold being discovered in the streams. She had heard of legendary cowboys and outlaws living free and irresponsible lives in the wild west and she wanted it for herself. She dreamed of experiencing life in the west and leaving Boston behind but she didn't want to speak of it to Charlie.

Charlie realized she was sad but he couldn't seem to talk her out of her doldrums.

A terrifying crash of lightning shook the tavern about then, followed by thunder. She stumbled back from the window.

"Are ye all right?" Charlie asked.

"Aye, all is well," she replied. The tavern had only a few patrons but more and more were hurrying in now to escape another downpour. "Charlie, since I failed to bring either cloak or umbrella and I'm feelin' a bit down, could Nicky and I stay the night here? I'd like not to be alone."

Charlie scowled. He hated having her sleeping on the floor. Stubbornly, he shook his head then busied himself with other things.

A second flash of lightning, closer now, produced a pungent smell of burning wood. Patrons rushed to the windows to see if a fire had started but they saw nothing. Moments later, the door swung open to allow three men to burst inside, their laughter loud and brash. They brushed rain off their clothes while looking around for a table near the fire. Maggie took their drink orders.

"Ah, we meet again," one of the three men said, reaching out to take hold of her hand. "Remember me? David Burdan?"

Maggie paused to look more closely at his face. "Oh, it's you," she replied coldly, recognizing the man as being one of Nicky's tormentors from her first day on the wharf. She pulled her hand away and headed for the counter to fill their orders. She returned with a tray of tankards expertly balanced on her fingertips. She had hardly finished setting the first mug down than lightning again crashed nearby, followed by a loud rumble of thunder. Startled, Maggie stepped backward, tripping and losing her balance. The two remaining mugs fell into David's lap, drenching him in ale.

Startled, he leaped out of his chair, unwittingly hitting Maggie with his elbow that sent her tumbling to the floor. She sat there stunned, her legs bared and her petticoats visible to all.

Silence engulfed the room as all eyes focused on Maggie then on Charlie who was thundering like an enraged bull across the room to where Maggie was on the floor.

"Ye struck m' girl?" he challenged David, his thick fists clenched and ready to do battle. "No man touches m' lassie and lives t' tell of it," he bellowed, his eyes bulging out of his head.

David, oblivious as to what had happened other than his getting drenched in ale, stared at Charlie, then turned to see Maggie sprawled on the floor.

"I did not strike her," he sputtered, stretching out a hand to help her up. "It was not my fault. She spilled the ale on me."

An embarrassed Maggie accepted David's hand and stood up. She brushed at her clothes then pushed wild curls back out of her eyes. "Well, that was a surprise," she forced a smile. "Now, if ye blokes have had yer fill of laughin' at me, 'tis time to get back to drinkin'."

"Did he hurt ye, Lassie? Just give the word and they're out of here. I'll not tolerate uppities behavin' badly with ye."

"'Twas no fault of theirs, Uncle. 'Twas the thunder what startled me." Maggie removed her apron and offered it to David to dry himself. "M' apologies. There'll be no charge fer the spilled drinks."

Charlie took a deep breath to try to calm himself as Maggie hurried off for fresh ale. She returned in minutes with tankards she set carefully onto the table.

"Notice, mates, no mishaps!"

David forced a smile. "Are we even yet?"

"It seems our encounters are destined to be unpleasant," Maggie replied. "Perhaps that's an omen." She arched her brow as though asking a question then walked away.

Later in the night the rain seemed to ease up. Customers that had been growing more and more rowdy left while at David's table there were no efforts to depart.

"What's yer name?" David kept asking Maggie, reaching for her arm every time she came near. His friends kept grabbing at her skirts, which was becoming very annoying.

"Why won't she tell me her name?" David asked Charlie, his eyes drowsy with drunkenness.

"'Cuz she's no interest in sharing it with ye," Charlie snapped. He had taken over servicing the table so the men would leave Maggie alone. "Finish yer drinks and be on yer way. We're closin'."

"One more round," they insisted, ordering whiskey to top off the evening. They were all very inebriated and noisy.

Maggie brought the bottle to the table, poured drinks, then turned to leave as one of David's friends grabbed her again. Charlie saw it all.

"That's it!" he exploded. "Ye're out of here. Simon, help me throw 'em out. I'm tired of 'em lookin' at the girl like she's a lamb and they're wolves!"

"Charlie!" Maggie giggled, squeezing his arm. "Ye're thinkin' I'm a lamb?" Her eyes twinkled.

"Aye and they're the wolves!" Charlie replied.

"I'd pay handsomely for time with you," David whispered just before Simon reached the table with his back up of sailors ready to toss them into the street. David had a lewd grin pasted across his face.

Stung by the implication of his words, Maggie stiffened. "I am not a harlot," she snapped.

Just then, Charlie and Simon yanked the men to their feet and shoved them toward the door.

David threw Maggie a gold coin. "I'll be back, darling," he winked.

"Not to this pub, ye won't," Charlie bellowed, shoving him and his friends into the rain and slamming the door behind them.

Chapter 7

Within the hour, the rains were pouring down heavier than before. The tavern was nearly empty and Simon was one of the last to leave.

"Well, darlin', as much as I love yer dear company, the walk home is a long one so I must be a-goin'." He patted her on the shoulder, smiling a half-sided smile. "Even us rats have to go into hiding on nights like this. It makes a man long fer the warmth of a lady's bed."

Charlie urged Maggie out, too, even though he knew she was still harboring the notion of staying at the tavern. "'Tis time to go, Lassie," he insisted, feigning a yawn. "Walk quickly," he urged, pushing her out the door.

"Well, that idea failed, did it not?" she asked Nicky who was trotting along in head of her. They hadn't gone far before Maggie heard footsteps splashing through the puddles. Nicky growled and took up a position between her and the approaching stranger.

"Simon, we're all right," Maggie said loudly, fully expecting to see her burly friend approach. Then she realized it wasn't Simon. It was someone else and he was holding an opened umbrella.

"May I walk with you?" the man asked. "I have a fine umbrella I'm more than willing to share."

"I'm all right without an umbrella. Who are ye?"

"David Burdan—the man you bathed in ale," he replied. "I've been waiting for you so I can apologize again for my bad manners. Seems that's my fate where you're concerned. Always apologizing."

Nicky growled.

"M' thinks m' dog has no good memories of ye either," Maggie observed. "Fer yer own sake, stay a step back. Ye shouldn't be skulking around anyways after dark. And why are ye standing in the rain? Have ye no good sense?"

"First of all, I am not skulking. I'm waiting for you. Aren't good intentions worth something?" His eyes glanced down at Nicky. "If you aren't interested, just say so."

"How long ye been waitin'?" she asked.

"Long enough to be catching a chill," he replied, cautiously moving closer.

"Ye called me a trollop, Mr. Burdan. I've not forgotten nor have I forgiven ye."

"I did not call you a trollop. I simply asked for time with you."

Raindrops began to fall.

"Do you want to share my umbrella or not?" he repeated. "If not, I'll be on my way." He turned to walk away as the rains fell harder.

"All right," she laughed, "I'll be givin' ye one more chance. Don't mess it up." She ran to the shelter of his open umbrella then held his arm while they sprinted to her boarding house then up to her apartment. "Would ye care fer a hot rum?" she asked."

He nodded, shaking the rain off his coat and hat then hanging them on a peg near the door. She tossed him a small blanket to dry himself with.

"How did ye get back to the pub? Did ye walk?" she asked, bending down with a rag to rub the rain off Nicky's fur. "I know ye don't live close by."

"My friends took the carriage and left me."

"Ah, ye should wonder about friends who would leave ye behind in the rain."

"They probably never gave it a thought. They're good at thinking only of themselves." He scowled at the truthfulness of his words.

"Don't be thinkin' I'm offerin' ye anything more than hot rum," Maggie assured him when she handed him the cup of hot rum heated in a kettle over a small burner on the wash table. "'Tis improper fer girls to entertain gentlemen in their rooms but this is an exception

49

since ye risked yer well-being to spare me from Mother Nature. Just talk softly or Madame Forrest will be tellin' all of Boston that I've got loose morals. David looks like you, Nicky—a near-drowned puppy," she teased. Nicky shook himself and lay down close to her feet.

While David sipped the hot drink, Maggie disappeared behind a brocade curtain separating her sleeping cot from the rest of the room. When she returned she was wrapped in a blanket that covered her flannel sleep gown from neck to toes. When he saw her, David's mouth dropped open.

"Well, that's not the most attractive frock I've ever seen," he observed sourly.

"It's not meant to impress ye. It's to warm m' self. Ye're not exactly a show stopper yerself, what with yer hair pokin' up like ye just seen a ghost. Do ye need a coverlet to warm yerself? Ye're shiverin'.'"

Without waiting for an answer, she brought a coverlet from off the cot and dropped it over his shoulders.

"You're a sassy wench, aren't you," he muttered, gratefully accepting the covering.

Padding barefoot to the sideboard, Maggie brought out a couple of sweet biscuits and offered one to David before tossing a piece down to Nicky. Then she sat down beside David and slowly munched on her own biscuit.

Even dressed shabbily, Maggie was beautiful, David decided. Her thick, golden hair hung loose and wild around her face.

"What are ye starin' at?" she asked. "M' hair?" She ruffled the curls even more. "It's m' hair most people admire. Da calls it Maggie's Gold. M' cousin calls me Goldilocks 'cuz of the color." She smiled at the thought of the two men she adored so much. "M' cousin Nicholas—he's m' best friend, ye know—his curls are tawny red like a forest cat's. Da says a rovin' Gypsy lord must have caught Nick's mum when she was hangin' out the wash." They both laughed.

For the next two hours, David and Maggie enjoyed idle talk, sharing stories of their lives while sipping on warm rum drinks.

"I thought all Irish girls had green eyes," David observed, "but yours are blue. Why is that?"

"Leprechauns have green eyes," she replied, "or so I hear. Never seen one fer m'self. Truth is, some Irish girls have green eyes but others have blue or brown eyes. M' own eyes are from m' Da. I told him once I wanted green dragon eyes but he told me he forbid anything but sapphire blues, so that's what I got. I miss him…" Her face turned sad.

David directed their talk toward politics and the western expansion, noting that the nation's future depended on settling the west as quickly as possible. Other countries had their sights set on some of the regions of the west. The Spanish made no secret of their wanting the southern reaches.

"I'm goin' west one of these days. Do ye ever long to go west?" she asked.

"Heavens no. I've no interest in those lawless regions. I like civilization."

"It's good to talk with someone m' own age," she admitted. "I've not had the chance to meet many people outside the tavern." She told him about her life in Ireland then asked about his family but he kept skirting the subject.

Maggie was growing tired, her eyes drooping shut as she rested her head in the crook of her arm at the back of the sofa.

"Is Charlie really your uncle?"

"Not by blood. He's m' Da's best friend," she answered sleepily.

"Why did you run away from Ireland?" he asked, toying with his sideburns.

"I didn't run away. Da paid m' way. He's a goldsmith, y' know. He made this ring fer me." She held out her hand to show him the serpent ring.

"That is fine craftsmanship," David agreed, his fingers tracing the lines on the band. "The sapphires match your eyes."

"Aye, 'twas as he planned." Maggie's eyes closed.

"Did you miss me when I left the tavern?" David asked, touching her arm with his fingers.

"'Nay, 'twas no concern of mine where ye went," she replied, her eyes suddenly popping open. She jerked her arm away. "M' time is too busy to give thoughts to pompous Yankees who kick little dogs." She smiled smugly.

"Ah, that again," he sighed. "How many times must I apologize?"

"Until Nicky stops hating ye, I suppose. Now, what about yerself? Ye keep avoidin' m' questions. Are ye ashamed of yer family?"

"Would it offend you if I said my family is rich?"

"Should it?" she asked.

"My father is a foppish fellow who only loves money. Mother's a socialite. Neither of them talks to me except to say "good morning." I'm a bother, I suppose. They'd faint dead away if they knew I was in a barmaid's room at three in the morning about to say "I love you." His waited for Maggie's reaction.

"M' thinks you've had too much rum," Maggie replied sleepily.

"You don't believe me, do you? It's true, though. From the first moment I saw you, I've been in love with you." He leaned toward her and traced her cheek with his finger. She was suddenly wide awake.

"Ye're drunk, David. Besides, I've been in America over a year yet it took ye 'til tonight to find me? Don't sound like love t' me," she snorted. "Now, it's time for ye to leave. I'm needin' m' sleep." She stood up and walked to the door. Taking his coat from the hook, she held it out for him.

"I love you, Maggie," David repeated, making no effort to leave.

"Go home, David. I'm tired."

"You're lucky," David went on. "Your family loves you while I grew up with everything money can buy but my family doesn't care what I do. I get a generous allowance to spend as I choose so long as I don't bother anyone. My life has no real purpose but now I'd like you to be my life's purpose."

He stood up and walked toward her but Nicky blocked him off with a warning growl.

"David, go home. It's late."

"My parents are snobs. They would never approve of you."

"Approve of me? What are ye saying?" Maggie's voice turned cold. "Yer parents don't even know me so how can they pass judgment? Is it because I'm Irish or 'cuz I work as a barmaid? Never mind, ye need not answer since I care not a whit if they approve of me or not. The bigger question is why do they treat their own child as if he were a poor stepchild?"

"You don't understand. It isn't you as a person. It's what you represent?"

"And what might that be?" Maggie shoved David's coat into his hands then propped her fists on her hips.

"It's Ireland. To them, Ireland means poverty and lower classes. My family despises people of low class. They think the Irish are polluting America's society." He shrugged.

"And do ye share their feelings? Is that why ye thought me to be a whore?" she snapped, losing control of her temper. "Is that why ye kicked m' dog?"

"That's not what I meant. You asked about my family so I'm telling you."

"Let me save some time then. Aye, I'm Irish and fiercely proud of it. M' parents are the finest people I know. As fer wantin' to get involved with the likes of ye, I'd rather be a simple sailor's lover than the wife of a swaggering, pompous dandy who can't seem to earn his own way. 'Tis not the gold in yer pocket nor yer puffed-up sense of self-importance that would ever capture m' affections, Mr. Burdan. 'Twould be the purity of yer heart I'd find most dear. Now go home before Madame Forrest wakes up."

Maggie was highly annoyed with David. She swung open the door and gestured for him to leave.

"I've hit a nerve again. I'm good at that," David muttered as he stepped out the door.

"Don't mock me, David. Ye're here 'cuz I've a soft place in m' heart for wet dogs. I'd have offered shelter to any mutt off the street."

"Calm down, Maggie," he said quietly. "You asked about my family so I told you, and yes, I am irresponsible. Lord knows father tells me often enough."

"Then be a man and find yer own way in life. Stop leanin' on yer father," Maggie suggested unsympathetically.

"I intend to marry you, Maggie. You'll see I'm serious." He slipped on his coat, took up his umbrella and left without another word.

"By daylight, ye will have forgotten all this," she called after him. She locked the door then turned to Nicky who was licking his fur. No longer a dirty mongrel, the dog had cleaned himself to where he was now silver in color.

"Come here, little one," she crooned. "Ye are the man of m' life." She lifted him to the foot of her bed, crawled beneath the covers, and was soon fast asleep.

Chapter 8

6 September 1874

Dearest Mum and Da,
    The leaves of autumn are bright with color.
Almost as lovely as the emerald fields of Ireland. I
am so lonely for you both. I am hoping Nicholas
found happiness. I am still searching for mine.

Your daughter,
Maggie

DESPITE CHARLIE'S ORDER THAT DAVID stay away from the
tavern, he kept coming back. His behavior, however, was much
improved. He arrived alone, behaved like a perfect gentleman, and
spoke only to Maggie. When work was done, he escorted her home
in his horse-drawn buggy, much to Maggie's delight.

"What's the bloke up to?" Charlie asked.

"He's repenting," she grinned.

Secret smiles soon began passing between them but Charlie saw
it all. She was enjoying this flirtation with the dashing young man
but, even more unsettling, David was showing a deep infatuation
with her, too. Charlie kept warning her not to become too fond of
the wealthy young rogue for nothing good could come of it, but she
paid no heed.

Some nights after work, Maggie and David took long round-about routes to her boarding house. David once drove past Beacon Hill and pointed out his parents' mansion. Another time, he drove through the docks showing her the many warehouses owned by his father and the ships bearing the Burdan crest.

Always, when arriving at her apartment, David helped her out of the carriage before politely kissing her fingertips then heading on his way. They never spoke of marriage.

One evening, David's friends came to The Iron Ram looking for him. They were already drunk but knew he must be there somewhere since they'd searched every other tavern in Boston. Seeing him sitting in a corner near the fire, they rushed to him.

"Go on home," he growled. "Charlie will kick us all out if he sees you here."

"Why are you avoiding us, David?" they asked. "You're never around anymore. Why do you come to this dump anyway?"

Then one of them spotted Maggie.

"Aha, it's the wench," he chortled, slapping David on the shoulder. "You're stuck on the serving wench!"

"Oooh, does daddy know?" the other man teased, staring right at Maggie.

"Well, she is a beauty," they both agreed. "Why not just bed her and get it out of your system?"

That made David furious. When Maggie approached the table, one fellow grabbed her skirt, raising it up while uttering crude words loud enough for everyone to hear.

Maggie yanked her dress away, glaring at the man who had touched her. She looked to David for backup but he was busy pouting. Charlie stormed to the table ready to do battle. David abruptly stood up, grabbed his hat and stormed out the door followed by his obnoxious friends. Maggie just stared at them while Charlie muttered something about their good luck at having left before he broke their scrawny necks.

David didn't return, nor was he there when Maggie left work. Disappointed, she walked home alone wondering why he hadn't defended her honor. When she reached the apartment, he was there waiting.

"Maggie, we need to talk," he said, his voice slurred from too much drink.

"Ye reek of whiskey," she stated simply, not even trying to hide her annoyance.

"No one—no one should try to keep me from you, my darling. I love you so much," he stuttered, leaning heavily against the stair casing.

Maggie ran past him up the stairs to her apartment, refusing to speak to him.

At The Iron Ram the next morning, Charlie confronted her.

"Lassie, what's goin' on with ye? Ye're behavin' like a lovesick school girl."

"'Tis true, m' heart is fond of him, Uncle." She shrugged. "I didn't go lookin' fer this but I've got strong feelin's fer him."

"Ye love him? Lassie, yer uncle's here warnin' ye to back away from this bloke. He's naught but trouble. Rich folks got no regards for anybody but themselves. Ye'll get hurt, I feel it in m' bones."

"He's always a gentleman when we're together," she tried to explain. "And he's not the big bad wolf waitin' to eat me up." She smiled sweetly and tweaked Charlie's cheek.

"Girl, be careful. 'Tis a bad feeling I have."

"Ah, Charlie, m' thinks it would make no matter who it was, ye would always be worried about yer Maggie." Her brows arched as if waiting for a reply. Annoyed at the truthfulness of her words, Charlie turned away. She was right and he knew it.

Two days later, David showed up at The Iron Ram before it was opened.

"Maggie's not here," Charlie growled, "but, since ye're here, we'd best talk man to man. Ye best tell me yer intentions with m' niece, and don't be lyin' t' me. I don't take kindly to bein' lied to, especially where Maggie's concerned."

"Sir," David stuttered, intimidated by the tough little man. "I'm in love with her and want permission to marry her." He couldn't even meet Charlie's penetrating gaze so looked at his feet instead.

"Marry her?" Charlie bellowed, slamming his fist onto the counter. "And yer father approves? He knows she's a bar maid?"

"No, I haven't told him yet, but I will," David grimaced, his eyes darting around the room as though searching for an escape route.

"And if he says no, what then, Laddie? Will ye go against yer father?"

"I'll marry her anyway." David nodded, trying to stand up straighter.

"I'll kill the man what hurts Maggie, as God is m' witness!" Charlie shoved his face up next to David's.

David stepped backward, fully expecting Charlie to punch him in the nose. At that moment, the door opened and in walked Maggie. Both men whirled around to face her, surprise plastered across their faces.

"What's goin' on?" she asked, pausing in mid step. "Ye look like cats what ate the canaries. Are ye talkin' about me?"

"Go ahead, tell her," Charlie chided David.

"Maggie," David sputtered, "I want to marry you."

"Marry me?" she asked, looking first at Charlie then at David. "And ye thought ye should talk it over with Charlie first? Do ye not think ye should have asked me before m' uncle?" The scowl on her face made it clear to both of them that she was displeased.

"Well?" David asked.

"Well what?"

"Will you marry me?" He reached for her hand then smiled timidly.

Maggie looked at Charlie who was frowning.

"Charlie, I love ye dearly, ye know that, but this is m' own decision, is it not?"

Charlie looked away so Maggie turned to David. "Aye, I'll marry ye, David." A radiant smile lit up her face as she stepped into his open arms. David heaved a sigh of relief.

"Well then," Charlie stated flatly, "we'd best plan a wedding." His gut felt like an iron ball had been dropped into it. Waving his hand in dismissal, he suggested they go somewhere to plan the wedding.

Since Maggie insisted on a Catholic ceremony, they went directly to Father Francis to ask him to perform the ceremony.

"David, are ye Catholic?" he asked.

"No, I'm Protestant," David replied.

"Then we must begin instruction immediately. Either ye can be baptized or ye take instruction to learn the requirements of our faith."

"How long do the instructions take?"

"Three, maybe four weeks. Do ye have a date set for the wedding?"

"This week," David replied, glancing at Maggie who was taken by surprise. They hadn't discussed a wedding date.

"So quickly?" asked Father Francis. "Maggie, are ye in the family way?"

"No, Father, we've not been intimate," Maggie blushed.

"Then why rush? Marriage is a serious commitment. It can wait while David takes instruction. Of course, baptism would circumvent the need fer classes," the priest explained

"No, I don't want to be a Catholic, and, no, we won't wait three weeks," David insisted. "If you don't want to marry us, we'll go before a justice."

"David, I want to marry here," Maggie whispered, gripping his arm.

"If ye feel so strongly about a hasty wedding, yer marriage will start off badly 'cuz ye will be offending yer bride," the priest warned. "Is that what ye want, son?" He leaned forward, looking directly into David's face as he tried to impose upon him the severity of his decision.

"We're in love," David insisted.

"It's important to Maggie fer God to have a place in yer lives, and unity in faith is vital to a couple's happiness. Ye should discuss this together. Just know that without instruction or baptism, I cannot perform a marriage ceremony fer ye. Maggie, yer opinion matters so speak up. Are ye ready to abandon yer faith fer a hasty wedding?" The priest had drawn a line in the sand.

"Father, please?" Maggie begged. "Can ye not make an exception? It's always been m' dream to be married in the church."

"I am bound by God's law," he replied sadly. "'Tis not m' own rules but the rules of God himself."

It was a sad young woman that walked with her betrothed out of the church that day. Neither spoke for quite some time but when they did, David made it clear he would not wait three weeks. The wedding would take place on Saturday.

Maggie went back alone to tell Father Francis.

"I'm sorry he refused," the priest told her. "Just let me warn ye, yer marriage will be troubled if only David makes the decisions. 'Tis a partnership, marriage is. Ye must have yer voice."

Maggie cried all the way back to the boarding house where David was waiting. He was completely unsympathetic and insisted she prepare for a Saturday wedding. He would make the necessary arrangements.

October 11 turned out to be a magnificent fall day. The skies were clear and bright with sunshine. Autumn colors were painted on the trees and flowers and birds chirped merrily in the trees. It was as though the world was smiling on Maggie's wedding day.

Maggie rose at dawn, too nervous to sleep. Madame Forrest was at her door as soon as she heard Maggie moving around. She brought a freshly baked croissant filled with jelly to start off Maggie's day but the girl was too nervous to eat. Knowing Maggie's parents were still in Ireland, Madame Forrest offered herself as a helper, delighted to share in the joy of the day. With patient fingers, she helped Maggie into the delicate ivory gown Charlie had purchased for her and clucked happily as she fastened the pearl buttons down the back. Around her neck she clasped a pearl necklace that matched her earrings, both items gifts from her mother back in Ireland. Maggie's hair was brushed then piled high upon her head, tied in place by ribbons adorned with yellow rose buds and white daisies plucked from Madame Forrest's garden.

"Ah, ye look perfect," the madam exclaimed.

Maggie slipped the serpent ring onto her right hand, whispering to her absent father, "Da, if only ye could be here to share m' joy."

Charlie arrived ready to stand in beside Maggie as witness and was met at the door by Madame Forrest. Her face was beaming at the handsomely-dressed man in his fashionable brown tweed suit pulled tightly over a bulky chest. Ruffles peeked out from beneath his jacket at the neck and wrists. He wore a black tie, and his hair and sideburns were neatly trimmed.

"Oh, Charlie, ye are so handsome!" Maggie exclaimed, hugging him affectionately. "I'll be so proud havin' ye standin' beside me. Do ye like the beautiful dress?"

"Aye, tis lovely," Charlie mused "but it's yer own beauty what takes m' breath away." He choked up as he looked at the radiant young woman.

Maggie plucked a daisy from the bouquet Madame Forrest had arranged for her to hold, tucked it into his lapel, and then gave one to Madame Forrest to wear.

"Please come with us," she asked the lady.

Madame Forrest was completely beside herself at being invited to witness the marriage. She nodded energetically then excused herself to dash back to her room to change into more appropriate clothes.

Maggie tied a yellow ribbon around Nicky's neck since wherever she went, Nicky was welcome, especially at her wedding. Nicky wagged his tail then sat down and tried to scratch off the ribbon with his hind leg. Everyone laughed.

"Am I making a mistake, Charlie?" Maggie asked while Madame Forrest was gone. "Father Francis says there will be trouble since I don't know David well enough. Perhaps m' heart has taken control of m' common sense."

"Darlin', if he's the one what sets yer heart t' fluttering, then he's most likely yer true love. Only time will tell if the love will last. We kin only pray it will."

Those were the words she had been waiting for.

Madame Forrest returned in minutes, an air of energy and excitement arriving with her. "It's going to be a wonderful day," she crooned.

"Both of ye are beautiful ladies," Charlie announced, "and it's time to go. The groom has a fine carriage waiting." Extending his elbows, each woman took hold so he could escort them down the stairs.

Across town, David, too, was preening. His heart was fluttering and his stomach was in knots. Today he would take a wife and his life would change. If only he could keep the news from his father. But then, he dared not dwell on that just now. What mattered today was making Maggie Hall his bride.

In the mirror, he checked out the fit of his nutmeg brown suit, the ruffles on his shirt and the tie around his neck. His moustache had been trimmed and waxed, his hair cut, and a dash of cologne patted onto his face. He smiled approvingly at his reflection then took up his hat and cane and walked briskly out the door to await Maggie's arrival at the courthouse.

Right on schedule, the carriage pulled up. David was there waiting and hurried to open the door to help Maggie down. When she smiled at him, she took his breath away. He nodded politely to Charlie and to Madame Forrest then possessively tucked Maggie's hand beneath his elbow and led them all to the Justice's chambers.

The ceremony lasted only minutes. When it was over, David slipped a magnificent sapphire ring encircled by diamonds onto her finger and waited as the Justice pronounce them man and wife. Only then did he kiss her for the first time.

"From this day forward," he whispered.

"Now and forever," she replied softly.

Chapter 9

Late October 1874

28 October 1874

Dearest family,

Wonderful news. On 11 October I married David Patrick Burdan. I wish you could have been here but Charlie stood with me in your place. David promises we will visit Ireland soon. Please tell Nicholas I too have found my true love and it's just as he said it would be. Wonderful.

Your daughter,
Maggie Burdan

Pressure for Maggie to quit working began almost immediately but she stubbornly resisted David's arguments. Once his family was told of the marriage, she promised, she would discuss no longer working for Charlie. Until then they needed the assurance of income in case David's father made good on cutting off his allowance. David felt, however, that the allowance provided them with much more than they needed to live on so she had no need to work.

Since Maggie wouldn't quit working and David dared not hang out with his friends in case he slipped and told them of his marriage, he turned his attentions to moving Maggie's meager belongings from the boarding house to his lavish apartment downtown. Madame Forrest was heartbroken when Maggie moved, not only because she adored the girl but also because Charlie maybe would no longer come visiting. Once Maggie's things were moved, David refurnished the apartment in ways he felt would please Maggie. He bought Turkish rugs for the floors, Irish-green settees, walnut tables, silk sheets for the bed, and colorful new dinnerware. Nicky got a soft new pillow so he would stop trying to sleep on their bed but Nicky would have nothing to do with it. He still growled every time David passed by, which was a continual annoyance. Maggie laughed it off saying David had earned Nicky's distrust so he should deal with it or find a way to get Nicky to give up his grievances.

David stopped visiting his parents. He was afraid he might slip and mention Maggie's name. When his friends came looking for him, he hid, refusing to answer the door.

Maggie was delighted each time David bought something new for her. She loved being spoiled and the gifts proved how much he loved her.

After refurnishing their home, David turned to buying jewels, perfumes, and fancy gowns for her to wear. He introduced her to fashionable hats that would eventually become her most delightful fetish in life—especially those with broad brims and fluffy feathers attached. The gowns were gorgeous, too, and soon filled the wardrobe.

After a while, Maggie began to stress over his extravagances. She dared not wear the gowns and jewels to work so they sat, unused, in the closet.

"David, the gowns are lovely but I've nowhere to wear them. We don't go to theater, we don't even go for walks together since yer father or his friends might notice. Ye should not spend so much on the clothes. Why not save that money in case yer father disowns ye as ye fear?"

Her blunt honesty was unnerving and made David cross. "Why must you always talk about my family?" he asked. "Can't you just accept the gifts I bring?"

Maggie was stunned by his reply. She simply stared at him wondering what to say that wouldn't make him angrier.

"If you can't wear the gowns in public, at least you might try dressing up for me at night," he said.

So she did.

But the jewels and gifts kept coming. Again she chastised his wastefulness.

"Darling, ye must save yer money. We might need it."

"Before you came into my life," he snapped, "money meant nothing. It was for spending, that's all. Now I have you to spoil. Am I not allowed to spoil the woman I love?"

It was true. As newlyweds, they were happy together and their love seemed solid and secure despite their disagreements over his spending habits.

One evening as they rode home in the carriage, David pulled over beneath a street lamp and presented her with a carefully wrapped parcel. He was grinning broadly knowing she would be thrilled with the gift. His fingers helped remove the parcel's wrappings to reveal a magnificent King James Bible bound in tooled crimson leather with the name "Molly Burdan" etched in gold at the top. Inside the front was written their names and their marriage date.

Maggie was completely surprised. She ran her fingers slowly down across the cover. "I've never seen a Bible so grand. 'Tis sad m' name is written wrong. It says Molly, not Maggie."

"It's no mistake, darling," he explained. "It's as I requested. Maggie is such a common name, I thought Molly would be more American."

"Ye dislike m' name, David?" she asked, stung by his words. "M' Da christened me Margaret after m' mum, then gave t' me the pet name of Maggie."

"Maggie, darling, it isn't that I dislike your name. I love your name but it's so…plain. When my parents meet you, your name will be important. Molly will be more acceptable. It's more dignified. Say the names together, Maggie—Molly. They aren't so different now are they?"

The prophetic words of Father Francis flashed through Maggie's mind. "Be wary," he had warned.

"Are ye ashamed of m' heritage? Is that what this is all about? M' name, m' parents, m' homeland? I know how much ye dislike m' work and Charlie. Tell me, what else do ye object to?" She pushed the Bible from her lap as hot tears broke free and slid down her cheeks causing her to turn away from him.

"It isn't like that, sweetheart," he stammered.

"I'm not ashamed of who I am, David, nor will I ever be." His words had hurt her deeply.

"It's only for appearances, love," he pleaded, trying to calm her down so she would look at him again. He knew he was in trouble but felt certain he could swing her over to his way of thinking. "It's for our future. In private, you'll still be my sweet Maggie. You'll always be the girl I fell in love with no matter the name." His fingers turned her face back to him where he tried to kiss away her tears.

"How many other things about m'self are ye wanting to change?" she asked, pulling back. She stared beyond him to the street lamp, almost afraid to hear his reply.

"There is one other thing," he confessed. "It's time you spoke proper English."

"What?" she snapped. "Ye don't like the way I speak either? And must I stop singin' Irish tunes, too? Or should I simply start at the top and disown everything about m'self that reminds ye of Ireland? Are m' parents an embarrassment even though ye don't even know 'em? Take me home, David, and keep yer Bible until ye decide what's truly important in yer life. Me or yer money?"

"Maggie, you're making too much of this. Proper English is important in America. You already have a fine education. You just need discipline when you speak. As for your parents, we simply won't tell father they're from Ireland—and we certainly won't tell him you're a bar maid!" He chortled as though it was all a joke.

"Ye don't think he'll ask questions, David?" Maggie glared at him, surprised at his ignorance.

"We're living in one of Boston's finest neighborhoods," he continued, ignoring her words. "Here people stroll about with their children, walking their poodles, discussing religion and politics openly. You want to fit in, don't you?"

"Right now I'm wishin' I was back in Ireland!" she snarled, her hurt turning now to anger. She wiped away her tears then slid away from him on the seat.

"Take me home, David, before I decide to walk." She reached for the door handle.

"Maggie, what is wrong with you?" he asked. "Haven't I given you everything you could possibly want? Are these simple requests so difficult for you?"

Maggie grew quiet. She had to admit her life had changed since their marriage. David was not only loving and kind, he also provided for her every whim and bought lavish gifts she had never even dreamed of. Were her only thanks given out to him as demands in the one area that concerned him most—his family? Perhaps she was being unfair. Changing her name, after all, would not change who she was.

"All right," she decided, sitting back in her seat. She immediately dropped the Irish lilt from her voice. "I'll be a proper Boston lady, if you wish, and I'll answer to Molly Burdan. I'll try to behave the way you want, husband, but be aware, what you are asking of me is offensive and I'll never be content to pretend I'm not Irish." Ice dripped from her words and she recoiled when he reached for her.

After that, their relationship grew strained. David had wounded her pride when he attacked her heritage, and he knew it.

A week later, David presented her with a second Bible, this one done up in black leather and engraved with the names of her parents, Thomas and Margaret Hall. Inside the cover, perfectly penned in David's own hand, was written:

> David Patrick Burdan married Maggie Hall
> 11 October 1874
> Boston Commonwealth
> State of Massachusetts
> May they live happily ever after.

"It's beautiful," Maggie whispered, surprised by his thoughtfulness. "My parents will be happy."

"I'll send it tomorrow," he promised, and he did.

That evening, after telling Charlie she would not be in to work, Maggie prepared an intimate meal for David as a surprise. She baked croissants, sliced up assorted cheeses and set out fresh orange marmalade as appetizers. The main meal was braised beef simmered in wine, with steamed, spiced potatoes. A rich, blueberry cheesecake provided dessert. She dressed herself in a shimmering blue satin gown that hung low exposing her bare shoulders. Her necklace and diamond earrings glistened in the candlelight.

"Molly, you are magnificent," David exclaimed.

Maggie rankled at the name he used but bit back her impulse to say anything. She had accepted the name Molly and that's how she would be known except at Charlie's tavern and with her family.

After dinner, they danced together, caught up in the intimacy of the moment. As the fire burned low, she took up her fiddle and played her favorite tunes.

> At Boolavogue as the sun was setting o'er the bright May meadows of Shelmalier, a rebel hand set the heather blazing and brought the neighbors from far and near. Then Father Murphy from Old Kilcormac spurred up the rock with a warning cry, "arm, arm" he cried for I've come to lead you, for Ireland's freedom we'll fight or die.

David's smile was strained as he pretended to enjoy the tunes she loved so much but inwardly he cringed. To him, the words were crude and offensive, and he detested Irish music.

Chapter 10

Late November 1874

20 November 1874

Dearest Mum and Da,

I never realized the need for such compromise in marriage. I've so much to learn. Sometimes I feel overwhelmed yet I've been a bride only a month. I wake up wondering how you were so successful at keeping happiness. Write and tell me your secrets.

Lovingly,
Maggie

As winter tiptoed into Boston, David focused all his attentions on convincing Molly to take a lengthy cruise into warmer climates near Mexico or in the Caribbean. There were so many places to see, he insisted. All she need do was tell Charlie she was quitting.

The idea of seeing more of the world was enticing to Molly since she secretly longed for more adventure. The problem was in knowing David still insisted on hiding their marriage. Until it was brought into the open, she would not abandon Charlie and the guaranteed income her work provided. David, of course, was disappointed and began to nag her daily about being so stubborn.

The Iron Ram's popularity had grown steadily since Molly's arrival. Between her personality and Charlie's character, business was booming. Charlie suggested she hire a helper.

Kitt was an attractive young woman with sultry dark eyes nearly as black as her hair. She was a quick study, had a spontaneous smile, and was youthful and anxious to please. Still, even with her help, the business kept all three of them working well into the night.

With Molly gone so much, David grew sullen and bored. He returned to hanging out with his friends, drinking and gambling until time to fetch Molly from work. On night he completely forgot her. Molly worried how to get home so Charlie insisted Simon escort her, which he did.

"Where have you been?" she chastised David the following morning. He had been out all night. "Simon had to escort me home—and that's a far distance!"

David just shrugged. "I lost track of time." He dropped his clothes onto the floor and climbed onto the bed, exhausted. Molly was furious. Not even an apology had been offered.

For a few evenings, he was dutiful in waiting for her to finish work, partly because he was enjoying watching Kitt. Since she didn't know he and Molly were married, she enjoyed flirting with him. After a while, however, David's boredom at the tavern took him back to the company of his friends. Rumors trickled back to Charlie and Simon that David was heavily into gambling and was now a regular user of opium, a popular narcotic. Charlie kept the rumors from Molly, confronting David with them instead.

"Why is it ye call yer wife Molly?" Charlie demanded. "Her God-given name is Maggie, not Molly."

"It was her choice," he replied, his eyes following Kitt. "Molly wants to be more American. It's not your concern anyway," he scoffed.

"Everything concerning Maggie is m' concern, ye insolent young cur," Charlie growled, keeping his voice low so Maggie wouldn't hear. "Gambling and drinking while she works is a big concern t' me, too, especially since ye're not man enough to own up to yer marriage. Why ain't ye got the gumption to tell yer parents? Are ye ashamed of yer bride? And if ye say yes, I'll throw ye out of here, Maggie or no."

"I'm not doing anything to hurt my wife," David replied. "Remember, old man, she is my wife, not yours."

Charlie's anger boiled over. He grabbed David's shirt in one hand and gripped a fist with the other, ready to punch him in the nose. That's when Molly walked up.

"Are you two arguing again?" She had long ago realized Charlie and David would never get along.

David shrugged and looked away.

"We were discussing when yer husband is goin' to man up and tell the world he's married. When do ye think that might be, David?" Charlie asked, feigning a smile.

David glared at Charlie. "When are you planning to stop interfering in our lives, old man?" he spat back.

"Charlie's right, David," Molly interjected. "Sooner or later, the truth will come out."

"Now you're both harping at me!" he snarled. Everyone in the pub stopped what they were doing to stare. "Neither of you has the faintest idea what will happen when Father finds out," he whispered. "He's a vindictive fellow and I'll be disowned without a second's thought."

"Maggie knows she always has work here," Charlie said. "She has security with me."

"I'm not willing to live like a pauper," David snapped back. "I enjoy what money can buy!"

"Then find yerself a job or tighten yer belt and stop wastin' yer money. Gamblin's nothing but wasteful, and ye should know that without me havin' to tell ye."

"Who told you I'm gambling?" David asked, glancing nervously at Molly.

"Everybody knows."

David saw Molly frown and realized even she knew what he was up to when he wasn't with her.

"If we start saving now, we'll be prepared if your father cuts you off," she volunteered, smiling slightly.

"We'll lose everything," David replied. "The apartment, the furniture. Everything. Quite frankly, the thought of it scares me to death."

Kitt approached the table then, smiling sweetly at David as she offered him another beer. "Do you still want to meet after work?" she asked innocently. "Charlie says I can leave early if business is slow."

David's face turned pale. He tried to stammer out an intelligible response but it was apparent both Charlie and Molly had heard. Without answering, he abruptly stood up and stormed out of the tavern.

"Why did he leave?" Kitt asked innocently.

"Because he's my husband," Molly replied, her words icy cold.

"Your husband?" she gasped. "Oh, Maggie, I didn't know, I didn't know." Embarrassed, she burst into tears and dashed to the back room.

Molly couldn't even bear to look at Charlie. She was visibly shaken by what had just happened. Not only was David gambling and using opiates but he was openly pursuing Kitt.

"Charlie, do you think he's bedding other women?"

"Ye need to ask him, Lassie. I cannot tell ye what ye aren't ready to hear. Only yer husband can answer that question."

"Did you know?" she asked, tears trickling down her cheeks.

"Aye, the rumors have been getting' t' me," he answered. "Maybe ye should go home early tonight, get things straight with him."

Slowly, she untied her apron, placed it on the counter, called to Nicky, and left the tavern. She walked all the way across town but David wasn't there. He didn't come home that night.

The next morning, Molly walked all the way back across town and stopped off at the boarding house where she poured out her misery to Madame Forrest. They decided Molly should take a secret room at the boarding house in case he kept failing to come for her after work. It would be a much closer walking distance.

She didn't go to work that day nor did she return to the apartment. She holed up in the room at the boarding house forbidding Madame Forrest from telling anyone but Charlie or Simon where she was. She needed time to think and get her head straight.

After three days, David sought Charlie out to find out why Molly had not been home but Charlie said he hadn't seen her since the night he stormed out of the tavern. He didn't tell David where Molly was staying. David went back to the apartment to wait, worrying himself into a drunken stupor with the whiskey he took with him.

When Molly finally did return to the apartment, it was just after dawn. David was sitting in a chair, half-a-dozen empty whiskey bottles close by. He hadn't slept in days and his eyes showed it, all red and bloodshot. His clothes were wrinkled and soiled.

"Where have you been?" he asked heavily. "I've been worried sick."

Molly didn't say anything. She just stared at him as he staggered across the room, unbuttoned his shirt, and dropped heavily onto the bed, drunk and exhausted. In minutes, he was sound asleep.

Molly pulled a blanket over him then watched and waited until his breathing grew steady. With a pitiful shake of her head, she stood up and walked to the window overlooking the park. The stench of his clothes had confirmed where he had been while she was away.

In the days before, she had gone through painful self-analysis, agonizing over where their lives had gone in the past weeks. Where once they had been happy, now they were distrustful and argumentative. Molly's love for him was fading. She realized part of the fault belonged to her but she gave little slack to him where his father was concerned. She needed someone to confide in, someone that could give her counsel. Father Francis, she knew, would only chastise her more so she dared not go to him. Instead, she decided to talk to Charlie. He was the closest thing to a father figure that she had.

With Nicky at her heels, she left the apartment and walked along in the cold morning air, enjoying how it cleared her thoughts. The walk took them through the park where Molly saw a child playing near the bushes. She was probably no more than nine years old and was dressed in rags. Nicky ran right to her, licking her face as though he recognized her from another time or place. The child laughed and hugged the dog, delighted to see him. When Molly approached, the girl ran away.

"Wait," Molly called out. "Come back, I won't harm you," but the girl was gone.

How can a child survive out here, Molly wondered? The wind was cold and the girl's clothes were shabby. Her father's words came back to her. "Where will you go, who will care for you?" It was then she realized the only difference between her and that orphaned child was Charlie. At that realization, her perspective returned. Charlie was her guardian and her salvation. She could never abandon him nor would he abandon her. David, the man who should have taken on that role in her life, was not her salvation, nor would he ever be.

Charlie was relieved to see her and happily went about preparing strong tea for them both.

"Are ye here to cook up some of yer delicious clam chowder?" he beamed. "The men been missin' yer cookin'."

"There was an orphan in the park, Charlie," Molly confided. "She was cold and frightened, probably starving. I called to her but she wouldn't come."

"'Tis the way of things, Maggie. There be hundreds of homeless urchins on the streets. Sadly, we can't save 'em all. Is that what's brought ye here, worry about an orphan?"

"No, 'tis not the reason," Molly answered quietly, tears welling up in her eyes. Even though she had found new resolve, the situation with David was terribly painful for her to talk about.

"Tell me, Lassie," Charlie insisted, patting her on the shoulder.

"My marriage is failing," she confessed. "We argue, we disagree on everything, he hates my work, he only wants to be with his friends. Sometime he doesn't even come home. I don't know what to do."

Charlie puffed on his pipe, listening sympathetically as circles of smoke drifted up over his head. "'Tis not you what's at fault," he advised. "'Tis the deceit. The truth is wantin' to be known but keepin' it locked away is woundin' yer marriage. Lies are chippin' away at it."

"He gets so angry when I suggest we go to his father," she whispered.

"He doesn't hurt ye, does he?" Charlie bristled.

"No, he doesn't mistreat me in that way. He just pulls away. He doesn't even touch me anymore."

"The longer ye wait, the more difficult the task will be. Sooner or later, the father will know—and that should be his real worry. The man might forgive yer hasty marriage but it's doubtful he'll forgive not being told. 'Tis a father's right to know when a child marries."

Charlie insisted Molly return to the apartment to try again to talk to David so she left the tavern, hailed a carriage, and returned to the apartment. Snow was starting to fall and a wind had come up.

David was awake when she returned. "Where have you been?" he asked. "Let me guess, with your uncle? Your husband walks the streets looking for you but you go straight to Charlie. Did you ever think I might be worried?"

Maggie set aside her coat and hat on a nearby chair, trying to hold back her temper. She noticed David was freshly bathed and cleanly shaven, ready for a day of activity—somewhere.

"Where I've been doesn't really matter. What matters is that we have a problem in our marriage, David, and unless we deal with it, the marriage will fail. Yes, I talked with Charlie. He's the only one I seem able to communicate with since you're seldom around."

David started to speak then decided not. He just kept looking at her, searching her face for blame. Seeing none, he reached for her hand.

"Look, Sweetheart, let's take a vacation. We can leave right away and stay gone until spring, if you want. We need time together."

"That would be nice," Molly sighed, laying her head on his shoulder. It had been weeks since they were able to share even a few moments of intimacy and she missed the closeness of him.

"Would you like to visit your parents first?" he smiled. "Or shall we sail to the south where it's warm and wait for spring before going to Ireland. I'll book the tickets today." He was happily encouraged by her words.

"Book the tickets for tomorrow, David. Today, we'll go to your parents." Her voice was soft as she raised her head to await his reaction.

He exploded with rage, shoving her away.

"Molly, why are you doing this? Do you want me to be disinherited?"

"It's time, for honesty, David. We can't keep avoiding the inevitable. It's the lies that are hurting our marriage."

"Charlie put you up to this, didn't he?" David yelled, his face next to hers. "Why can't he just leave us alone?"

"Charlie isn't the problem. It's us. If you love me as you say you do, show it by telling the world about me. If you're ashamed of me, then don't. Your actions will be proof provided. I'd follow you to the ends of the earth—starting tomorrow if I know you care enough to proclaim our marriage. I just won't keep hiding. I want you in my life, I want to have children, I want to grow old with you. Don't you want those things too?" Her eyes were pleading for understanding.

David stood at the window keeping his back to her. When she touched him on the shoulder, he yanked himself away, shutting her out.

Sighing heavily, Molly turned away and began dressing for work.

"All right, then. I presume your silence is the answer I was waiting for. Good-bye, dear heart."

She called to Nicky then left the apartment. She hailed a buggy to drive her to the tavern and arranged for him to pick her up at midnight. No longer would she wait for David to arrive, nor would she saddle Simon with David's responsibility. She would take care of herself. From the window, David watched, his heart in turmoil between going after the woman he loved or facing a vindictive father who would most assuredly disinherit him. He chose not to call out to Molly. Instead, he watched her drive away.

At the tavern, Charlie realized things had not gone well. Molly never spoke of David but went right to work. Before long, soup was bubbling over the fire and bread was baking. Soon, patrons began arriving, delighted to see her again and anxious for a hot meal on a cold, blustery day. Molly realized those people had become not only her friends but her family. They accepted her for who she was, and they loved her unconditionally. Even Kitt, who arrived later, wanted to be her friend but she was embarrassed and kept avoiding Molly.

"I hold no anger with you, Kitt," Molly explained. "David is having troubling giving up his bachelor ways." She smiled warmly at Kitt. "Please don't tell anyone what you know. David's not ready."

It was a surprise when David showed up at the tavern, whistling and pretending nothing was out of the ordinary. He winked at Molly when she set a mug of hot ale before him.

"I do love you, Molly," he whispered, reaching for her hand and raising it to his lips. "We'll work through this, all right?"

Molly's heart began to beat as though it were a captured baby bird, fluttering and excited. Charlie's face lit up when he saw how happy she was. He nodded approvingly at David and was pleased when David nodded and smiled back. Charlie suggested Molly sit a while with David and share supper with him, which she did. Everyone in the tavern sensed they were happy again.

Then the door opened and his friends strolled in. They went straight to where David and Molly were sitting. Molly excused herself but they immediately began badgering David.

"We always seem to find you here," they scolded him. "You avoiding us again?" Both laughed.

"You've been drinking too much," he told them. "You better go."

"What is it about that little tart that keeps you coming back here?" one fellow asked. "Or is it that little darkie that's got your eye now?" Both men ogled Kitt.

"She is a beauty," David replied. "I got my eye on her so don't be cutting in," he lied. He hoped to divert attention away from Molly.

Kitt, eager to make amends with Molly, flirted with his friends, trying to get them to focus their attentions on her rather than on Molly. One of the men beckoned Molly to the table.

"If you can find another friend, the three of us could go out and have some fun tonight," he laughed. He grinned at Kitt. "Come here then, sweet thing, and share your sugar with us. We're all friends, you know, so we'll like you as much as he does." He then tried to pull Molly onto his lap.

Molly slammed her elbow into the man's neck causing him to yell out.

"Get your hands off me," she snarled.

"Leave my wife alone," David chipped in, standing up to pull Molly away. Then he realized what he had said.

"Your wife?" the friend grinned, rubbing his throat. "You're married to this wench?"

Before David could answer, Charlie and Simon were shoving the men to the door. "Does Daddy know? He's gonna be really surprised!" one man called back seconds before the door slammed shut behind them.

A deathly cold silence enveloped the room as all eyes turned to David, then to Molly. Charlie walked over to them, his face nearly as pale as David's.

"Well, the secret's out," he stated simply. "And now ye have a real problem."

Chapter 11

30 November 1874

THEY WERE SUMMONED TO BEACON Hill. The carriage arrived early to carry them to the Burdan mansion. David sat as though frozen to the seat, trying his best to decide what to say to his father. Molly, strangely enough, was relieved the secret was out. She had been waiting for this day, confident she had done everything to make her presentation to the parents acceptable. She was stylishly dressed, her English was proper, her education was evident, and her love for David was apparent, or so she believed. She glanced at David who was sitting beside her, properly dressed and handsome as always. David glanced back, a brave smile flashing across his face. Today, the charade would end.

The redbrick Burdan mansion was covered in winter-darkened ivy that clung tenaciously to the iron fence works on every side. A single oak tree over-shadowed the snow-covered lawn. At the door, a butler stood waiting, shivering in the cold but ready to help the visitors from the carriage. Once inside, they were ushered into a study area then left to wait.

Molly took a seat next to an over-sized walnut desk, her hand resting near a bronze replica of one of the Burdan ships in the harbor. Not far away a fire crackled in the fireplace radiating warmth into the massive room. Heavy brocade draperies covered the windows helping to hold out the cold. Molly noticed hundreds of books lining the enormous bookshelves.

They waited nervously for nearly an hour, then realized Joshua Burdan had been silently watching them from a side door. When he realized they knew he was there, he shuffled toward them with a limping step.

He was a small man, bony and slender, a full head shorter than David. His face was heavily pocked, his hair thin and gray, and his eyes darted around as though he was expecting something creepy to appear without warning.

"Hm," he muttered, squinting at Molly. "Is this your wife?" Only then did he face David who nodded but didn't speak. Joshua took a seat behind the desk then withdrew an envelope that he placed in front of him face down.

"Does she have a name?" he asked David, still staring at Molly who boldly met his gaze and held it. She knew he was judging her.

"Father, this is Molly. We were married in October," David told him.

"Hmm," Joshua murmured again, rising up out of his chair to limp toward Molly. He was surprised at her attractiveness and the perfection of her appearance. She was dressed in a wine-colored gown that matched her stylish hat, and beneath the hat were her golden curls. Her only jewelry appeared to be a strand of pearls and a matching broach.

Joshua's hands reached out, fluttering just above her curls as though he wanted to touch them but dared not. Instead, he grabbed her hand and examined the sapphire wedding ring.

"He does have expensive tastes, does he not?" he blurted out, his eyes darting to David then back.

"It is beautiful," she smiled sweetly, pulling her hand away. She looked adoringly at David then held out her hand to him since he still couldn't seem to find his tongue.

"Bought with my money, of course," Joshua muttered. "Too bad you couldn't invite us to the wedding." He glared at David, his lips pursed in annoyance.

"It was a quick decision," David sputtered.

"Oh, she's in the family way," Joshua chortled. "That explains a lot of things."

"I'm not in the family way," Molly corrected him, frowning up at David. "We were in love and didn't want to delay our wedding."

"You met this trollop at a tavern, I hear."

David nodded.

"Sir, I take offense at your words," Molly blurted out, rising to her feet. "You've no cause to insult me." Her eyes grew dark with anger.

"Ah, a wench with attitude," Joshua laughed wickedly. "That's something in your favor, Son. I guess you thought you caught a rich one, didn't you?" He faced Molly, determined to insult her.

Molly looked to David for back up but realized he was so intimidated by his father that he had no intention of defending her honor.

"Mr. Burdan, your son and I fell in love and were lawfully wed. We only want your acceptance."

"Not my money? You knew he was rich, didn't you?" Joshua went on. "Well, little Miss, I'm sorry to tell you my son is worth nothing. All he has in the world is what I give him. His allowance keeps him out from under my feet. What do you suppose will happen when I cut off that allowance? Will you still "love" him? Will love buy food for your table?"

"We'll get by," she replied.

"Oh, Molly-Molly, he's a worthless boy, can't you see that? God forbid if you add a string of runny-nosed brats to the family."

Molly was stunned by Joshua's bitter words. She kept looking to David but he just stood there behind her chair, his expression pale and cold. Finally, she couldn't contain her anger any longer. She marched right up to Joshua.

"What terrible words you speak," she spat. "David is your son and deserves some respect. Why do you speak so badly of your child?"

"Who are you to talk to me about my son?" Joshua snapped. "Has he tried to find honorable work? No, I'd guess not. He won't even learn the family business."

"Have you tried teaching him?"

"Why waste my time?" Joshua snapped.

"Perhaps he could learn if he had someone to teach him, a competent teacher," she replied coldly. "Students are only as good as their teachers are. But then a man of your obvious stature knows the importance of proper instruction. Perhaps it's you that needs more training."

David gasped at the sharpness of her words and Joshua appeared dumbstruck.

"You're an arrogant wench," he shouted, his face turning crimson red. Little drops of spittle formed at the corners of his mouth. "For your information, David never showed any interest in the family business."

"Was he given a chance? How would you know if you failed to spend time with him?"

"I've no need to justify my actions to you," Joshua snapped back. "Perhaps you should explain your own background, Missy."

Molly began speaking in fluent French then switched to Latin as she recited proverbs from the Bible about people loving one another. After that, she spoke in German, then in Spanish.

"Do you agree?" she asked sweetly, suspecting he had no understanding of anything she had said. "I'm certain you know many languages, do you not? You must be educated…or perhaps I should translate." She smiled coldly at the squirming little man who now seemed speechless.

"You are out of line, Missy," he stuttered.

"As for my credentials, you need only to know I am your son's wife and we're here to seek your blessing. Do we have that?"

"You want my blessing?" Joshua squealed. "You want my blessing?" He stood of tiptoes, his face shoved up next to Molly's. "She's sweet, David, but does she know how fickle you are? Let's see, it was the Torrence girl you were in love with last year, then the Hartwell girl before that, and Janie Adams before that." A cold laugh escaped Joshua's lips allowing the droplets of spittle to break free and trickle down his chin.

Molly slipped her arm possessively through David's but didn't respond.

"You denied your mother the opportunity of hosting a proper wedding celebration," Joshua raged on, waving his hands in the air like a foppish dandy. "Your Mother likes a good party but now she's been embarrassed by her only son. Did she deserve that? Why couldn't you have chosen someone other than a barmaid, a cheap little harlot!"

Without thinking, Molly slapped Joshua right across the face causing him to gasp and stumble back against the desk, his hand covering the spot where she had struck him.

"Do not call me a harlot, you sniveling little man," Molly snarled. "I am your son's wife, a woman of honorable Irish heritage, a Burdan whether you like it or not. I make no excuse to anyone about my background, least of all to a pompous, egotistical, mean-spirited, hateful little man blinded by gold. You're missing out on the true treasure of life, a good and worthy son. All of the trappings bought by your gold cannot buy the love and respect he would freely give if only you showed him some affection. Children thrive on love, you should know that," she ranted on, her arm making a wide sweep around the room, indicating the lavish furnishings. "These are not true treasures. Wealth is in the children!"

"Spoken like true Irish riff-raff," Joshua spat. "Well, David, you made your bed, now sleep in it."

With that, he circled around the desk, snatched up the envelope and made good on his threat. The envelope contained the legal papers of disinheritance.

"Please don't do this, father," David begged, rushing to the desk and leaning forward to push away the papers his father was signing. "I don't know how we'll live without an allowance."

"Oh, for heaven's sake, David, stop sniveling. You knew this would happen. You should have considered the consequences before marrying this tramp." Joshua flinched in case Molly might be considering striking him again.

"At least give me a temporary allowance until I can find work," David whimpered.

"Get out, David, and stay out. As for you, Ms. Molly-Molly, ply your trade well. There are men who will pay handsomely to bed you." He snorted again.

"'Tis little wonder David despises you, you evil little troll," Molly replied quietly.

Joshua glared at Molly, still taken aback by her boldness. "I admit, she has more spunk than you ever had, David." Rubbing his still-stinging cheek, he hobbled out of the study, slamming the door behind.

Scarcely had the door closed than David's mother, Mellina, entered. She was a short lady, buxomy in appearance but gentle looking. Her silver hair was stylishly braided and coiled atop her head. Sequined combs held the braids in place.

"Mother, you heard?" David cried out, rushing into her open arms. "I am so sorry I hurt you. Father disowned me. Whatever shall we do?"

"I heard. First, introduce me to your bride." Mellina pushed him away and extended a limp hand to Molly.

"This is Molly. She's wonderful," David beamed. "You'll like her, I know."

"I'm pleased to meet you, child," said Mellina.

Molly smiled brightly. "I am happy to meet you, too. David speaks warmly of you."

"He does? I'm surprised. He hasn't been to see me in weeks." She eased herself into a chair near the desk. "Please forgive me for sitting but my hips are troublesome of late.

"David, I am saddened that I will not get to know your wife. When Joshua renounced you, he intended you be barred from this house as well. The days ahead of you are going to be difficult."

"Is there nothing you can do?" he pleaded.

"Nothing. If I interfere, your father will freeze my funds as well. I might sneak a coin to you now and again but nothing of size enough to help you. He will be watching us both."

"Would Grandfather intervene in our behalf?"

"You can approach him if you wish but don't expect much. He doesn't like arguing with your father either so I'm afraid no one can help you."

"What if the marriage were annulled?" David asked, avoiding Molly's eyes.

"David?" Molly gasped, grabbing onto his arm.

"I must go now," she told them, struggling to stand. "I'm on orders not to speak with you." A cold smile found its way to her lips. "Things are not easy for me, either. Joshua is a hard man to live with."

Mellina hugged David briefly, smiled at Molly, then shuffled out of the room.

"An annulment?" Molly asked as they left the house but David didn't reply.

Chapter 12

December 1874

14 December 1874

Dearest parents,
    Winter has come to Boston and into my heart as well. Already my marriage is troubled. David's father disowned him and we are destitute. Only my work keeps us in food. Charlie, once again, is my benefactor, and I am so grateful.

Your daughter,
Maggie

MOLLY WAS OVERCOME BY DESPAIR. In the two weeks since meeting with David's parents, David had stopped speaking to her completely. She knew he somehow blamed her for the disinheritance. If she had controlled her tongue perhaps this would not have happened. Sullen and cross, David turned his anger on everyone, particularly Molly and Charlie. At the tavern, the patrons blamed David so he dared not go there since they made no bones about their views on the subject. David stopped coming in and only returned to the apartment when he knew Molly would be at work. During the hours when she was away, he began selling off everything, even her clothes. Molly carefully kept her earnings hidden, certain he would use those, too, to drink and gamble with.

Molly started staying at Madame Forrest's every night. She no longer could afford renting a carriage and refused to have Simon escorting her home. She kept Nicky with her, afraid that David might harm him out of spite. To help out, Charlie increased her pay, for which Molly was grateful.

One morning Molly showed up early at the tavern only to find the door unlocked. The building was dark and silent. Concerned, she called Charlie's name but got no answer. Suddenly Nicky dashed toward the back room where they found Charlie laying on the floor.

"Charlie!" Molly cried out, dropping to her knees beside him. "Are you all right?" She patted his face, urging him to open his eyes.

"Molly?" he asked hoarsely, his eyes fluttering open. "What ye doin' here?"

"I'm here to work. What happened, Charlie? Are you ill?" Molly's heart was pounding.

"Ah, no," he smiled crookedly. "Too much rum. Kin ye help me up?" His arms reached for her support as he struggled to sit up, then to climb up onto the bed.

"Mercy, Girl, ye frightened me," he mumbled, running his fingers through his wild hair.

"I frightened you? I thought you had been killed. The door was unlocked. Someone could have robbed you, or worse."

"My, my, ye sound just like m' mother," Charlie retorted, wrapping his arms around her in a weak hug. The smell of rum and sweat overwhelmed her.

"Truth is," he explained, "Madame Forrest was here. Such a fine lady, she is. We had a party." He grinned sheepishly. "After she left, I got all melancholy. 'Twas this time of year when m' dear wife passed. I still miss her." Tears welled up in his eyes as his head drooped down. "I didn't want to be alone so I kept m' cup filled 'til m' brain went numb. I kept thinkin' how lonely I'll be when m' Molly leaves me, too." His tired, sad eyes looked up to Molly, causing her to cry.

"I'll never leave you all alone," she promised, hugging him tightly.

"Now, what are ye doing here so early?" he asked, patting her hands then rubbing the sadness from his eyes.

"From rags to riches and back to rags again," she replied sadly. "David doesn't come home anymore so I stay at Madame Forrest's, as you know. He's selling everything for gambling money and drink. He'd wrench the rings off my fingers if he could."

"Mabel's delighted ye stay with her. She's thinkin' ye're her daughter," Charlie laughed.

"Mabel? Perhaps she's going to become the companion you're wanting," Molly teased. "As for David, it's probably my fault as much as his. I shouldn't have said such mean things to his father. I just couldn't control my tongue when he started on about my Mum and Da."

"Mabel's naught but a dear friend," Charlie winked. "As fer the old man, his mind was made up long before ye got there, little one," Charlie tried to comfort her. "Don't blame yerself. It was bound to happen this way. Ease yer mind, ye'll not go hungry, not while I'm alive and kickin'."

"I love you, Old Bear," Molly exclaimed. "You always brighten my spirits. Perhaps when spring comes, things will be better. I'll see if I can find that pot of gold on Saint Patty's day, and maybe there'll be a rainbow there, too."

The next morning, Molly went back to the apartment for whatever clothes and belongings she hoped hadn't been sold yet. To her surprise, David was there.

"Where have you been?" he demanded. "Got a new lover, do you?" He was seated near the window, one leg crossed over the over as though he had been waiting all night.

"I took a room at the boarding house. It's too far for me to walk here every night." She was in no mood to argue.

"I've been worried about you," he said quietly. "I miss you even though I don't show it." He approached her with open arms but she turned away. "I hate knowing you work in a place where wharf rats can manhandle you. They don't care if you're a married woman."

"I never forget I'm married. It's you I fear that's forgotten. Do you not think I can smell another woman's perfume on your clothes—like now?" She pushed him away then picked up one of his shirts from off the floor, sniffed it once, held it at arm's length and dropped it back to the floor.

"Molly, I know I'm a failure," he whimpered, walking back to the window. "You'd be better off without me."

"We're married, David, for good or bad, but if we can't talk civilized, what kind of marriage will this be? It's growing weaker by the day."

She sat down on the bed and looked around. The apartment was nearly void of furniture now, all except for the bed and a few chairs.

"You think I'm afraid to find work, aren't you? You harp on my failures so much it's no wonder I hate coming home." His mood had swung again. It was the opium still in his system.

"I do not criticize you," she gasped, reaching out her hand. "I understand, I really do."

Roughly, David slapped her hand away then stormed out of the apartment again.

Molly spent the night at the apartment. It was a bone-chilling cold morning when he returned, his coat missing, his clothes reeking of whiskey and perfume. He fell onto the bed beside her and was instantly asleep. Molly slipped from beneath the covers and gently covered him with warm blankets before crawling back in beside him. She lay there awake, watching him sleep, engulfed in guilt and remorse, wondering how she might have done things differently. Nicholas had warned her about always wanting to be right. She began to cry for their lost happiness, for ever having left Ireland, for offending Nicholas, for believing her marriage to be invincible even against his father. Exhausted, she wrapped her arms around her sleeping husband then fell asleep. When she woke, he was gone.

Chapter 13

March 1875

1 March 1875

Dearest Family,
    Alas, all is not well. Since David's disinheritance, he has stopped caring for me. Please, pray for me. Tell me what to do.

Your daughter,
Maggie

DAVID CLOSED UP THE APARTMENT during the dead of night, unable to pay the rent. He moved in with Molly at Madame Forrest's place. Molly vowed to keep the rent paid so as to not take advantage of Madame Forrest's kindness. She budgeted her earnings carefully so rent money was available. She skimped on food, choosing instead to take meals at The Iron Ram as Charlie insisted. After all, he insisted, Molly did all the cooking.

In David's mind, they were now poverty stricken, a situation so humiliating he couldn't speak of it. It didn't concern him, however, to beg drinks and money off his friends. Molly kept her earnings hidden so they wouldn't tempt him. She no longer waited up for him, caring little at all if he even came home.

Then one morning, he arrived home early, whistling happily and in seemingly fine spirits.

"Good morning, sweetheart," he said when he saw Molly dressing for work.

"You're home. What a surprise," she replied sarcastically.

David ignored her tone of voice, stepping up behind her and hugging her tightly.

"Are you angry with me?" he whispered as he nuzzled her neck.

"Stop, David," she snapped, spinning around. "I'm leaving for work."

"Do you have a minute to talk?" he asked. "I've found a solution to our financial needs."

"And what solution might that be?"

Taking her by the hand, David led her to the edge of the bed, sat down, and pulled her onto his lap. His sleep-deprived, bloodshot eyes searched her face even as his fingertips toyed with her soft hair.

"You are so beautiful," he told her.

"David, what is it? I need to leave." Inwardly, she was angry with him and had no wish to sit on his lap and pass idle talk.

"I went to my father and begged for work but he threw me out—again. That sour old man called me a wharf rat. Nonetheless, I went groveling to grandfather, too, but he could only give me a few coins. Such a fine family, don't you agree?" He laughed sourly.

"Your solution is begging money from your grandfather?"

"I know, it's belittling—but so is being kept by my wife."

Molly pushed away from him. She was in no mood for his self-pity.

"You dream of wealth without work. There is no such thing, don't you know that?"

"There's a warrant out for me," he stated simply. "I'm going to Debtor's Prison if I don't pay our past debts."

"What?" Molly gasped. "Debtor's prison? I assumed you used the money from the sale of our belongings to pay your debts."

"I lost it all on the tables," he declared. For some reason, he wasn't even upset about the possibility of prison.

"What will we do?" she asked, sitting back down beside him. "I don't want you to go to prison. Should I talk to Charlie about a loan? Will it help if we sell my wedding ring? Tell me what to do."

"I met a man, a very wealthy man, who offered to give me enough money to pay the rent and still have money left over to pay our debts. I'd never even consider such a thing if I weren't so desperate, but I'm here to ask your help. Please, darling, keep in mind that I love you, no matter what I've said or done. I will always love you, I swear it."

"What are you saying?" she asked suspiciously.

"What I am asking of you will bring in a lot of money for us. More than you can imagine."

"Tell me, what is it, David?"

David took a deep breath then faced Molly straight on. "The man is waiting downstairs and wants only an hour with you—an hour during which you will submit to him."

Molly was stunned. She stood up and backed away trying to catch her breath. Her fingers were pressed to her lips.

"What are you saying? You want me to be a whore? You've sold me?" she gasped.

"It won't be so bad, Molly. Just pretend it's me, your loving husband. When it's over, we'll be able to pay the rent. It will keep me out of prison."

Too stricken to speak, Molly could only stare at him, tears welling up in her eyes.

"You are the only man I have ever been with," she whispered.

"We need the money, Darling, otherwise, I would never ask such a thing. He promised he would be gentle. Molly, I don't want to be thrown in prison."

"Adultery is a sin against God!" Molly's mind was reeling. She couldn't even face him.

When she turned back to him, he was sitting on the bed, hunched over and sobbing into his hands. His body was shaking with anguish over what he was asking of her. Overcome by compassion for his misery, she went to him and knelt down at his side, her hands gently placed on either side of his face. She smoothed back his hair, stroked his cheeks, then kissed him on the forehead.

"Tell him to come up, David. I'll be waiting."

Chapter 14

July 1875

3 July 1875

Dear Parents,

Things are better now but I am still learning how difficult marriage can be. I have made many mistakes and I'm afraid there are more to come. I live for your comforting letters.

Lovingly,
Maggie

ONCE DAVID REALIZED HOW EASY it was to convince Molly to prostitute herself, he knew he had found the answer to their money problems. Every night thereafter, he lined up more clients then played on Molly's emotions to get her to give in to other men. Because of her beauty, she became a popular prostitute and the fees he charged, though steep, were willingly paid. He kept a schedule of appointments just to keep up with the demand. Most of the men became return customers willing to pay any price just to be with her.

Molly sometimes heard men bartering with David over fees. Her clients confided she was already the highest paid prostitute in Boston. Some days, five or six men could be seen waiting outside the boarding house hoping for time with her.

Frustrated, Molly finally refused to see any more men until David backed the schedule off. She would service two men a day, no more—and Sundays were off limits.

David happily agreed. That would make her even more valuable.

Molly stopped working at The Iron Ram. David had finally succeeded in getting her away from Charlie. She sent a message to Charlie asking patience and understanding and insisted he not worry. She never told him why. Suspicious, Charlie sent Simon to see what was happening but David turned him away. He insisted Molly was in good health but wanted privacy. Besides, they were moving to a larger place.

Madame Forrest suspected what was happening when she saw men traipsing up and down the stairs at all hours. She went straight to Charlie to voice her suspicions. He asked her to seek Molly out, to find out for certain if Molly was being prostituted. It was inconceivable to him that she would do such a thing on her own but, then again, her worthless husband was capable of doing almost anything to avoid working.

It was days before Madame Forrest was able to find Molly home alone. David had left the house so Mabel hurried up the stairs, knocking loudly on the door. When Molly saw her, she burst into tears and rushed into her open arms, sobbing uncontrollably. When she was finally cried out, they sat together on the sofa, their arms around each other while Molly begged Mabel not to think unkindly of her. The decision had been her own.

"Please make Charlie understand," she begged.

When she left, Madame Forrest insisted Molly remember there was sanctuary for her if she needed to run away from David, and Molly was grateful for that. Charlie, however, was not at all understanding. Crazed with anger, he stormed to the apartment ready to do battle for Molly's honor, but he arrived too late. They had already moved.

The new place was spacious and tasteful despite being garishly decorated with reds and golds purposely selected to stir men's passions. Molly hated the colors but said nothing. Her life was spiraling out of control. Every day she recalled Joshua Burdan's prophecy that she could easily become a highly paid prostitute. His words had been prophetic and she hated him even more. In her mind, she was now damned forever since Father Francis made that abundantly clear the first time she went to confession. He promised she would be excommunicated if she continued down that path, and so she was. David scoffed when she told him, assuring her the church would always willingly accept their money, even if it came from whoring activities.

Once in the new place, David went about crating Nicky whenever clients arrived. He hated the dog's growling at the high-paying clients. Either Nicky was crated or he would dispose of the dog, he informed Molly.

"If the dog disappears or is hurt, this arrangement stops," she informed him, stomping her foot. "If you dare touch Nicky, I swear to God I will leave you!" The subject never came up again.

Within months, David and Molly were wealthy once more. Molly, however, was withdrawing into a sullen, dark person. The light in her eyes grew dim, her view of the world bleak and sad. She admitted her love for David was gone forever but David seemed happier than ever, showering her with jewels and high fashions. He deliberately overlooked her changing personality.

Simon stormed right into the apartment one afternoon, physically shoving his way past David.

"It took me a week t' find ye," he bellowed at David as he pinned him against a wall. "Let m' see the girl or I'll break ye in half. Ye filthy cur, I'll see the girl privately, too, and if ye cross me up, spawn of Lucifer, I'll throw ye out that window!"

Trembling with fear, David knew Simon would do just that so he called for Molly then ran from the apartment.

"Molly, girl, come out here," Simon yelled.

Molly ran into his open arms, her eyes swollen from crying. The gruff old sailor held her tight against his chest, crooning into her ear.

"There, there, Lassie. Simon's here, Simon's here. I'll not let anyone hurt ye anymore."

He lifted her into his arms and carried her to the sofa where she sat on his lap, her face buried in his hair. His brows were furrowed with concern.

"Molly, what's happened to ye?" he asked tenderly. "Ye can tell me. I'll not judge."

"Simon, I'm a whore, a fallen woman. I thought I could handle that one time when David begged it of me but now I'm in so entrenched I can never go back. I've sold my soul to the Devil."

"Aye, and the devil's name is David Burdan," Simon replied. Molly kept crying, releasing her frustrations as Simon held her and rocked her back and forth like a little child.

"Git yer things. Ye're coming back with me to the tavern—to the family what loves ye. We'll take care of ye." He tried to help her stand but Molly refused.

"'Tis too late for me. The damage is done. There's no redemption for women like me, Simon."

"Lassie, being a whore doesn't make ye a bad person. Yer heart is still good, people love ye fer who ye are, not what ye've done. Let me help ye," he pleaded. "Charlie's beside himself with worry."

"Ah, dear friend, you've lifted my spirits," she replied, wiping away her tears. "I needed to see you to find hope again. You've given me hope but you can't undo what's been done. My course is set, I fear. Just promise me you won't forget me, and tell Charlie I'll adore him 'til the day I die."

When he stood to leave, she raised up on tiptoes and kissed Simon on the cheek. "I'll love you, too, for as long as I live."

Letting him go without her was the hardest thing she ever did. When the door closed, she backed up against it and closed her eyes. "Maggie Hall," she asked herself, "what has happened to you?"

Subsequent soul searching brought her to the conclusion that she could only blame David for half of what had happened. In truth, she could have said no but she hadn't done that so the blame belonged to her as well. Where her life went from here, however, was up to her. She looked around at the lavish furnishings of the apartment, at the closets full of fashionable gowns, at the jewels and hats. What would Nicholas say, she wondered. Then she knew what he would say. "Take care of yer own self and remember who ye are and where ye came from."

It was time to take back her life, one way or another but she needed a plan.

On a late summer day, Molly took a long walk to the park where she had once seen the orphan girl. There she was, playing alone in the shadows, watching the other children. Molly sat down on a bench and watched as Nicky bounded over to the girl and began to lick her excitedly. He lay down on the ground, inviting her to play.

"Come here," Molly called out. "I have a peppermint stick in my pocket just for you." She set it on the bench beside her. "Come get it before the dog eats it. He loves candy."

Cautiously, the child approached the bench then reached for the candy.

"Would you mind keeping me company?" Molly asked. "I brought a sandwich but I hate to eat alone. I'll share it if you'll sit by me."

To her surprise, the girl came up and reached for the sandwich then knelt on the grass to eat it, sharing bits with Nicky.

"If you're hungry, Nicky can wait for his supper," she said. "He doesn't need your food."

"It's okay, lady. I'm used to not eating," she replied.

Molly's heart lurched. The child was hungry but still wanted to share her food with the dog.

"It's a lovely day, don't you think?" Molly said, gazing out over the park. "Is your mom somewhere close?"

"No, she's dead." The girl focused on the sandwich.

"I'm Molly. Do you have a name? It can't be Goldilocks since that's what my cousin calls me. Are you Rapunzel maybe?"

"Who's Rapunzel?"

Molly laughed. The child's brown eyes seemed suddenly brighter, less guarded.

"Becca is my name," she replied.

"Are you an orphan, Becca?"

Becca shrugged but didn't answer. Her attentions were centered on Nicky who was tugging on the corner of her tattered dress.

"I know someone who lost his little girl. His wife died trying to have a baby. Would you like to be adopted, Becca?"

Becca turned wary, her eyes darting back and forth as she prepared to run. Molly touched her gently on the shoulder.

"I won't hurt you, Becca, I promise. I just hate to see children alone in the world. The man is my uncle and he needs someone to take care of him since I have to go away. He's very nice but if you don't like him, I promise you don't have to stay with him."

"Is he mean?" Becca asked, desperately wanting to trust someone. "My stepfather was mean. He pushed me out in the cold then locked the door so I couldn't get back in. It was raining, and I was afraid."

"No, little one, he is not mean. He acts gruff but everyone knows he has the heart of a puppy, a puppy just like Nicky. His name is Charlie, and he's very lonely. Want to see for yourself?"

For a few brief moments, Becca studied Molly's face. Then, in a leap of faith, she took hold of Molly's hand and they walked together across town to The Iron Ram. Nicky stayed right on their heels.

When Molly left the tavern an hour later, her eyes red from crying, she left behind a child who would fill the void she had created in Charlie's life. Charlie had gruffly agreed to give Becca a "temporary" home but Molly knew he was already captivated by the homeless little girl. Molly had found the perfect way to repay Charlie for his kindness. She had given him a daughter of his own.

The next morning, she sat quietly at her dressing table brushing her hair before working the curls into a stylish coif at the back of her head. She fussed with a new feather-plumed hat David had brought home to her, pulling the feather down over her eyes and across one cheek.

"Very nice," David commented.

"David," she said, setting the hat aside, "we must talk about our arrangement. Adjustments are needed."

David sat down on a stool close to her, ready to hear her out.

"For some time now, you have found much pride in this business venture you so carefully arranged." Her words were unemotional. "We're partners, are we not? You make appointments, I provide my services. Do you agree?" She turned around in her chair and smiled sweetly.

"Yes, I suppose we are partners," he replied. "What are you getting at?"

"I've been doing a lot of thinking lately. The point is, I never wanted to be a prostitute. It was never my life's ambitions. Truth is, I detested prostitutes but now I am one. I'm entrenched in a business I despise and it's all for money to keep us in luxuries and gambling money."

David began to squirm. He didn't like the direction this conversation was taking. "I thought you liked the things I buy," he tried to explain but Molly waved him off.

"My dream when I met you was to be your wife, perhaps a mother to your children. Now I know that dream is gone. We don't behave like married people anymore. We aren't even lovers." Her face was sober.

"Is that what's bothering you, Darling?" he asked, relieved. "I'll resume my husbandly duties anytime you want."

"What I'm saying is this. I don't feel like your wife anymore. Everything has changed between us."

Molly turned away to tie a colorful blue ribbon around her throat, one that matched her satin gown. She spritzed perfume into her hair, preparing for her next client.

"I've come to a decision, David—one that won't please you, I'm certain, but this is how it will be from now on. You, David, can share my bed anytime but only as a paying client," she stated flatly. "You will pay me just as you pay your other whores."

"What? Molly, you're my wife! And I don't patronize other women, you know that," he gasped.

"Please, dear, no lying," she chastised him. "Remember, I've been excommunicated because of my actions so, in the eyes of God, I can only look forward to a life in Hell no matter what I do, so if I must experience Hell, so should you."

"You can't turn away your husband," he stammered.

"Ah, Love, I can, and I will—unless, of course, you pay the price. But there's more. Starting today, I will control the money. The men will pay me, and I will give you an allowance, just like your father did." Her smile was cold.

"Molly, this is outrageous. I'm the one who lines the men up. You can't put me on an allowance!" His face turned bright red with frustration. He took Molly by the shoulders and shook her roughly. "You cannot do this to me!"

Molly's temper exploded. Never before had he laid a hand on her. She stood up abruptly and pushed him away.

"Perhaps you think it gives me pleasure to see you squander the money I earn by submitting myself to strange and often repulsive men knowing all the while you are out spending the money on other women. My insides gnarl up over your cavalier attitude while I must accept that my soul has been doomed forever. There will be no children for me, no happy marriage. My dreams have been dashed forever."

"Who told you there are other women, Molly? You're the only woman I love."

"Perfume doesn't lie, darling. Nonetheless, it's no longer of concern. As I said, from today on I'll manage our funds and you can either get used to it or find yourself a new job. I could walk away from this business without even looking back, you know that, so, do you want to do it my way or not do it at all?"

David didn't know what to say. The ultimatum was clear but he was stunned by her declarations. She placed a platonic kiss on his cheek, gathered up her skirts and stepped around him, whistling for Nicky.

"Make appointments for me as you wish, Darling," she called back over her shoulder. "I'll be back in an hour."

Chapter 15

July 1877

4 July 1877

Dearest Mum and Da,

Adventure calls so I am headed west. David is no longer with me so where I shall end up, I do not know. It is wonderful to finally be moving on.

Your daughter,
Maggie

AMERICA DURING THE 1860S HAD already undergone enormous changes, mostly due to the actions of the gangly young Illinois politician named Abraham Lincoln. His election to the presidency happened during a very tumultuous time, and about that time, gold was discovered in Colorado and Nevada. With the enthusiastic encouragement of the government, thousands of people turned their sights to the west to escape the aftermath of the war or perhaps to find new lives for themselves. Mostly, however, it was to experience the lure of easy fortunes that might be found in the gold fields of the west.

The Transcontinental Railroad spent thousands of dollars promoting the rush to the west although their motives were somewhat different. They needed help finishing the railroad. To find laborers, they touted free land, limitless business opportunities, and gold a-plenty for people willing to take on the challenge of moving to the frontier. The headlines of the newspapers all across the east promised work and high wages working for the railroads. Even romance was capitalized upon.

The Matrimonial News, a San Francisco match-making newspaper catering to lonely men and desperate women, advertised regularly for mail-order brides. A few women were brave enough to answer the calls but overall the recruitment efforts failed dismally. Regardless, men like Asa Mercer of Puget Sound kept up the efforts to find brave, refined women willing to head west to pair up with lonely, desperate men. His efforts were honorable, to be certain, but finding women willing to give up security for questionable match ups were difficult at best. Still, he lobbied tirelessly for the men, arguing that the men could not populate the west if there were no women to be had.

Molly was captivated by the ads but had no interest in marriage. She wanted adventure, plain and simple. The prospect of life on the lawless frontier didn't frighten her at all since, to her way of thinking, the only persons capable of surviving were those with enough pluck and courage to make it work, and she knew she was just such a person.

Leaving David was easy enough. One day she just picked up her bags, said good-bye, and walked out the door. She took with her a sizeable bank account, a chest full of jewels and fancy gowns, and her best friend, Nicky.

By rail she traveled to Chicago, New York, Portland, San Francisco, then east again to St. Paul, Minnesota. Her stays in each city were brief since she wanted to discover everything. As she traveled, she soaked up the talk she heard about government land giveaways in the west, the big ranches being opened up for homesteading, rich mining claims that went to whoever could stake a claim first, and enormous timber stands in the Pacific Northwest just waiting to be harvested by ambitious lumbermen. Lumber was even in higher demand than gold since there were entrepreneurs flooding west to set up businesses that would feed upon those looking for easy fortunes.

Trappers, miners, cowboys, prostitutes, Indians, and businessmen became plentiful.

Each town along the rails had houses of ill repute, as the town founders called them. Rail workers kept their crews aware of where they were by placing bright red lanterns in the cabin windows thereby spawning the references of "red lanterns" as being houses of prostitution. The symbolism caught on quickly.

Prostitutes were everywhere. They were in parlor houses, mansions, boarding houses, shacks, and rooms above the saloons. The doves, as the women were called, came in every size, shape and color, with some being gentle and refined while others were brutish and crude. Payment for their services might be anything of value—gold dust, jewelry, horses, and even single shots of whiskey.

In the larger cities like Salt Lake City, San Francisco, Denver, and Portland small, cramped enclosures called cribs sprung up everywhere, even on streets and alleys. They were often inhabited by children brought in as opium- and whiskey-addicted child-slaves forced to sell themselves for mere pittances. Their voices could be heard day and night begging men to lay with them just for the price of a drink of whiskey or a taste of opium. Needless to say, those girls' lives were always short and desperate.

Doves like Molly were of a different class. They were those who considered themselves financially independent, so to speak, and with voices as to who they would or would not bed. For them, clean lodging, high fees, and fancy dresses were the norm.

Denver was where Molly met Mattie Silks,[2] a madam with a formidable reputation. She had moved west from Chicago, spending time in Abilene, Texas; Hays City, Kansas; and Georgetown, Colorado before opening her parlor at 501 Holladay Street. The sign above the door said it all: "Men taken in and done for."

---

[2] Mattie Silks came to Denver in 1866, establishing herself as a proper madam owning many high-class bordellos. She married Cort Thompson in 1886, adopted and raised his grandchild. After his death in 1900, at the age of seventy-six, married John Ready. She died in 1929 and was buried near Cort under the name of Mattie Ready.

Mattie's parlor boasted twenty-three rooms, each one magnificent enough to outshine even the governor's mansion. The ladies wore expensive silk gowns adorned by feathers, diamonds, pearls, topaz, and emeralds. Clients willingly paid top dollar to be with Mattie's women, either by the hour or by the day, and they received royal treatment while there—including musical entertainment, Cuban cigars, fine wines and expensive, imported liquors.

Mattie was every bit as beautiful as was Molly. They were, in truth, quite similar. Both had silky blonde hair that glistened in the candlelight, sparkling blue eyes, and strong personalities. Mattie, however, was an already established shrewd and calculating businesswomen when Molly arrived. Since she owned a number of places all around town, she kept on the lookout for exceptionally attractive women who would help to boost her income. From the moment she met Molly, she knew Molly belonged in the main bordello. It would be better to have Molly with her than competing against her.

A huge party was thrown to welcome Molly into Mattie's group. Embossed invitations were printed up for hand delivery to every male of importance in town, including prominent politicians and judges. New gowns were purchased for all the girls; a sixteen-piece brass band was hired to play loud, brash music; crystal goblets and chinaware were brought out; and foods extravagant enough to impress a king's court were spread out across a dozen tables throughout the building. So much champagne was served that even the servers lost count of how many bottles were opened and summarily emptied.

To say Molly was impressed would be a gross understatement. In Molly's mind, Mattie was not only classy and cunning but she was the highest paid game in town. When Mattie strolled through a room, fights routinely broke out amongst her many suitors all vying for her attention. Mattie loved it and fueled the fires at every opportunity—unless Cort Thompson happened to be in the room.

Mattie was in love with Cort, and he loved her.

"Cort's my man," Mattie warned Molly right at the start. "Claim any gent you want but keep your hands off my Cort." She pointed a finger right at Molly's nose to make her point then smiled sweetly, rolling her eyes as though she was nothing but a sweet, gentle kitten. "I don't share him, not with anyone."

"He must be quite a fellow," Molly replied. "It's not often one man captures a madam's heart then keeps it."

"Oh, I do adore that man," she chirped. "He won me over the very first day we met and now I love him so much he's all I think of. Surely you've been in love, haven't you Molly?"

"Only once," Molly replied. "That was enough." She dropped her eyes, not wanting to talk about David.

Cort was everything Mattie said he was: handsome, charming, tall and slender, firmly muscled, and impeccable in his dress. His sandy-blonde handlebar moustache matched his shoulder length thick, curly hair.

"You bear more than a slight resemblance to my cousin Nicholas in Ireland," Molly confided after she got more acquainted with him. "Your smile and mannerisms are so similar I can't help but stare."

"Just don't stare too much, darlin'," Mattie reminded her. "Cort is such a tease he might think you're wanting his attentions."

Cort laughed nervously. His job was to keep Mattie happy because if she was happy she was extremely generous with him in every way. If she found reason to be jealous, all hell would break loose. Firing up her temper could lead to his being cut off from her money. Mattie demanded his loyalty despite the fact he was still married to a woman who refused to divorce him so he could marry Mattie.

"Mattie knows all my vices," he whispered into Molly's ear, loud enough for Mattie to hear. "She knows I gamble and I drink too much, don't I, Sweetheart, but I never cheat on her." He grinned at Mattie then added, "Did she tell you I love a good foot race?"

"That he does," Mattie laughed. "He's a fine racer always looking to challenge someone to a race. He never loses, you know." She winked at Cort, then possessively took hold of his arm, pulling him close so she could kiss him repeatedly on the neck. "He especially likes spending my money, don't you darling?"

Cort's face grew flushed. They obviously knew each other well and it took no time at all for Molly to find out Cort did, indeed, enjoy spending Mattie's money. Surprisingly, most of it was spent on her. Only recently he had surprised Mattie with three magnificent new Arabian horses to add to her stables.

A few weeks after arriving in Denver, Molly was talking with Mattie when Cort strode into the room.

"Mattie, honey, we need to talk," he told her rather abruptly. "You listen, too, Molly." He pointed to the couch and insisted they sit down. "There's too much crime these days and I'm concerned for your safety, Sweetheart. Molly's, too, of course. I've decided to teach you gals to protect yourselves."

He opened up a small wooden case and presented Mattie with a shiny new ivory-handled .38 Colt revolver engraved with her name. He had a .38 Colt revolver, Dragoon model, for Molly but it was nowhere close to being as stunning as Mattie's gun.

"Starting this afternoon, we will practice shooting over near the creek beyond the edge of town," he stated matter-of-factly. With that, he stood up and left the parlor leaving both women speechless and wondering what had brought this on.

Both women became excellent students. Skill and accuracy were critical, he explained, and no amount of complaining could get them out of their lessons. In no way was he willing to see his Mattie attacked and unable to defend herself. Nor he insisted, should Molly need to worry. To Molly, it was like being back with Nicholas. He, too, had always been overly protective.

Not long after Cort declared the two of them competent with firearms, cause for his concern rode into town in the form of a plump little fairy-belle named Katie Fulton. She rode right up to the saloon where Cort was drinking and playing faro and quickly became enamored with him. Before the night was over, she announced to everyone that Cort was hers.

Like wildfire, the news spread to Mattie's ears. Storming into the saloon like a mad cat, Mattie walked straight over to Cort, shoved Katie off his lap, and took her place. She kissed him so long and hard it left no doubt to anyone that Cort was already taken. Cort's face turned flame red even as Katie's blood began to boil. She demanded Mattie remove herself from Cort's lap but Mattie just laughed in her face. Cort squirmed nervously. Something bad was sure to happen, and he knew it.

When it became obvious to Katie that Mattie wasn't about to surrender Cort, Katie slapped her right across the face then challenged her to a duel.

Cort was just as stunned as Mattie was. He'd never been party to a duel much less been the cause of one. It was all kind of exciting, though, so he blurted out that he would be Mattie's second.

Katie grabbed Sam Thatcher, a gambler seated next to Cort, and informed him that he would be her second.

Within minutes, the whole town was abuzz over the impending fight between two whores over Cort Thompson's affections.

The day of the duel brought hundreds of spectators out at dawn to watch and bet on the outcome. Thousands of dollars of wagers were laid down and drinks flowed like water. Weapons were chosen. Mattie selected the pistol Cort had purchased for her.

Soberly, the two doves paced off the necessary thirty paces, their skirts whirling around their ankles as they spun around to fire. The sounds of gunfire broke the silence split seconds before Cort screamed out in pain, wounded in the neck by Katie's shot. He fell to the ground, blood spurting from his neck.

Mattie went crazy, tossing her pistol to the ground as she ran screaming to her lover's side.

"Get the doc, get the doc," she cried, lifting Cort's head into her lap and shoving her hands down over the spurting blood.

Seeing her opportunity, Katie leveled her pistol at the back of Mattie's head but before she could pull the trigger, she felt the cold steel of another pistol shoved up against her own head. Cautiously, she turned to see Molly standing behind her.

"Don't," was all Molly said as she cocked her gun. Nicky was standing next to her, growling fiercely.

Katie dropped her weapon then ran helter-skelter to her carriage, scrambling inside and whipping the horse into a gallop toward the city limits.

Fortunately, Cort's wound was not fatal. He recovered completely, thanks in no small part to Mattie's personal nursing efforts.

She stayed with him day and night, lamenting over their good fortune that he had survived. Nevertheless, the near miss gave her cause to change her priorities. From now on, caring for Cort would take precedence over everything. To keep her businesses running, she tapped Molly to take over management until Cort recovered.

Delighted at such an opportunity, Molly accepted wholeheartedly. Soon she was focusing all her attention on learning every aspect of managing bordellos. A welcome side benefit was knowing she could now reduce the numbers of clients she needed in order to keep a steady flow of personal money coming in. As a manager, she would receive a share of all the other girls' earnings. It was a perfect arrangement.

Weeks passed by as Molly became more and more proficient at running the bordello just as Mattie had done. She also found more free time to explore Denver and discover its secrets. It was during that time that she met Jennie Rogers,[3] another popular dove.

Jennie was a quiet girl, extremely handsome with her chestnut hair and enormous brown eyes. Her clients were numerous and generous enough that she was able to buy lavish furnishings for her small parlor house. One of her most prized possessions was a grand piano that she played regularly for her guests.

Molly and Jennie met by accident while shopping in a wine store. Before long, they were sharing drinks together, usually Irish whiskey. That's when Jennie told Molly about her difficult start in Denver.

"Mattie sold me one of her buildings," she explained. "I tried to get financing to fix the place but no one would loan me any money. I was quite desperate, you see, since I had no wish to go back to St. Louis. It was a low time for me so I confided in a friend back there—a policeman—and he offered to come help."

[3.] Jennie Rogers opened the Temple of Aphrodite in 1880. It was a two-story magnificent structure with five faces carved in rose stone on the exterior around a full bosomed lady above a leering man winking up at her. Jennie was kindhearted and gave homes to the destitute. She died in 1909.

Molly learned Jennie's friend headed straight for one of Jennie's politically ambitious customers and asked him to loan her the money she needed. The man refused so the friend decided to force the politician's hand. By dead of night, he crept onto the politician's grounds, buried an Indian skull in a corner of the yard, and then confronted the politician the next day with a fabricated story about having seen a murder committed on his property. Stuttering and stammering, the politician denied any such thing but the lawman went straight to the burial place and unearthed the skull. Now threatened with hanging, the politician became desperate to find a way out of his predicament.

"Maybe if you help my friend Jennie with the money she needs, I can overlook this dastardly deed," the officer suggested.

Relieved, the tycoon nearly fell over himself agreeing with the arrangement. Jennie could have all the money she wanted, he promised.

The policeman quietly returned to St. Louis so Jennie was able to take on her ambitious task of turning her place into the show-stopping business she nicknamed the Temple of Aphrodite. A horseshoe-shaped enclosure filled with bright flowers led right to the front door.

Molly stayed on at Mattie's place for several months but when Mattie returned to work, Molly decided to move on. Next stop: Dodge City.

Chapter 16

May 1878

May 21, 1878

Dearest Da and Mum,
Life is good. I have been training as a business manager. You would be proud. I've met some unusual people here in the west. Some I even call friends.

Lovingly,
Maggie

In the early days of settlement of the Old West, Dodge City, Kansas earned the reputation of being the true beating heart of the untamed frontier. Established in 1865 to provide safety from marauding Indians, Fort Dodge quickly evolved into being the commercial stopover for travelers headed to or from Missouri and New Mexico. An old rancher, Henry Stitler, was first to build himself a sod house east of the fort where traders and buffalo hunters could stop and rest a bit but, within a year, a town grew up around him and was named after Richard Irving Dodge. The town was known as the buffalo capital of the world up until the huge bovines were slaughtered nearly to extinction. After that came the longhorn cattle era when herds arrived for marketing from all points south along the Chisholm Trail. But it was the arrival of the Atchison, Topeka and Santa Fe Railroad that catapulted Dodge City into being a thriving, exciting city filled with shops, restaurants, blacksmith shops, medical offices, and dozens of dance halls catering to rowdy travelers wanting to drink, gamble and carouse. Cowboys, soldiers and railway workers were brought together in what could only be considered a bad mix in every aspect. Front Street was wild and lawless. Fighting was routine with shootouts and killings that left bodies littering the ground. At first they were buried where they fell but that practice became a problem. Boot Hill, so named because gunfight victims were buried with their boots still on, was finally designated as a better burial place high on a barren, windswept hilltop overlooking the town.

Law and order arrived wearing the names of legendary lawmen Wyatt Earp[4], Bat Masterson and Charlie Bassett. Wyatt had the reputation of being a fast shooter and a hard fighter despite being a naturally amiable fellow when not riled. He was good natured and attended church regularly, always distinctively dressed in a black overcoat covering a white shirt and black tie. He wore a black Stetson hat and had a trademark handlebar moustache.

Wyatt's brothers were much like him, always on the move back and forth across the west, restless and driven. When not working as lawmen, they drove horse and mule teams carrying heavy equipment or rode shotgun on stagecoaches carrying passengers and gold. On occasion they hired on as manual labor for the Union Pacific Railroad and plowed the earth so rails could be set into place. Their reputations, however, came from bringing in lawmen, especially in towns that previously had none.

Lawmen weren't exactly welcome in Dodge. The locals rather enjoyed getting drunk and shooting up the town whenever they felt like it. When Bat Masterson was hired as the first sheriff, he realized the job was bigger than himself so he sent for backup. Wyatt and Morgan Earp came to help, as did Basset.

Front Street was declared weapon free. No guns would be allowed along either side of the "deadline," as the railway tracks were known. To the south of town, however, lawlessness went on as usual.

---

4. The Earp brothers were close friends with Molly, especially during their time in Murray, Idaho.

The red lantern district was also overlooked since there wasn't a man in town that didn't enjoy the pleasures of the "fairy belles" of Dodge.

It was during one of the town's many skirmishes that Wyatt found himself in big trouble, outnumbered by rowdies determined to do him in. Fortunately, a notorious gunman named Doc Holiday was watching from inside a saloon. Doc, already dying from tuberculosis, had no fear of death so stormed out of the Long Branch Saloon, guns blazing, to back Wyatt up. That brave deed cemented a deep and lasting friendship that endured for the remainder of Doc's life.

Dodge City's many saloons were open around the clock, well stocked with the finest in whiskeys, brandies, and liqueurs, all cooled down with ice. They brought in caviar, fresh fish, and exotic cheeses to serve at special performances presented by traveling entertainers from St. Paul, New York City, and Boston, and at the gambling tables, pots routinely exceeded a thousand dollars.

To Molly, this city was everything she had dreamed of and hoped for. Free, wild, exciting, and brimming with adventure. For a short time she had a room above the Long Branch Saloon. The owner hoped to make a deal with her to work right out of the saloon and, in return, she would have free room and board, a clothing allowance, and even a percentage of the saloon's daily take. Molly, flattered by the offer, declined. After having worked in Mattie Silk's bordello, everything else paled by comparison.

As it turned out, Kate Rowdy's[5] place did appeal to her. It was a small, fashionably-furnished parlor with a reputation of honesty and class. Kate was a handsome woman, tall and extremely beautiful with flaming red hair, piercing hazel-green eyes, a sharp nose, and a lopsided smile that exposed a charming gap between her two front teeth. The smile enchanted men so completely that she had all the business she could handle. Usually, she explained to Molly, she worked alone but she was in need of a partner. Perhaps Molly could help solve a problem she was having.

[5.] Kate Rowdy arrived in Dodge City in 1871. She had a soft spot for orphans and saw to it that they were cared for and well educated. She died a wealthy woman.

"Here's the straight of it. I'm a married woman but my man, Rowdy Joe Lowe, shot a cowboy down in Fort Worth and got sent to prison. I miss him terribly so I need someone to take care of my business here while I visit him. Conjugal visits are allowed in Texas. You interested in helping me?"

To Molly, the arrangement was perfect. It would enable her to once again pick and choose clients while still earning money so she agreed to the arrangement. Kate left immediately for Fort Worth.

Wyatt Earp heard of the beautiful blonde fairy-belle working out of Kate's place so decided to check her out. His usual companion, Mattie Blaylock, was away and he felt the need to spend the night with a pretty woman. He strolled into the bordello with spurs jingling, his two polished pistols hanging low on his hips barely concealed beneath the black topcoat. Molly sensed his raw energy and immediately knew who he was. Wyatt had a reputation with the ladies.

"Ms. Molly?" he asked politely, pulling off his Stetson. "I heard you're new to Dodge City so I came to introduce myself. Now I seen ya, I know the rumors to be true. You're prettier than an angel." He twisted his hat slowly in his hands then reached up to run his fingers through his dark hair. Molly liked him instantly. They become lovers that day but, more importantly, they became lifelong friends.

"I lost my wife years ago," he confided to her. "Typhoid took her and our baby. Can't seem to get over losin' 'em both. I vowed never to marry again, swore that to her on her grave. 'Course that ain't to say I don't enjoy spendin' time with ladies like yerself," he grinned.

"You fixin' to stay in Dodge?" she asked, enjoying their unhurried conversation.

"For a while. Then I'll move on. I just keep travelin' around, findin' new places, learnin' new trades. I guess I got a wanderlust in my veins so I gotta keep moving."

Molly understood completely since she felt that way, too. In a sense, they seemed to be soul mates.

Several weeks later, Kate sent word that she was headed back to Dodge after spending quality time with Joe. She was thinking of shutting down her place in Dodge and moving closer to Fort Worth so she could see him more often. They had always planned to start a family but now, with him locked up, the chances of that were nearly nonexistent so all they had together was the time she spent with him in a prison cell. She suggested Molly might want to buy the parlor house. Molly wasn't too keen on that idea, however. The last thing she wanted was to be tied down again.

As the stage Kate was riding neared Dodge City, she spotted a pretty, freckle-faced young girl walking barefoot down the road.

"Driver, stop!" she yelled, pounding on the coach door to get his attention.

Once they were stopped, Kate swung open the door and called for the girl to climb aboard before signaling for the driver to continue on.

"What's your name, youngster?" Kate asked. "And what you doing out here all alone? Where's your family?"

"Name's Eleanor," the girl replied. "Got no family 'cept for a mean cuss of an uncle who beats me all the time. I couldn't stand it no more so I run off." She flicked her tawny braids back across her shoulders.

"Where you headed, and how you planning to live? You can't be more than fourteen."

"I ain't got no idea how I'll earn my way," the girl shrugged. "Somebody told me Dodge City's always needin' dance hall girls. They wear pretty clothes and sparkly jewels. I'd like that. Reckon I'll be a dancer."

"You're just a child, Eleanor. That's no life for a youngster."

"It's the only life I ever heard of. Got no education so can't do much else. Uncle says I'm only good sprawled on my back with m' legs spread—and he done gave me plenty of practice doing that. I'll like it in the city, I suspect. It can't be worse than what I ran away from."

As they rode into Dodge City, Eleanor's eyes lit up at the sight of so much activity. Kate patted her on the knee then decided to offer her a choice. If she were interested, Katie would take her in as a ward.

"Let me give you a good life," she offered. "I'll get schooling for you, provide you with a home, and take care of you until you're grown. All you have to do is treat me like I'm your mother or your aunt."

Eleanor immediately grew suspicious. "Why would you do that for me? You don't know nothin' about me."

"My man's locked up in prison. We never got the chance to have young'uns of our own but I always wanted a daughter. If you'll be my girl, I'll make sure you're raised proper. If you hate the arrangement, you can leave at any time. You interested?"

Eleanor's smile gave her the answer she wanted.

Once things were settled and business returned to normal at the parlor house, Molly teased Kate by calling her a softhearted madam. "I hope there's a place in heaven for people like you," she added. "It's good what you're doing."

"The arrangement will benefit us both," Kate smiled. "Up until I found Eleanor, I was ready to leave Dodge. Now I think I'll stay. As for heaven, I doubt God will give me credit for much but maybe Eleanor will grow up with choices. I never had many in my life, did you?"

Molly didn't answer. Instead she asked Kate about something else that kept bothering her. "Does it matter to you that we're gonna burn in Hell because we're whores?" Her eyes looked beyond Kate to the boardwalk below and the many pedestrians.

"I don't think on it much. Ain't got the time nor the inclination. I tried being a regular church goer once upon a time but I realize now it probably doesn't do much good to pray for God's mercy if I'm just gonna keep on whoring. Used to be that Joe took care of me but when he got into trouble it left me on my own. Now, come Hell or high water, I am what I am. At least I know where my next meal's comin' from and where I'll sleep each night. Didn't plan things this way but life gets in the way." Kate smiled sadly then grew quiet, lost in her thoughts.

"How come you're a fairy-belle?" she asked Molly after a while. "You're smart and pretty. Why did you pick this life? Why ain't you a school marm or a married woman with a passel of young 'uns?"

"This life wasn't my choice either," Molly admitted. "It was my husband's doings. He wanted more money coming in."

"Is he dead?" Kate laughed loudly. "If my man did that to me, he'd be dead!"

Molly laughed. "He is dead—to me. Probably went back to living off his rich daddy. It'd serve him right. They belong together."

The women clicked their brandy glasses together in a hearty salute.

Molly was in the Long Branch Saloon a few months later when Wyatt strolled up and asked her if she wanted to meet another of Dodge's notorious madams, Fannie Keenan.[6] Molly agreed.

Fannie was like no other prostitute Molly would ever know. She was not only beautiful and soft spoken but gracious and kind hearted as well. By day she was known as Dora Hand, a somber-dressed humanitarian with pinned-back braids who roamed around town administering to the needy as Lady Bountiful. At night she became Fannie Keenan, one of Dodge's highest paid prostitutes. She was singing the first time Molly saw her and her voice was like an angels. Often, she learned, Fannie wandered from saloon to saloon just singing and showering men with her attentions. They called her the Queen of Fairy Bells, and none adored her more than did Wyatt. He was always close to her, fawning over her like a lovesick puppy even when Mattie Blaylock was with him. It so annoyed Mattie that she took to ingesting laudanum on a regular basis, so much so that she developed a severe dependence on the drug.

"Fannie is every man's fantasy," Molly teased Wyatt one night as they sat together listening to Fannie sing. "She certainly is your fantasy, is she not?"

Wyatt seemed mesmerized by her and admitted as much. Something about Fannie captivated him. "She's wonderful, that's all I know," he admitted. "But then, you're every man's fantasy, too,

---

6. Fannie Keenan, also known as Dora Hand, had two separate identities, one as Queen of Dodge City's fairy belles, the other as Lady Bountiful, helping the poor and downtrodden. In 1878, she was killed by a jealous lover.

Darlin'," he grinned, always ready with flattery. "It's just that, well, when Fannie sings, my heart melts."

"Fannie, your voice is magnificent," Molly exclaimed when Fannie came to sit with them. "I've never heard such lovely singing."

"It's my opera training," Fannie replied, perching herself lightly on Wyatt's knee. "I studied opera abroad. I must admit, however, my greatest joy comes in singing with the North Side Church choir." She mischievously tweaked Wyatt's ear then whispered so both could hear. "The parishioners know me as Dora Hand so don't give away my secret," she giggled.

"Wyatt's in love with you," Molly announced. "Aren't you, Wyatt?"

Wyatt smiled. "I love you both," he chuckled. "And as often as I can."

"Oh, Molly, Wyatt loves my voice, not me," Fannie beamed. "As far as pretty women go, the rascal really does love all of us but tomorrow he'll be off loving some other pretty face, won't you, Wyatt?" Her melodic laughter was so infectious they all laughed.

Molly's friendship with Fannie was sincere. She admired Fannie's tenacity at being able to maintain two different lifestyles so perfectly.

After a while, Molly noticed trouble brewing amongst Fannie's admirers. As long as Wyatt was close by to defuse the heated arguments, order was always restored but Molly began to wonder what would happen if ever Wyatt wasn't there.

"Fannie, you should get yourself a gun," Molly warned her. "Learn to defend yourself. The arguments among the men are getting more heated."

"I'm a lover, not a fighter," Fannie smiled. "Anyway, I would probably get so flustered I wouldn't remember what to do with a gun. My life's in God's hands, same as yours is. I trust Him to take care of me but if He's busy, maybe Wyatt will stand in for Him. You've got a nice little dog to protect you. I have Wyatt." She seemed so naïve that Molly began to truly fear for her.

Unfortunately, Wyatt did leave Dodge City for a quick trip to Abilene, and that's when Fannie needed him most.

Mayor James Kelley was fond of Fannie, showering her with money, gifts and everything else money could buy. Spike Kennedy, son of a wealthy Texas cattleman, was also obsessed with her. Several times, the two got into vicious fistfights over her. Fannie tried to defuse the arguments but with limited success but the hatred between the two men grew stronger. Molly rushed to the saloon one evening ready to defend Fannie, if need be, since rumors of a violent argument between the mayor and Spike had reached epic proportions. With pistol in pocket, she burst into the saloon only to learn Mayor Kelley had already banished Spike from the town. He figured Spike needed time to cool off so the vigilantes escorted him away.

"Come stay at our place," Molly insisted. "You aren't safe here."

"Spike's gone. I'll be all right," Fannie insisted. "Besides, the mayor's ill and in the hospital so I'll be staying at his place. He has a maid servant to keep me company."

Spike, however, wasn't about to let things be. Just after dawn, to rode back into Dodge fully intending to kill the mayor. He rode up to the mayor's house, pounded on the door until it began to open, then shot his pistol right through the door, emptying it on the poor unfortunate on the other side. With the deed done, he leaped onto his horse and rode out of town, laughing at how he had killed the mayor. Sadly, it was Fannie who lay dead on the floor.

The vigilantes captured Spike and brought him back to Dodge City to stand trial but without any corroborating witnesses, and with the help of his father's money, he was found innocent and set free.

Wyatt was in the courtroom when the verdict came down. Enraged, he shouted to Spike that he was a dead man. Wyatt promised to kill him for what he had done to Fannie. Terrified, Spike dashed to his horse and high-tailed it to Mexico while vigilantes held Wyatt at bay to keep him from carrying out his threat. No one saw Spike again after that but rumors eventually came back to Dodge months later that the Wyatt Brothers found him in Arizona and exacted their revenge.

Meanwhile, the distraught citizens of Dodge City wept openly over the death of their beloved Dora Hand. Her death was viewed as a tragic, senseless loss.

On the day of her funeral, hundreds of mourners lined the streets. Wyatt stood as a pallbearer alongside Doc Holiday, Charlie Bassett, and Bat Masterson who also had adored Fannie. At the cemetery, Molly watched solemnly as the simple wooden coffin was lowered into the ground in Pauper's Field. The town clergy refused to allow burial of a harlot in hallowed ground alongside proper folk. No matter the kind deeds, to them she was a sinner, plain and simple.

"Is there nowhere on earth where doves can be judged by the goodness of their hearts rather than their occupations?" Molly asked Wyatt. He glanced at her from the corner of his eye.

"'Fraid not. Nor will there be forgiveness for gunslingers like me. I guess we'll enter through Hell's gates together, Sweetheart," was all he said.

Within the week, Wyatt Earp left Dodge City for Tombstone, and Molly and Nicky headed west.

Chapter 17

July 1879

28 July 1879

Dearest Parents,
My dear friend was senselessly killed and I am heartbroken. Why is the world so cruel? I could not bear staying in Dodge City any longer and be reminded of what happened. I miss you both and long to see you again.

Your daughter,
Maggie

DRIVEN BY GROWING FRUSTRATION OVER the injustices mankind heaped upon one another, particularly prostitutes, Molly resumed her search for a place where she might be accepted as a person with a good heart rather than by her occupation. She felt women like herself were being betrayed by society for practicing a profession so highly in demand yet outside the realms of what many deemed as proper. If it was so improper, why did so many men pay so much to participate, and why were the women held responsible? Prostitution was sometimes the only way for women to earn money to live on. The rules seemed unfair and weighed heavily on Molly's mind. At the very least, Fannie deserved a proper burial.

Molly moved often, sometimes spending only days in a particular town. Always she asked where Pauper's Field was located so she could walk amongst the graves to pay her respects to forgotten doves buried there, mostly in unmarked graves. She visited Seattle, then turned south to Portland, then San Francisco. Disillusionment made her more cynical. Her only light moments came when she received mail from home.

Nicholas' father, she learned from her parents, had passed away leaving Nicholas as owner of the family business. He and his wife now had five children, including twin girls, Maggie and Nicholai. She was pleased with the names despite being disappointed that Nicholas would probably never come to America now. Not with his increasing responsibilities in Dublin. More than anyone else, it was he she longed to see, to talk to, to ask for suggestions on how to find her place in life. Only Nicholas understood the way she felt and what she longed for. During this time, Molly felt terribly alone.

The City by the Sea, San Francisco, was the tenth largest city in America during this time in history. It was a true melting pot for emigrants with its harbors jammed with vessels from every country. Shorebirds circled overhead despite constant, low-hanging clouds that kept a constant chill in the air except during the short summer months when the air turned hot and humid. Amongst the rolling hills beyond the harbor lay the city with its many businesses and enterprises being too numerous to count even in a single day.

Molly hadn't seen many Chinese laborers before coming to San Francisco. Here they made up a large part of the city's population, most having been recruited from China to work the gold mines or lay tracks for railroads linking the east to the west. The workers were industrious, thrifty and hard working—and that annoyed the non-Chinese inhabitants. The cause was the habit of the shy Chinamen keeping to themselves in tight little communities and hoarding their earnings to send back to their families in China. The whites resented the earnings being sent elsewhere rather than being spent in America. It caused strong feelings that often led to violence. Even the vigilantes turned blind eyes to atrocities committed against the Chinese. No one minded, however, when Chinese children were brought in as sex slaves. Some girls came by choice but most were bought, sold, or kidnapped into slavery by opportunistic slave traders taking advantage of desperate families having too many mouths to feed. Children as young as six often arrived as indentured servants to be sold at auctions for prices as high as $300 apiece. The younger the girl, the higher the price.

By coincidence, Molly happened upon a slave auction shortly after arriving in San Francisco. It was a cold, windy day but a rowdy crowd had formed around an auction platform where a naked child was being bid upon by several affluent-looking businessmen and a single oriental woman named Madame Ah Toy.[7]

One fellow standing near Molly explained that the girl was probably about ten years old and was indentured for ten years. Most likely, she would belong to the winner for the rest of her life. It was a very attractive deal.

"Are you saying she can be set free in ten years but will still never be free? That makes no sense," Molly exclaimed.

The man laughed. "Lady, those contracts never get paid off. Penalties are written in for everything. If a girl gets sick, if she has an accident, if she breaks a dish, all of those things add up to more and more penalties. After a while, they become greater than the original contract." He seemed proud of the fact.

"What pigs!" Molly declared loudly, causing heads to turn.

"The girls or buyers?" the man asked. "Lady, some beautiful girls walk across this sale block."

"No, you fool, it's men that are pigs!" she snapped. "Children aren't chattel. Why do you treat them that way?"

"Because they're Chinese, don't you know that? They expect this. And who are you, anyway? Some religious zealot? You sound just like Madame Ah Toy, always trying to save the innocents." The man's face turned sour.

"I'm a human being who believes everyone is entitled to dignity, especially innocent children." Turning on her heel, she clicked

---

[7.] Selina Ah Toy owned brothels in San Francisco, Sacramento, and all down the coast. Supposedly, she was the first Chinese prostitute in the area during the 1880s.

her tongue for Nicky to follow as she stomped away, sick inside over what she had seen.

Molly secured a hotel room near the beach overlooking the great Pacific Ocean. Watching the waves pounding over the sand brought back fond memories of Ireland and her life there. It would be so easy to go back home to be with loving, caring people. As it was now, Nicky was her only true friend.

At dinner one evening, she struck up a conversation with some of the locals and inquired as to who were the most successful businesswomen in San Francisco. To her surprise, all of them were prostitutes, with Selina Ah Toy being the most successful. She was the same woman Molly had seen bidding on the child at the auction block.

Madame Ah Toy, she was told, had once been a slave prostitute herself but eventually was able to buy her freedom. Since prostitution was the only life she had ever known, she decided to continue whoring. Soon she owned her own brothel. Systematically, she opened up more and more places until she owned parlors all down the coast toward Los Angeles. She brought in girls from China, Mexico, Peru, and Chili to work the houses. Unlike many other madams, Madame Ah Toy insisted on kindness and fair pay. Rather than objecting to their paying off their contracts, she encouraged it. After all, there were hundreds of other girls waiting to come to America.

Molly decided to pay Selina Ah Toy a visit.

The door was answered by a polite young servant girl dressed in a black satin kimono. She led Molly to a luxurious waiting room then disappeared behind a partitioned wall.

Moments later, Madame Ah Toy appeared.

She was a tiny woman, olive-skinned and breathtakingly beautiful despite her advancing age. Though slightly bent, she seemed surprisingly agile and was impeccably dressed in an embroidered black satin kimono adorned with silver- and blood-red threads. A lacquered cloisonné brooch was clipped onto her thick, waist-long braided hair.

"Come, sit," she said softly, motioning for Molly to sit beside her on the floor on red-satin cushioned seats. She rang a tiny brass bell to summon a servant girl into the room bearing a silver tea service and a plate of small almond cookies.

"Your home is elegant," Molly remarked, impressed by the heavy tapestries, thick rugs and extensive bamboo furnishings. Jade statuettes were everywhere, as were intricate woodcarvings and fragile paper lanterns that glistened in the lamplight. A pungent-yet-illusive scent of incense clung to the air.

"You are most kind," Madame Ah Toy replied, nodding her head up and down. "What brings you to my house?"

"Your reputation is that of a woman who provides pleasure to men."

"Ah, you are a whore, also?."

"Yes, I am. I came from Ireland."

"Are you wanting work?" she asked.

"I don't really know," Molly replied honestly. "I'm on a quest to find my destiny, wherever that might be."

"In San Francisco, business opportunities for men are great but few come to women. Men believe women worthy of one thing only. Giving them pleasure. Businessmen pay well for time with me but believe I have little worth beyond being a whore."

"Are you happy?" Molly asked, leaning forward to look deep into the woman's eyes.

Madame Ah Toy looked away, searching for the right words to answer Molly's question. "Happiness is elusive emotion found only in one's heart," she said at last. "Contentment is better word. Contentment brings one closest to true happiness. Neither can be bought with gold, that I know." Her shy smile bespoke of the wisdom of her simple words.

For over an hour, they talked and became acquainted as best they could with so little time. When it came time to leave, Madame Ah Toy toddled to the door in that rolling motion unique to oriental women whose feet had been bound since infancy in lotus fashion to keep them small.

"There is woman you should meet," Madame Ah Toy told her. She wrote a name onto a piece of paper. "She prophecies destinies. She maybe helps with your quest."

Reaching down, she touched Nicky's ear gently, causing his tail to wag vigorously. From her pocket she withdrew a small sweet cracker and offered it to him.

"Is this your true friend?" she asked sweetly as Nicky chomped the cracker down in one bite.

"My only true friend, I'm afraid," said Molly.

"May I touch ring?" she asked, admiring the serpent ring Molly now wore on her left hand. Molly held up her hand and allowed Madame Ah Toy to trace the finger's curves and jeweled eyes.

"From someone who loves you?"

"Aye, it was a gift from my father."

"Perhaps happiness is in Ireland. America is hard place for women."

Molly nodded. She had been thinking about going home again. Spontaneously, she took Madame Ah Toy's hand in her own and squeezed it gently before stepping back out onto the streets of San Francisco.

Mary Ellen Pleasant[8] was the name written on the paper. She, like Madame Ah Toy, was also a prostitute, but she was a trained voodoo priestess as well. She was born to a free Negress and a Cherokee father.

Right from their first meeting, Molly was awestruck by the woman's exceptional beauty and flawless mulatto complexion that made her midnight-black eyes so captivating. Her hourglass figure was breathtaking to behold, even to other women. Madame Pleasant personally answered the door to her bordello dressed in a tight fitting copper-toned gown heavily trimmed in brown and gray feathers. Molly arrived dressed in a blue satin gown that set off her blue eyes and golden curls partially hidden by her feather-adorned hat.

"Welcome to my cottage," Madame Pleasant laughed since the cottage was actually a two-story mansion lavishly decorated from

---

8. Mary Ellen Pleasant was a beautiful Philadelphia born mulatto who moved to San Francisco in 1850. She practiced voodoo and black magic. She was personal mentor to Francis Bell until his mysterious death in 1892 of voodoo magic. Madame Pleasant died at age ninety-two.

top to bottom in rainbow colors and scores of ruby-red baubles that hung down from the high ceilings. All of the windows were done up in painted glass as well. The pungent smell of incense was highly noticeable.

"Come in, little hound," she said, clicking her tongue at Nicky who immediately liked her.

"What a magnificent palace," Molly exclaimed.

"Thank you," the woman laughed, her eyes twinkling. Molly couldn't help but smile.

They sat beside a crackling fire that seemed to hold back the chill of the day.

"Do you need a potion, perhaps a spell placed on someone?" she asked, her face growing serious. Even more than prostitution, she loved voodoo spell casting.

"No, I am looking for a brothel with room in it for another dove. Me."

"Why would you want a room when you despise whoring so much?" she responded, already tuning in to Molly's emotions and concerns. "I sense you are not really looking for a room but rather are looking for enlightenment. Is that true?" Her dark eyes were suddenly penetrating and sober.

"It was not my first choice in life," Molly said.

"What was your first choice?"

The question caught Molly by surprise. She hadn't considered the type of life she would have chosen if things had gone differently.

"I'm an adventurer. That's what gives me happiness. Sadly, it doesn't buy me food and shelter." Molly felt oddly uncomfortable now since Madame Pleasant was studying her intensely. She seemed to be learning more by watching her than Molly wanted her to know.

The Madame leaned forward, taking hold of Molly's hand and turned it palm-side up. She traced the lines with her finely-manicured fingertips. "Hm, I see why you are so unsettled, Ms. Molly. There has been much turmoil in your life, and there is much more to come. Still, I see a line leading toward love and commitment." She raised her eyes to meet Molly's. "Are you ready for that love?"

Molly could only sputter, shaking her head defiantly. "No, I'm not ready to love anyone. Love only leads to betrayal." Her eyes gave away her deepest fears.

Madame Pleasant released her hand and stared at Molly for several long minutes. Then, shaking her head as though dislodging strange thoughts, she ordered a strong tea brought in to allow her time to study Molly further.

"My talent is in setting up love matches," she whispered to Molly. "It's what I do best. Even better than pleasuring men. The millionaire Thomas Bell was one of my most well-known clients. I set him up with an enchanting young fairly-belle named Teresa Clingan. Of course he was smitten with her immediately and begged to have her as his own personal mistress. It was a perfect match.

"There have been many others as well. Only one turned out poorly. If the stupid girl had only minded her behavior, that one would have been perfect, too." She scowled then shook her head in disgust. "Sarah Hill was matched up with the owner of a large hotel owned by Senator William Sharon. The foolish girl had a loose tongue that spoiled an otherwise perfect union. Everyone, including me and the Senator, grew tired of her sassiness. He kicked her right out onto the street. I offered use of voodoo to fix things but the little fool didn't trust my spells. People should never distrust my spells." Her face turned stone serious when she said that.

Talking with Madame Pleasant was not only a fascinating experience but an informative one as well. She exhibited a personality completely different from any she had known. No one Molly knew had such a passion about a second occupation as did this woman.

"Do you believe in voodoo, Molly Burdan?"

"I know nothing about voodoo. Is it witchcraft?"

"Mercy, no! Where did you hear such nonsense? Voodoo is much more powerful than witchcraft. It affects people's minds as well as their actions. If you ever need a spell cast, come to me. I am the best voodoo priestess in the west."

Her eyes locked with Molly's as she raised a smoldering incense closer to her nostrils, inhaling deeply of its vapors. Her eyes rolled back in her head.

"I see troubled times ahead for you, Molly. Disappointments, danger. You distrust men and that will cause you to push away the one who truly desires to love and protect you. Be wary. Your destiny will be bound to his as is your hope for happiness."

Suddenly, her eyes were open again and she stood to escort Molly to the door.

"Your stay in San Francisco will be short. Go to Bertha Kahn. She will provide you with a time of rest and seclusion. Beyond that, you must go where destiny leads. If you need a voodoo spell, call on me." A bright smile flashed across her face then was instantly gone. Molly left her house with a sense of uneasiness.

Bertha Kahn's[9] parlor was unlike any Molly had yet experienced but, like Madame Pleasant predicted, it was a place of peace and harmony. It was a plain white parlor house with a grandmother figure as its owner.

Bertha, as she insisted on being called, was large and plump with a sweet smile that produced tiny wrinkles at the corners of her baby-blue eyes. Her thin silver hair was meticulously braided and pinned back just above the nape of her neck above the high collar of her gingham gown. She appeared to be more of a pioneer woman than a guardian of young prostitutes yet she maintained firm control over all her charges.

"Thirty sisters live here," she told Molly after passing pleasantries with her in the waiting room. "Everyone dresses similarly and all the girls behave properly."

Indeed, the young women were all freshly bathed and dressed in white-lace nightgowns with simple red accessories. They padded around the parlor in bare feet waiting for gentlemen callers to arrive. When they did, a tiny golden bell summoned all the giggling girls to the common area where they sat properly while the men paced back and forth in front of them trying to decide which one to spend time with. Once the selection was made, Bertha whispered into the chosen girl's ear that a man wished to speak with her in private. Only

---

[9]. Bertha Kahn lived in San Francisco in the 1870s. Her parlor offered only doves of genteel nature, refined and proper.

then would the girl shyly ascend the stairs to wait for her gentleman to follow. As he approached the stairs, Bertha collected payment.

"If you wish to work here, are you willing to dress like the other girls?" Bertha asked Molly, her eyes looking over Molly's attire.

"I'm afraid I would be most uncomfortable doing that," Molly replied. "This is the way I've always dressed." She looked down at her midnight-blue gown with its many rows of lace.

"Do you have any talents, perhaps musical?"

"I can fiddle," Molly replied.

"Then it's settled," Bertha beamed. "Sunday is our day of rest. We read, sing and simply enjoy ourselves during the family time, as we call it. If you care to play for us, you may join our family and wear whatever type of clothing you choose."

The weeks that followed were as Madame Pleasant promised. Times of rest and healing.

Chapter 18

April 1880

14 April 1880

Dearest Parents,
    The curse of wanderlust is upon me again.
Why I am so driven, I do not understand. If ever
I find my place in the world, I shall want you to
come immediately to visit me.

Your daughter,
Maggie

I N LESS THAN A YEAR, Molly and Nicky left San Francisco for the gold mining town of Virginia City, Nevada. While dining at the Gold Nugget Saloon, she met Julia Bulette.[10] Like birds of a feather, they were instantly drawn together by shared interests and ambitions, and the bond was not only instant but deep.

Julia was stunningly beautiful, with a full, voluptuous figure and a Creole complexion so flawless people would stop her on the street just to admire her. Walnut-brown eyes looked out at the world from beneath lengthy lashes as dark as her chestnut brown hair. She exhibited such a genuine warmth and bright outlook on the world

---

[10.] Julia Bulette was born in 1832 in England, arriving in Virginia City in 1859. She was a kind, generous dove brutally murdered in 1867 for her belongings. The ladies of the city brought gifts to her killer's cell to thank him for killing her.

that people, especially men, couldn't help but like her. She was called the darling of Virginia City, even amongst some women.

When she offered Molly a room at Julia's Palace, Molly accepted immediately. Julia's Palace was simple but well furnished with furniture and gifts given to her by adoring customers. She placed small value on worldly things but reveled in displaying gifts her men brought to her, particularly the music boxes and crystal figures. The gifts represented love, not wealth.

The men of Virginia City nicknamed Julia the "dark-skinned beauty" and Molly the "fair-haired fairy belle." Both women were very popular.

"How do you like my town?" Julia asked after Molly had been there a few weeks. "Do you like my place?"

Molly nodded. It wasn't the largest parlor she had ever seen but it radiated good taste.

"What you see are the simple things that give me pleasure," she explained. "My favorite is this locket from my darling Tom." She rubbed her fingers across it then toyed with the golden chain.

"Have you read all those books?" Molly asked, gesturing toward the bookcases.

"Oh, no," she smiled. "I'm a poor reader. I just enjoy looking at them so I can pretend I'm educated and worldly."

With Julia, Molly found a new sense of happiness. She became such a positive role model that Molly couldn't help but respond. She smiled more, she welcomed back the sunshine, she indulged herself in taking lengthy horseback rides across the desert just to witness the cactus blossoms in bloom. But mostly, she basked in the light of a growing friendship with the woman she considered to be more of a sister than a friend.

Julia's determination to help those less fortunate was another trait rubbing off on Molly. At Julia's insistence, they both spent daylight hours searching out needy souls who lacked food, shelter, or caring. Orphaned youngsters took top priority.

"Why did ye come to this little minin' town?" Molly asked Julia one morning, allowing an Irish lilt to slip back into her speech. "Why not Denver or Portland or some other large city?"

"Oh, that's easy to explain," said Julia, her eyes turning wistful as she watched the breeze playing with the leaves of a tree outside her parlor window. The sweet scent of apple blossoms blended with that of new tulips poking through the earth. "People like me here. They accept me even though I'm a fallen dove." She laughed at her words. "Let me amend that statement. The men accept me and a few of the women do, too, even though most of them probably would be happier if I weren't around.

"I traveled the world before I came here. Europe, Spain, the Orient, even Ireland. I visited ancient cathedrals, touched golden idols, and even rode on the back of an elephant in India. I've seen more in my short life than most people experience in a lifetime—yet this is the place where I feel I belong. I'm appreciated here and that makes me happy. Do you understand?"

"I'm tryin'," Molly answered. "I guess I'm jealous of what ye found. I'm still lookin' fer m' own place. Are ye plannin' to retire from pleasurin' men someday?"

"Never," Julia laughed. "I chose this life, it didn't choose me. Making men happy makes me happy, and I'm grateful when they want to give me gifts of appreciation. They don't have to but they want to because they love me. That means a great deal. Besides, being a prostitute lets me enjoy things other women only dream of—unbridled passion, love, wealth, freedom, even security.

"And what skeletons does Molly keep so carefully hidden? You hide your emotions well, Molly. Are you ever gonna tell me what it is that bothers you so much?"

For the first time since leaving Boston, Molly told her story beginning with her disappointment in Nicholas for not coming with her to America, then David's betrayal. She even faulted the church for abandoning her in her hour of greatest need. Rather than helping her, it had excommunicated her and promised her a life in Hell. She even told of her guilt for abandoning Charlie, especially after he had helped her so much. Mostly, however, Molly voiced her anger at the world in general for judging women like herself whose hearts were good and their deeds admirable.

"You didn't abandon your uncle," Julia replied. "You found him an orphan girl to fill your spot. That's important, surely you know that. You helped his business grow. I know money doesn't drive you, Molly, but it matters to some people. I'm suspecting it isn't the world you're mad at. It's David. You trusted him but he betrayed you so you can't forgive him. Maybe it's time to put the past to rest once and for all. It's gone. Let it go. Besides, if all of those things hadn't happened, you and I would never have met! How sad would that be?" She squeezed Molly's arm.

"Ye think I'm blamin' it all on David?" Molly asked, somewhat taken aback by Julia's analysis.

"Maybe."

"He was a charmin' devil, I'll give ye that," Molly laughed.

"Do you trust me?" Julia asked suddenly.

"Aye, I trust ye, but then ye're no man." They locked eyes then burst into laughter.

"We'll just have to build new dreams for you and set the old ones free to fly away like spring butterflies," Julia decided, fluttering around the room with arms waving up and down and skirts twirling. "We will set Molly free, free, free," she sang.

Summer gave way to autumn as Molly came to terms with her new emotions. Then winter came and went, surrendering to spring and the desert wildflowers that burst into bloom, brilliantly painted by Mother Nature's pallet. Sadly, with it came the wanderlust that always seemed to plague Molly when she felt she was settling into a permanent life. Nicky felt it, too, and paced the floor, sniffing under the door and barking at every sound.

"Molly, dear, forgive me for saying this but you're behaving like a caged feline. Are you thinking of moving on?" Julia asked one morning as the two women sat together enjoying tea and biscuits. They were both casually dressed in satin sleeping gowns, Julia in her favorite deep purple and Molly in scarlet. Their locks hung free, still rumpled from sleep, but they didn't care since gentlemen callers never came this early.

"Spring does this to me," Molly admitted. She stirred the minted tea, waiting for it to cool. Julia had a passion for dark tea, especially when sweetened with honey and fresh cream.

Julia's cat, Fluff, lay on her lap playfully swiping a paw down at Nicky who watched warily from beneath Molly's chair. "Are you planning to leave me?" Julia asked Molly.

"Aye, m' soul is yearning to move on," Molly replied. "It's leavin' ye behind that's causin' me stress. I've come to love ye like a sister, and I've not had a sister before."

"Then stay with me," Julia pleaded, reaching out to cover Molly's hand with her own. "You've a place here always, you know that don't you?"

"I do, and that means more t' me than anythin'." Molly poured more tea from the porcelain teapot and refreshed it with cream, stirring it slowly before adding a jigger of Irish whiskey. "Ye taught me to enjoy tea, that's what ye've done," she commented as she raised the cup to her lips. "Before now, I only thought of m'self as a whiskey drinkin' girl."

"Molly, I'm serious. Stay with me," Julia coaxed. "'Tis not an offer I make lightly. My heart will break if you leave."

"'Tis that what keeps me here. I'll miss seeing ye in purple silks and fur, that's for certain. No one wears purple like ye do."

"Diamonds are good, too," Julia laughed, flipping open the lid on a gilded music box given to her by Tom, her favorite lover. She withdrew a brilliant topaz ring set in a bed of diamonds and slid it onto her finger. "I tell you this in strictest confidence. I wear purple because it reminds the pious biddies of this town how much their men like pretty ladies. If they wanted to keep their men at home, they would be taking lessons from us and dressing as we do. A bit of naughty behavior in the bedroom wouldn't hurt either. It would keep their men in their own beds—but then, it would put us out of work, right?"

The two women were still giggling when the bell above the door signaled the arrival of a client. With a heavy sigh, Julia pushed the kitten off her lap and padded to the door.

"Who could be calling at this hour?" she wondered, faking annoyance. "I never take clients before midday." Peering through the curtains, she recognized Tom.

"Oh, it's just my darling Tom," she said as she swung open the door and hugged him warmly.

Molly politely dismissed herself but not until she graced Tom with a smile as she brushed past him.

"If ye weren't already taken, ye'd be my man," she whispered, chucking him under the chin.

Tom's face turn beet red as he nervously glanced over at Julia who was faking a dark scowl.

"Get to your room, you hussy," she told Molly, "or I'll have to scratch your eyes out."

They all laughed.

Alone in her room, Molly resumed pacing from window to door and back again. She lifted the curtain at the window and stared down to the boardwalk and the bustling hoards of incoming miners and restless cowboys. With a heavy sigh, she sat down on the bed, coaxed Nicky up beside her.

"It's time to move on, little one, as much as I hate to. The question is, where shall we go? North to Utah Territory or into Idaho or Montana? What do ye think?"

Nicky s eyes were closed in sleep.

A week later, when the stage bound for Utah Territory pulled up, Julia and Molly hugged each other good-bye. Both women were crying.

"I fear I shall never see ye again," Molly wept. "Will ye visit me when I find a place?"

"I will. And no matter what, we are friends forever, bound in spirit as well as soul. If we don't meet again in this life, we'll meet in the next." Julia leaned back against Tom for moral support.

As the coach rolled away with Molly in it, she turned and waved one last time to Julia Bulette.

Chapter 19

May 1882

19 May 1882

Dear Mum and Da,
    I left Nevada for the goldfields of Montana. Sadly, my dearest friend is still in Nevada and I miss her terribly. She is like a sister to me. I wish you could meet her.

Your loving daughter,
Maggie

U PON REACHING OGDEN IN UTAH Territory, Molly secured a stagecoach ticket to Virginia City, Montana. Riding the stage was notably more uncomfortable than traveling by rail but Molly enjoyed it since it allowed her more time to experience the countryside with its sage-covered prairies and miles of tall desert grasses that waved so gracefully in the wind.

The trail took them into Idaho Territory past several small Mormon settlements before entering a mountain-surrounded valley where a small settlement was still in its earliest infancy. Pocatello Junction, named after a warring Shoshone Indian chief based high in the Salmon River country, was a stage station where the Utah and Northern railroads merged together in 1879. Through the center of town meandered a river known as the Portneuf.

Riding in the coach with Molly were two somber, heavily-bearded Amish elders who sat in stoic silence, their eyes always focused on the countryside. Nicky lay across their shoes but they didn't seem to mind. The ride was unusually rough this early in the year so the passengers continually rocked back and forth, holding tight to the door railings and dodging loose parcels that bounced around on the floors and seats.

The stagecoach drivers were young fellows, their faces darkly tanned by constant exposure to the sun. The coating of dust they also wore gave them a ghostly hue. Snapping the whips and reins, they kept the horses moving fast while still watching for renegade Shoshones. One of the drivers bore had a striking resemblance to Wyatt's brother, Morgan, so Molly kept an eye on him. He sat with a rifle on his lap, ready to use if need be. The other driver was the one that kept the whip cracking over the rumps of the sweating horses.

"To the west's the Snake River," the Morgan-look-alike yelled down. "See the antelope?"

Craning her neck, Molly leaned to the window to see a herd of over fifty antelopes grazing on the open plains. Always curious, the pronghorns raised their heads to watch the stagecoach career past. Long-eared jackrabbits dashed across the trail followed by a coyote half again the size of Nicky.

"Where are the buffalo?" Molly asked the men.

"Gone. Killed off by buffalo hunters and redskins. A sinful waste," one of the Amish men replied.

"A real shame," the other parroted.

Molly had hoped to see bison. She'd heard about them even before leaving Ireland.

Her musings were interrupted by their arrival at Fort Hall Trading Post where thousands of west-bound emigrants had once passed through headed for Utah, Oregon and California. The fort was built near the river by the military to keep out hostile Indians. It housed living quarters, stables, extra horses, and supply rooms.

"Ya can git a cold drink here," the Earp-look-a-like suggested, politely tipping his hat to Molly before going about his business. A flock of yellow-headed blackbirds swarmed out of a patch of wild sunflowers as he strode toward the trading post.

Molly stood in awe as she watched the enormous Snake River flowing by. The grasses along the banks were bright green and grew clear down into the willows near the water. "It's no wonder immigrants found relief here," she said to herself. "This place is an oasis!"

A few grubby, near-naked Indian children played in the dirt just outside the spiked fence surrounding the fort. Their parents were seated nearby in the shade keeping watch. They didn't move much nor did they react when the passengers and drivers walked by.

After finishing their tasks, the drivers plunged their heads deep into the horse-watering trough to cool down, shook off the water, then dipped a metal cup into a bucket of cold well water, drinking deeply before ordering the passengers back on board.

"Next stop, Eagle Rock!"

The Amish men decided to stay a while at the trading post but a handsome Indian woman and her two small daughters climbed in beside Molly just before the stage pulled out.

As the stage rolled on down the trail, Molly wondered about two unusual hills jutting up in the far distance.

As if in answer to a question, one of the drivers yelled down that the hills were dormant volcanoes that spilled molten lava onto the plains thousands of years ago. "You'll see the dried lava right soon now. It's jagged and hostile and can tear a man's boots to pieces."

True to those words, the lava beds soon appeared. Molly was surprised by the tiny wildflowers and cactus blooms growing in amongst the harsh crevices as though showing off in the midst of an extremely hostile environment.

Thick stands of poplar trees came into view as the stage neared the settlement of Eagle Rock. The trees were occupied by a number of Bald eagles.

"This town used to be Hunter's Ferry," the driver said. "Now it's called Eagle Rock because of all the eagles. See the one on the cliff in the river? Eagles don't share well so their nests are where they can be protected from scavengers."

Fascinated by the enormous birds, Molly watched as one having a wingspan of over six feet took to the air. The midday sun reflected off his white head as he rode the wind currents high into the sky, his keen eyes staring at the river waters below. Then a piercing, screeching call split the air and his wings folded back against his body as he plunged toward the river. Molly gasped. It was certain the eagle would crash into the blue-green waters but just he reached the river, his legs and talons shot forward into the water, his giant wings fanned out and beat effortlessly to carry him upward, a flopping silver trout clutched in his talons. He flew directly to the nest on the rock.

Molly was dumbstruck by the scenario that had played out right before her eyes. "Did you see that?" she declared excitedly. "That was marvelous! I've never seen anything like that, have you?" She clapped her hands joyfully and grinned at the wonder of it all.

The children giggled and the Indian woman smiled. "Eagles sacred to Indians," she said.

"This is amazing country," Molly exclaimed. "Wild creatures are everywhere." Perhaps, she thought to herself, she would stay a while and explore this marvelous country.

The stage braked to a stop in front of a small hotel where the driver explained there would be an overnight stop. A wheel hub was cracked and needed replacing. Tomorrow they would resume the journey into Montana. They then tossed the freight onto the ground, slapped the dust off their clothes, and headed toward the saloon for a drink. The day was already hot.

The door of the stagecoach was opened from the outside by a young man who extended a helping hand to Molly and the Indian family.

"Ma'am," said the tall half-breed standing at the door, "may I help you down?" His blue eyes locked with hers and held her captive with their brilliance. His deep bronze complexion was off-set by a thick head of curly black hair barely concealed by his hat.

Molly accepted his hand, instantly aware of the strength of his arms. When she stepped onto the ground, she repaid him with a dazzling smile.

He helped the Indian woman and the children disembark, too, then turned back to Molly.

"Welcome to Eagle Rock. I'm Sam Maddison. There are rooms to rent down the street," he said, pointing to the saloon, "or there is a boarding house down there. I'd take the boarding house," he whispered. "Fewer bedbugs." His face lit up with a bright smile causing Molly's heart to skip a beat.

"I think I'll choose the boarding house," she decided, slipping her hand beneath his elbow. "Do you suppose they furnish baths?"

"I'm sure of it," he grinned, escorting her down the dusty street. The Indians disappeared in the opposite direction.

Nicky was panting heavily. The day had turned exceptionally hot and he needed a drink. When he spotted a horse-watering trough, he ran on ahead, stretching up on his hind legs to reach the cool water. When he was finally sated, he ran back to where Molly and Samuel were watching so they could continue on to the boarding house.

"The dog has the right idea. Would you like a cool drink once you've freshened up?"

"You're a bit young to go into saloons, aren't you?" she asked sweetly, toying with him.

"I assure you, I'm old enough," he replied. "I'm twenty-nine."

"No!" she gasped playfully. "Well, in that case, yes, I'd love to have a drink with you."

An hour later, Molly entered the saloon where Sam was waiting. As usual, her entrance caused everyone to stop and stare. She was dressed in light blue cotton, her soft, golden curls piled back behind her neck. Sam's breath caught in his throat when he saw her standing in the doorway.

"You do know how to make an entrance," Sam grinned as he escorted her to his table. "Tell me, what would you like to drink?"

"Whiskey, straight up. The trip's been long and I am very thirsty." She sat down and brushed at the wrinkles in her dress.

"Bartender, the lady wants whiskey."

She downed the first drink in one fast swallow then motioned for another.

"Can't say I ever met a whiskey-drinking lady before," Sam confessed, humor in his expression.

"Who says I'm a lady?" she winked, leaning close to him. "Would you believe it if I told you I can box like an Irishman? Want a demonstration?"

"No, no, I'll just settle for a drink, if that's all right," he laughed. "What's your name, Girl?"

"I go by Molly Burdan."

"Are you married?"

"Not anymore, I'm happy to say. So is Eagle Rock your home, Mr. Maddison?"

"Sam's what people call me. And no, I don't live here. I'm looking for livestock. Mustangs, to be exact. They're tough little horses so I figure they'd add strong stock to my herd. What I don't keep I'll sell to other Mormon ranchers."

"You're a Mormon?" Molly asked. She had heard of the religious sect that was driven out of Missouri to settle in the Salt Lake valley. "Someone told me Mormons have green horns. Is that true?" Her fingers toyed with the whiskey glass, her eyes locked with his.

"Do you see any?" he asked, removing his hat and rumpling his curls.

"No, don't see any," she admitted, admiring his thick dark hair.

"That's good. I try to keep them pushed down." He set his hat on the table then grinned at her again. He couldn't seem to take his eyes off her.

Molly didn't board the stagecoach to Montana the next day, nor the day after. Instead, she spent every waking hour with Sam Maddison.

Sam, she learned, had a white father and a Nez Perce mother. When the father took a second wife and became a polygamist, Sam's mother threw him out of their house leaving Sam to assume responsibility for their horse-raising business. His father went on the run from the authorities searching for polygamist Mormons.

"I'll be needing a horse when I get to Montana," Molly declared, changing the subject. "Would you help me find one?"

"Can you ride?" he asked.

"Oh, yes, cowboy, this girl can ride," she laughed, spontaneously touching his hand.

They agreed to meet at the sale ring on the edge of town the next morning where a new batch of mustangs had just been brought in.

Sam was already there, perched on the lower pole of the corral looking over the horses when she arrived. She climbed up beside him, met his smile, then watched the horses milling nervously around. Molly extended her fingers hoping to entice a curious horse to come closer. And it worked. A small white mare with a half-black face took the bait and moved right up to Molly. She snuffled loudly as she smelled Molly's fingers but only flinched once when Molly tried to rub behind her ears. Molly tried again and this time succeeded. The mare enjoyed the feeling so pushed in closer.

The mare wasn't a very large horse but her freckled legs appeared strong and that pleased Molly. She would need a horse with endurance. She continued stroking the pony on the neck, nose and behind her ears. Another horse tried to muscle in and that caused the mare to turn sideways to keep the competition away. All the while she kept gazing up at Molly with innocent-looking chocolate-brown eyes. When the interloper horse tried again to get close, the white mare's ears lay back and she bared her teeth just before she kicked at the other horse, warning her to stay away. She was in no mood to share Molly's attentions. Nicky crawled under the fence to bark at the feisty little mare then quickly backed away when the mare kicked at him, too.

"What was that all about?" Molly laughed, leaning back from the fence. "You know, Sam, this mare has my personality. Can I ride her?"

"With or without a saddle," he chortled. "I presume you don't do side saddle."

"Not a chance," she grinned, hopping off the fence and hurrying for the gate.

The mare, Sam learned, had been ridden a few times already so probably could be ridden by someone with riding experience. Sam sensed Molly was no novice at riding so ordered the mare saddled up.

Minutes later, Molly had hold of the reins, hiked up her skirts, and effortlessly swung into the saddle. She took a moment to straighten her clothes then nodded toward the gate. After a bit of nervous fidgeting, the mare accepted the woman's weight and settled down.

"She's only been ridden a few times," the owner warned. "She may buck."

Molly nudged her heels gently into the mare's flank, cautiously circling the corral a few times before telling the men to drop the gate.

"We're going for a run!" she exclaimed.

"Molly, wait. She's not ready. It's too soon," Sam yelled but she was already at the gate.

When the top two poles hit the ground, the mare became airborne, effortlessly leaping over the poles in a headlong gallop toward the open prairie. Molly leaned into the gallop, giving the horse her head while Nicky yapped frantically as he tried to keep up. Soon the trio disappeared from view.

"You wanna go after her?" the owner asked.

"If you're worried about the mare, I'll follow. If you're worried about the woman, I don't think so. She's a helluva lady!"

An hour passed before the exhausted threesome returned to the holding pen. Molly's hair had fallen free down around her face. Her skirts were high above her thighs exposing her bare legs for all to see, but she didn't care. The ride had been exhilarating and the glow on her cheeks spoke more than words could say. She hadn't known such happiness since leaving Ireland.

"Oh, I have missed riding," Molly exclaimed breathlessly, falling out of the saddle right into Sam's outstretched arms. "Write up the bill of sale. She's mine, no matter the cost! Her name is Willow, by the way. Now, I need a drink."

In the days that followed, Molly and Sam rode together, walked arm in arm along the river, took their meals together, and allowed a bond to develop between them.

"I need to head back to Utah pretty soon," Sam told her one evening. "Mother will be wondering where I am."

"Where's your father?"

"Somewhere in Montana. We don't often hear from him but his reputation as a horse trader is so good I can always ask around and find out where he is. Somebody said he's working the timber fields in Idaho Territory right now."

"Aren't you angry at him for leaving?"

"No, anger's a wasted emotion. He did what he thought was right, that's about all there is to say about that. We were friends before he left and we're still friends. It's just that things are different now. He always was a good father. He taught me a lot."

"Doesn't it bother you he has two wives? I'd never share my husband with another women." Then she smiled to herself. David hadn't minded sharing her, however. Truth was, he rather enjoyed it. She blinked back the transient thought and turned her attentions back to Sam.

"Most Mormons don't practice polygamy. I never thought my father would either since he and mother seemed to love each other so much. When he took a Shoshone wife, all he said was there were reasons why he did so. He'd been away for a while so we never knew what had happened. Before I could quiz him about it, he was gone, and my mother's heart was broken. She's a hot-blooded Nez Perce, though, so she rose to the challenge of raising me and my siblings without help. He couldn't have brought his new wife into our house anyway. The Shoshone and Nez Perce tribes never have gotten along well."

Sam was quiet after that. When he spoke again, he asked about her family.

"Dublin's where I came from," she replied. "Mum is a fabulous cook and Da is a goldsmith. I've got cousins there, too. My best friend was my cousin Nicholas. Named the dog after him." She reached down and patted Nicky on the head.

"I don't think I could have left my family like that," Sam said.

"I always say it was my way of escaping the fighting and poverty but mostly I was after adventure. I've been here since '73. Lived a while in Boston with my Da's best friend. I was a barmaid. Then I headed west." She avoided telling him about David.

"There's more to this story, isn't there?" Sam suggested, seeing a hint of sadness on her face. "You were married?"

"Aye, there's more. Someday, I'll tell you the rest. Now, tell me, do you look like your Mum or your Da?"

"Both. Father's tall and blonde, has my blue eyes and curls. Mother's tall, too, but has thick black hair. I'm a true half breed, no question about that."

"I've never seen a blue-eyed half breed. Let me guess, you think Irish girls should all have green eyes."

"I'll admit, I did think that. You should have red hair, too, not blonde hair." He grinned.

"Someday," she confided, "I'll inherit my uncle's tavern in Boston. What do you think of that?" A mischievous smile teased her lips.

"I'm guessing you'll probably have the most popular place in town, what with that smile."

She grinned. For a brief moment she thought maybe it was time to return to Boston to check on Charlie and maybe to face David once more. "I may go back to visit someday," she admitted.

They rode the next day across the open plains, Sam taking the lead. He stopped near a thicket of willows along a small stream, dismounted then helped Molly down. The horses went right to grazing.

"Girl, I'm growing fond of you, you know that don't you?" he confided after a brief period of silence. "Would you consider staying here?"

His question caught Molly off guard. She knew there was a growing bond between them but she dared not consider it to be anything more than flirtatious. She was comfortable with flirtation but she wasn't open to love. Love was what men talked about when they wanted passion but to her it signaled commitment.

"Stay here with you?" she choked, setting aside the water canteen. The air suddenly felt hot and oppressive. "Sam, we've barely met."

"I feel as though I've known you always," he replied, reaching for her hand. "I think I've been searching for you all my life. That day when you stepped from the stagecoach, I felt in my gut that I'd found you at last. I know we've not known each other long but I also know I want to spend my life with you. I'm certain of it." Sam's face was somber.

Molly didn't know what to say. Her thoughts were reeling as Madame Pleasant's words flashed through her mind. Was this that once in a lifetime moment? Was Sam the one that would change her life? David's false promises kept grabbing hold of her, reminding her of betrayal.

"You're just infatuated with me. There's so much you don't know, where I've been, what I've done, who I've been with. If you're just wantin' to bed me, say so, but if you're wanting a commitment, I'm not sure I can give you that. I'm not ready. I have to keep moving. You don't want that, do you? A woman always on a quest to experience different places, different things?"

"I don't want to bed you, Molly," he replied, openly hurt by her suggestion. "That's not what I want, although I've considered it." A quick smile flashed across his face. "What I'm saying is that I'm falling in love with you, and whether you admit it or not, you're falling in love with me. It's written on your face. I can feel it here." He placed his hand over his heart.

"I'm not the marrying kind, Sam," she replied pulling his hand down. "I'm a prostitute. Haven't you figured that out yet? My job is pleasuring men."

Sam's expression was puzzled. Had he read her wrong?

"Do you think that matters to me? I see you as a beautiful, exciting woman but I'd feel the same if you were a plain and simple school marm." Sam was struggling to find the words he needed to convince her to stay.

"I'm leaving for Montana tomorrow, Sam," she lied, looking away.

"Girl, I don't know if I can let you go." His strong hands took hold of her shoulders and turned her around to face him.

"I'm a wanderer," she whispered, trying to avoid looking at him. Strange feelings were swirling around inside her making her feel terribly vulnerable.

"I care about you," he repeated. "I think I love you."

"I care for you, too, Sam but I'm not sure I love you. I've been hurt."

"Let me heal your wounds," he whispered, pulling her into his arms.

"I can't, not yet, not now," she cried, pushing away. "We need time apart. I can't do this, I can't."

"All right, I'll let you go but I'm coming after you after I take the herd back to Utah."

"Sam…," she tried to speak but he pressed his fingers to her lips, silencing her words.

"Molly, sometimes love happens when it's least expected. That's how it is. If by chance we've found something special, we owe it to ourselves not to let it escape. If we do, it may never come to us again. That would be tragic for both of us."

Again, Madame Pleasant's words flashed across her mind. Those had been her words, too. Don't push him away, she had warned, yet here she was, doing exactly what Madame Pleasant had warned her against.

"Go on to Montana, if you must," he told her. "Take time to think about us being together. I've got time since I've been waiting a while to find you, but I won't wait forever. I don't want to waste another day away from you. Just think about me and wait until I come for you. Will you do that?"

"I'll wait," she whispered, surprised by her answer.

Sam's kiss was gentle but only caused more confusion to Molly.

When the stagecoach rolled into Eagle Rock the next morning, Molly was there waiting but she was by no means anxious to leave. Sam quickly tethered Willow to the back of the stagecoach then gave the driver instructions not to wear the mare down and to keep her well watered. He paid the driver extra coins for the extra services. Then he faced Molly.

"It's been a pleasure, Girl," he smiled, lifting her fingers to his lips. "Watch for me in the fall, if not sooner. If you're not in Virginia City, I'll search to the ends of the earth 'til I find you."

Tears welled up in Molly's eyes.

"Don't cry, Girl. The time will pass quickly." He took Molly into his arms and held her close, stroking her soft hair, feeling the beating of her heart against his chest.

"I'll be waiting," she whispered in his ear. Bravely, she pushed him away, smiled sweetly and touched her fingers to her lips then to his.

"Don't forget me, cowboy."

Chapter 20

May 1882

24 May 1882

Dearest parents,
    I'm now in a rip-roaring mining town in Montana Territory. I met a young cowboy in Idaho Territory who wants to marry me. Wouldn't that be something? Maybe I could do it right the second time around. Nonetheless, I left him behind. I'm wondering already if that was a mistake.

Your daughter,
Maggie

O<small>N THE STAGE WITH</small> M<small>OLLY</small> was the Indian family that had ridden with her from Fort Hall. They sat quietly, the oldest child pressed to her mother's side, and the younger girl sitting at her feet playing with bird bones tied together with rawhide cords and bright, colorful ribbons. Nicky lay close to her welcoming a touch now and then.

"Are you Shoshone?" Molly asked, still speaking without the Irish lilt. She visually admired the mother's thick black hair, flawless complexion, and the meticulous buckskin dress she wore that was adorned in colorful glass beads similar to the ones on her knee-high moccasins.

The woman nodded. "I am Shoshone."

"Your daughters are beautiful," she continued, extending her hand to lightly touch the youngest child's head. "I think this girl is three?"

"Only two. The older child is five. Morning Dew," she said, touching the five-year old on the knee, "and Daisy." The toddler looked up when she heard her name and smiled sweetly at her mother, then at Molly. "I am Annie Blue, wife of Snow Buffalo," the mother said.

"I'm Molly. Your English is good," she replied, aware that most Indians were unschooled. "Sometimes I still fall back to my Irish brogue," she laughed.

"Husband teach us English. He is white man."

Since few Indian women rode stagecoaches, Molly wondered if her husband was wealthy or just considerate. The Indian men she had seen always had their women walking several steps behind with children at their sides or strapped into cradleboards on their backs. Annie Blue obviously was well respected by her man.

Molly tried to sleep since the night before had been restless as she anguished over leaving Sam Maddison behind. His blue eyes were always in her thoughts and she could still feel the strength of his touch, the tenderness of his kiss. The little things he did so naturally, like helping her step off the boardwalk, touching her shoulder when he wanted to show her a lovely cactus bloom, or complimenting her on her smile or her dress, stayed with her. She was pleased when he allowed Nicky to lay his head on his lap at the end of the day. Most importantly, talk of money and wealth never came up.

A feather-light touch from Daisy's hand on her knee caused her to open her eyes as the toddler scrambled into her lap, resting her head on Molly's shoulder before drifting off to sleep. Annie reached for her but Molly waved her off.

"Let me hold her," she said. "I don't often get to enjoy little ones." It felt wonderful to feel the child pressed against her breast, her soft breathing and angelic expression priceless beyond description. Molly wondered what it would have been like to be a mother.

She thought first of David, then of Sam as she lay her cheek against Daisy's soft hair and savored the moment.

It was stifling hot by the time the stage rolled into Virginia City amid a cloud of choking dust. Waves of heat radiated off the barren hillsides where not even a wisp of a breeze was felt. The nearest pines were miles away atop the imposing mountains, standing like sentinels over the long, narrow valley down below.

Annie Blue and the children were sad that Molly was getting off at Virginia City rather than traveling on to Missoula. Daisy grabbed Molly around the legs, hugging her tightly while Dew just smiled and timidly waved good-bye from behind her mother's skirt. Annie's eyes linked with Molly's and they smiled.

"Good luck," the driver said flatly, tossing her luggage onto the boardwalk. He handed her Willow's tether rope. "If this ain't a place to yer likin', try going on to Missoula or Coeur d'Alene. This place don't have much to offer a lady."

Molly thanked him for the advice then watched as the stage disappeared down the trail. After boarding Willow, she went looking for a room to rent. Sweat was already trickling down her chest and back.

The town was primitive and highly depressed in appearance. Despite the beauty of the Madison River and its willowed, grassy shores, the buildings were dirty and unkempt. On one of the hills stood Boot Hill with its wooden markers standing stark and lonely against the background of the sky.

"This place is nothing like Julia's Virginia City, is it?" Molly asked Nicky who was panting and nearly stepping on her heels.

Half-a-dozen tumbledown shacks stood across a meadow away from the main buildings. Molly assumed they were the houses of the soiled doves.

A small saloon offered rooms so Molly stepped inside. She was already fairly certain she wouldn't be staying here long. When she emerged from the hotel, she took greater stock of the town. People milled about, cowboys rode by on horseback, and greenhorn miners quizzed oldtimers about the supplies they would need to go panning for gold. The oldtimers' advice was free and extensive, colored with many warnings about being well prepared before embarking on an expedition into the Montana hills. More than one foolish miner had been caught unprepared by early storms that could come at any time.

In the space of minutes, Molly had covered the town from one end to the other counting three boarding houses, twelve saloons, three mercantile shops, a doctor's office, three churches, a news office, one livery stable, and three blacksmith shops.

Tired of walking, she sat down next to a grizzled old miner casually whittling on a piece of cedar wood. He told Molly the dilapidated old buildings actually housed hundreds of men when the cold weather set in. They packed in together like sardines in a can, not asking for anything more than a spot on the floor to sleep on. They bartered for money for food and drink, with drink taking precedence. When the cold was worst, usually in January, temperatures dropped far below zero causing fellows to drink just to stay awake so they didn't freeze. When they got too drunk, they got into fights. John Plummer was head of the vigilantes but he didn't care about the fighting since fighting relieved stress—and he was more focused on finding bank robbers and stagecoach thieves than breaking up fights.

At the end of a week, Molly was settled into a boarding house and had taken a clerking job at one of the mercantile shops. She told the owner she was waiting for her soldier husband to come for her.

To her surprise, she actually enjoyed working in the store. People were friendly enough and more than willing to point out the finer points of living in Virginia City. They told of other areas, too, and talked often about the gold fields of the Coeur d'Alenes.

On a whim one afternoon, Molly rode Willow up the canyon and into the hills to enjoy the colors of autumn that were already popping out. Nicky was full of energy, dashing after ground squirrels and chipmunks, and sometimes skunks. Molly knew little about those odorous little creatures until Nicky got too close to one.

"Nicky," she yelled as the dog took off in pursuit. "He isn't running. Something's wrong!"

He came back a much wiser dog.

"Oh, little one," she choked at the smell. "You're not sleeping in my bed tonight!"

She tried to wash the smell off in the icy-cold creek but Nicky was having no part in that. With her own clothes now soaking wet and the sun dropping in the west, she realized they would be spending the night on the mountain. Urging Willow toward a small cave beneath a rocky overhang, with an opening nearly obscured by pine trees, she wondered if her saddlebag had enough provisions to keep them warm and fed.

Inside the cave she found remnants of a campfire and some old animal bones. Moving quickly to beat the fast-approaching darkness, she unloaded the bedroll and the packet of meat, cheese and bread she had brought along. Scurrying in and out of the cave, she gathered limbs and bark to use for a fire before realizing she had nothing to start a fire with.

With only the bedroll for warmth, she huddled in the back corners of the cave with a smelly Nicky in her lap. She kept her pistol close at hand in case a grizzly bear or cougar decided to drop in. Frightening stories of grizzly bear attacks had already reached her ears.

Just after dark, a noise at the entrance brought her to instant alert, one hand gripping the pistol, the other holding onto Nicky.

"Who's there?" she called out.

"It is me, Shell Flower,[11]" said a woman's voice. "May I come in?"

Molly hollered yes then watched as a petite Indian woman entered the cave, her body wrapped in a warm buffalo robe.

"It is cold. May I share cave?" she asked. Molly nodded.

"Of course, share my cave. I don't have a fire, though."

"I am not lost, just on journey. I am peacemaker between tribes. Truckee of the Northern Pauite is my father. Do you know of him?"

"No," Molly admitted. "Is he with you?"

"No, I travel alone. Father is chief so stays always with tribe."

[11.] Shell Flower was another name for Sally Winnemucca, born in 1844 to Truckee, a well-known Northern Paiute. Sally became legendary for her peacemaking skills between whites and Indian tribes. She died in 1891.

She whistled for her pony to come inside, too. She knew first-hand about the grizzlies of Montana. She led Willow in, too.

"Shadow is good horse but is better for riding than for eating," she laughed. "We must tell that to the bears."

Shell Flower turned her attentions to making a fire after Molly explained she didn't know how to start one.

"Come, I show you," Shell Flower said, heading right to the pile of wood. Using a flint stone from her pack, she quickly teased sparks into the kindling and soon had a brisk fire blazing. The warmth felt wonderful to Molly who was shivering even with the bedroll blanket wrapped around her shoulders. Shell Flower hunched down beside her to enjoy the heat.

"What is your name? And why you in this cave?" Shell Flower asked they nibbled on the foods Molly provided.

"My name is Molly. I work in town but wanted to ride a while and enjoy nature. We rode too far so decided to sleep here. The dog found a skunk."

"Ah, yes, I could smell. It is easy to stray far from home, I know that well. I am always far from family but that is my job. Here, keep flint so you can start fire next time. Without fire, you can freeze." Shell Flower held out the flint and Molly gratefully accepted it.

"I will keep it with me always. Right here with my pistol." Molly patted her pocket then smiled at Shell Flower.

Shell Flower was a pretty woman, probably not much older than Molly but half a head shorter. Her thick dark hair hung in braids down her back with a white band encircling her head. The beadwork suggested stature and power.

"You are a peacemaker?" Molly asked.

"Yes, between whites and Indians. Whites call me Sarah Winnemucca, which is strange, I think, but that is name they give me. Some call me Sally. To my people I am Shell Flower."

After a while, they curled up near the fire and slept. The horses were tied at the rear of the cave behind them. Nicky positioned himself near the cave opening to warn if danger approached, either in the form of a bear, a cougar or a human.

When Molly awoke the next morning, the Indian girl and her horse were gone, and Molly hadn't heard a sound.

Back in town, Molly's employer got a hearty laugh out of Nicky's encounter with the skunk. He kept the dog tied outside so his skunk perfume didn't drive customers away and assured Molly the smell would last a week or more. Still, he got a cold bath in the river every night and had to sleep near the door of her room rather than on the bed.

When Molly mentioned having spent the night on the mountain and meeting up with Shell Flower, the shopkeeper was surprised. He hadn't realized she was even in the area. He told Molly she was a highly-admired woman, very popular with everyone.

It was late November when a rough-looking cowboy came galloping into town, all sweaty and agitated.

"Hey fellas, did ya hear? Some bastard killed Julia Bulette down in Nevada." He leapt out of the saddle even before the horse stopped running.

"What? Who did it?" another man asked, grabbing onto the horse's reins.

"Some drifter named John Millain. Folks say he was always hangin' around her, so much so old Tom had to keep running him off. Guess he broke into Julia's Palace during the night and beat her to death. Even stabbed her after she was dead. Why did he have to do that to Julia? She wouldn't hurt nobody."

Molly was near the door when she heard Julia's name. "Who you talking about?" she asked.

"Julia Bulette down in Nevada. She was murdered a week ago."

"Murdered?" Molly's heart leaped into her throat as her gut felt like a rock had dropped into it.

"Yeah, some low-life scoundrel did it. The whole town's up in arms. She was a good friend of mine," the cowboy went on, his face sad as he rolled a cigarette then took a few puffs.

"Tell me everything," Molly demanded, stunned by what she was hearing.

"Robbery, they say. That devil killed her right there in her bed while she slept. Then he stole everything. Her clothes, her jewels, her music boxes. After beating her to death, he stabbed her over and over."

Molly grew physically ill, unable to breathe, her legs weak and rubbery. "Was it Tom Peasley who did it?" she gasped.

"Oh, no, not Peasley. He adored her—even put up a thousand dollar reward to catch whoever did the dastardly deed. Says he'll kill the man himself if he gets the chance. Vigilantes told him it was probably that Frenchman John Millain who did it. Cagey damn fellow sat up all night by her coffin just weeping and wailing like a sad hound dog so as to throw off suspicion. Next day, he was out in town selling off her stuff. Even tried to sell her purple dresses. That's what gave him away. People knowed them was her clothes."

"Has he been arrested?" Molly asked, her legs trembling so bad she had to lean against a hitching post for support.

"Vigilantes are hot on his tail. He'll get hanged if Tom doesn't shoot him first. Poor Julia, she didn't deserve that even if she was a whore." The cowboy took another puff on the cigarette then realized what he'd said in front of Molly. "Sorry, Ma'am, didn't mean to talk so blunt."

"When did this happen?" Molly asked quietly.

"Over a week ago. The damn fool might have got away with it if he hadn't tried to rob another whore in town. She beat him off with a wooden broom then told the authorities. That's what sent the vigilantes to his room. It was full of Julia's things. He still had the shiny gold music box Tom gave her. Yup, he's gonna hang. Wish I could be the one to wrap the rope around his neck! Buried her the next day but them uppity churches wouldn't even give her a decent Christian burial. They dumped her in Pauper's field without even a wooden cross to mark the spot. Now that just ain't right! She deserved better." The cowboy shook his head in disgust and spat tobacco juice onto the dusty street.

Molly's thoughts were spinning. All she could see was Julia's smiling face as she waved good-bye the day Molly left Virginia City. She began to cry.

"One of them snooty women in town suggested the killer get a medal for what he did!" the cowboy said. "Can you believe it? Well, old Tom put a stop to that. Ordered a big wooden cross made up from a black walnut tree with her name carved in it, all at his own expense. He vowed to shoot any person who dared take the cross down, man or woman!"

Molly found comfort in that. Tom would see to it Julia was remembered.

"Lady, you all right?" one fellow asked when he saw Molly's tears. "You look pale. Did you know Julia?"

"She was my sister." Molly blurted out, wiping at her tears. Fighting back the urge to vomit, she turned and ran to the boarding house, pausing in the alley to heave and heave until her ribs ached. Once she was in her room, she sobbed long into the night. If she had stayed with Julia, she lamented, this wouldn't have happened. Maybe it was her fault.

By morning, she had made a decision.

"Nothing changes for us, does it, Nicky?" she asked as she stroked the dog's fur. "Is that what I'm destined for, too? An unmarked grave in Pauper's Field? If so, then that's how it will be. I'll accept my lot in life and, come Heaven or Hell, I'll meet Julia again even if it's beside the roaring fires of damnation."

Chapter 21

November 1882

29 November 1882

Dear parents.

I am going to Idaho Territory. I heard my dear friend Julia was ruthlessly murdered so my heart is grieving. She was so young, so special. Pray for me. My soul feels dark, my heart wounded. There's such evil In the world. Why must good people die at the hands of others?

Your daughter,
Maggie

MOLLY LEFT VIRGINIA CITY ABRUPTLY after hearing about Julia. She booked passage to Thompson Falls, Montana, the jumping off place for those wanting to reach the gold mining towns in the Coeur d'Alenes. Enroute, she met a legendary figure who would move in and out of her life dozens of times in the years to come. She was none other than Calamity Jane.[12]

The woman was dressed like a tough cowboy, even swaggering down the aisles to boldly sit down beside Molly. She tugged at her

---

[12.] Calamity Jane's real name was Martha Canary. She was born in 1852 and lived until 1903. She was exactly as depicted in this narrative and often associated with Molly, but they never became close friends.

soiled buckskin pants that were tied at the waist with a wide, tight-ly-cinched leather belt. Her boots were thin and shabby, the heels nearly worn off. A sweat-stained cowboy hat pulled low on her head did little to hide the greasy hair poking out beneath it. Squirming around on the seat, the woman tried to shift the two pistols hanging from her belt for better comfort. Next to her on the bench was her rifle.

"Where ya headed, lady?" she asked Molly, her eyes piercing and bold as her fingers worked at rolling a cigarette. Once it was lit, she blew smoke right into Molly's face.

"Murray's m' destination," Molly coughed.

"Well, boy howdy, we're headed to the same place!" the woman snorted, slapping her hand on her knee. "I'm goin' there to relieve some of them miners of that easy gold they brag about. Some say it grows right up out of the grass roots. Don't much care fer mining m'self but I sure do like talkin' them prospectors out of what they find. Yup, that's where I'm a-headed."

Molly didn't say anything so the woman kept talking nonstop.

"Let me guess. Ye're a school marm ain't ya. Well, that's good. Them ruffians need some learnin'. So damn many folks movin' in, there's gotta be a need fer gettin' smarter." She laughed at her own joke.

"I ain't no teacher," Molly replied bluntly, her eyes locking with the woman's.

"Blow me away, don't tell me yer a whore?" Calamity blurted out, the cigarette dangling from her lips.

Molly didn't answer.

"Ya got a name?" she asked. "People call me Calamity 'cuz I cause such a fuss wherever I go. Don't mean to but it just happens. Ya probably heard of me. I'm famous even if I do say so m'self. I kin shoot the fly off a dog's nose and never ruffle a hair." She glanced down at Nicky. "No worry, mutt, I ain't in the mood to shoot no flies today." She laughed coarsely.

"I'm Molly."

"Well, I'm pleased t' meet ya, Molly, even if ya are gonna be my competition. Ya goin' to Eagle City or Murray?"

"Murray."

For a while they eyed each other up, neither saying much.

"There ain't gonna be room fer the both of us in Murray," Calamity finally decided after a lengthy silence. "Hell, there ain't no man gonna pick me over you. Reckon I'll just keep on goin' back to Deadwood. Ol' Bill—Bill Hickock, he's my lover—he's in Deadwood and he's probably missin' me. I ain't seen him in a while and I'm kinda wantin' to see his handsome mug again. Deadwood's m' favorite spot, leastwise fer the time bein'. It keeps callin' me back. Ya ain't goin' there, are ya?" she asked suspiciously. "I'd be right upset if ya decided to go to Deadwood. That's my town."

"No, I'm not going to Deadwood," Molly assured her.

"Good. I need to find some work. M' purse is runnin' low. 'Course, I kin always find work. Just have to say m' name and somebody will give me a job. I'm a darn good muleskinner, just so's ya know. Don't need to do whorin' unless I get a hankerin' fer a tumble in the hay or need a bottle of whiskey if m' cash is low.

"Did I tell ya I kin ride shotgun on them stagecoaches, too. Bet ya didn't know that. Don't care if it's Indians or robbers, I kin shoot a fly off a horse's ear." She laughed then. "I told ya that already didn't I? Well, it's true. Even the Indians are skeered of me so drivers like it when I ride topside with 'em. Whorin's m' side job, like I told ya. It gets me a coin or two fer the faro tables."

"Do ye know Wyatt Earp?" Molly asked when there was a pause in Calamity's continuous dialogue.

"Hell yes, knowed him fer years. First time I saw him was in Abilene. He came dang near close to buying a place on Boot Hill last month down near Tombstone. Him and them brothers of his crossed up the Cowboys. Doc Holliday was there too. Doc, he's one fast gunslinger—even faster than me, and he don't miss. Slaps metal like he was born a-doin' it. Anyhow, the brothers got wounded but Wyatt and Doc came out okay. They sent them Cowboys a-packin' then he went after the ones what shot his brothers. Them that wasn't killed high-tailed it to Mexico, skeered fer their lives.

"He dumped that tagalong whore, too, but hooked up right away with a lady entertainer named Josie. Them two are closer than fleas now, that's what I hear."

Molly was pleased to hear about Wyatt and thought a lot about him while Calamity rambled on.

When their one-sided conversation lulled, Calamity gave a heavy sigh, leaned back, jammed the leather hat down tight on her head, took a final drag on the cigarette before dropping it to the floor, then closed her eyes. "Wake me at Thompson Falls," she muttered.

Thompson Falls was a small railroad jumping-off town with coal smoke belched out from the locomotives staining all the snow banks. Calamity woke with a start, sat up, brushed off her buckskins, then tipped her hat to Molly before hopping off the train and strutting off toward the ticket station, rifle in hand, to buy a ticket to the Dakotas.

Molly sighed heavily. The most intriguing thing about being in the west was witnessing the diversity of the people. Businessmen gave up profitable enterprises to go west; miners deserted their families to take up hermit-like existences in the hills; cowboys just wandered foot loose and fancy free anywhere they felt like going. Calamity fell into that category.

Winter storms had already deposited a thick blanket of snow on most of Montana by now. Thompson Falls and its few permanent structures stood as the last-stop for those heading into gold territory in the Coeur d'Alenes. Since Molly had arrived already well outfitted for the trip over the Bitterroot Mountain range, she needed only to secure passage with a mule train. She learned it would be forty miles of steep, treacherous mountain trails and passes made even more dangerous by the notorious bitter cold Montana winters. The captain of the mule team warned her the trip would be hazardous. Was she sure she wanted to take the chance?

Molly politely accepted the warning, assuring him she was not only mentally prepared but also physically capable.

At the crack of dawn on departure day, the mule train was ready to leave and so was Molly. Her baggage had been tightly secured to the back of a mule so Willow's load could be kept as light as possible.

Willow was a small horse so this trip would test her mettle in the most extreme of circumstances. A deep saddlebag strapped to the saddle would hold Nicky if the snow got too deep for him.

"Ya know that mare ain't gonna last goin' over them there mountains," the muleskinner cautioned her, turning his head to spit tobacco juice onto the packed snow. "Them mountains don't only kill people in winter. They kill horses, too."

"Willow's a mustang," Molly argued. "She was born into adversity."

The muleskinner grunted, looking the mare over like she was little more than an over-sized kitten. Nonetheless, Molly had no intention of riding any horse but Willow, and that was that.

"Hope ya know what yer doing, Lady. I'm tellin' ya, the mare won't make it," the skinner snapped.

Slowly, Molly removed her fur-lined glove then smiled sweetly as she slid her warm fingers down the side of the man's coarsely-bearded face then up around his ears.

"It will be all right, sweet man," she purred. "I know ye'll take care of me. If the horse seems to be faltering, I'll swap her out with another horse, maybe that big old stallion of yers. I feel so much safer knowin' ye're in charge."

She kissed him on the cheek, causing his face to flush bright red as he grinned a tobacco-stained grin, muttered something unintelligible, then galloped off to get the pack train ready to go.

With the crack of a dozen whips, the stoic lineup of thirty heavily-laden mules, twenty-two horses with and without riders, and nineteen burros pulling sleds or toboggans began to move. Shouts from the drivers broke the calm of the still-dark icy morning. Icicles hung sparkling with moonlight beneath the trees and rooftops. Before long the sun would chase back the stars and the mountain peaks would surrender to its warmth even though it probably couldn't raise the temperature much. By sunup, the mule train would already be entering the shadows of the imposing Bitterroot Range.

As promised, the lead skinner kept close check on Molly, often riding alongside her to share tidbits of the land's colorful history. He was born and raised in the Bitterroot Valley so knew things first hand. He warned her the ascent up to the high mountain pass would be difficult at best but the descent into Prichard Creek Valley would be fast if the weather cooperated.

"Murray's a boomin' town. Hundreds of people go flockin' there summer and winter. Most come by rail into Coeur d'Alene then by stage to Rathdrum and Coeur d'Alene City. Noisy place, that one, what with all the hammerin' and buildin' going on. Ain't seen nothin' like it. Rumor is the hotels got three beds or more in each room so's two people kin sleep in each bed, no matter if they be friends or not. Lots of folks sleep on the floors. Ain't many women, though, except fer whores." He smiled. He'd transported enough prostitutes to know a woman traveling alone, like Molly was, probably was headed to join the red light ladies. Not that he cared. He rather enjoyed sampling the ladies' charms himself.

"Camp Coeur d'Alene's got nine hundred acres on the north shore at the head of the Spokane River. It causes contentiousness when them soldiers git to shovin' up against the immigrants in the saloons. Always cussin' and fightin'. Anyhow, there's a steamboat what crosses the lake to the Old Cataldo mission. You Catholic?"

"Not anymore," she replied.

"When that lake freezes over, things get mighty risky fer steamers. The Indians keep firewood piled on the banks fer the steamers' fires. White folks are more'n happy to pay the Indians fer doing the wood cuttin' fer 'em, and the Indians like the gold."

"Tell me more," Molly begged.

"Well, it's about sixty miles by water from Coeur d'Alene to Cataldo. Once people get there they rent horses to git the twenty-five miles to Evolution Trail, then it's twenty-five more miles into Eagle City. It's easier goin' that way than 'tis this way 'cuz they don't git no twenty feet of snow like here. The wind blows there just like here, and that trail winds in and out of the woods. It's a narrow road always covered over with fallen trees. Git off the trail where ye cain't see the ax marks and ye're in a heap of trouble. People don't know where they're goin' to start with, much less when the trail markin's disappear. Some of them fools are dressed in nothin' more than rags to start with. They just keep ploddin' on 'til they either make it there or freeze to death tryin'. Kin ya imagine that? Wantin' gold so bad you don't care if ya freeze?"

"What about Eagle City?" she asked, veering off the depressing subject of people freezing to death on the trail.

"It started out as Hayes City but folks didn't go fer that so changed the name t' Eagle City 'cuz of the cliff where them eagles live. Others call it Stump Valley 'cuz the lumbermen done cut off all the trees and left nothin' but stumps." The muleskinner paused to yell profanities at one of the drivers who seemed to be slacking off.

"Is it bigger than Murray?"

"Yup, fer the moment, but that don't mean nothin'. Mining towns change overnight if the gold fizzles out. When it's gone in one place, it always crops up in another. Mule teams make the trip to Eagle every other day, that's how busy it is, but one of the big places, Evolution Mine, is already slowin' down, or so I heard."

"Is the town lawless?" She thought about Wyatt.

"Thievery ain't tolerated there 'cuz thieves get shot on the spot if they git caught. There's whores everywhere and gamblin' goes on day and night. Most popular place is Acion Saloon. It ain't much t' look at, just an oversized tent with a potbelly stove and wooden benches around the faro tables. Lamps hang from the ceiling so the place can stay open around the clock."

A shout from the front of the line caused the skinner to spur his horse ahead to check on the commotion leaving Molly to ponder all she had heard. He had told her more about Eagle City than about Murray but she didn't get to ask how close together the towns were.

Willow did good during the early part of the trip, valiantly keeping up with the other animals. Molly was pleased with the spirited little horse and tried to keep her on the packed trail where walking was easiest. Nicky kept up, too, but she kept a constant check on him in case he tired. She herself was well dressed in multiple layers of clothes all covered over by a heavily-lined, hooded fur coat that kept her toasty warm. Inside her rabbit-fur mittens were thick, woolen gloves for added warmth, and around her neck were scarves of soft wool that could easily be pulled up onto her face if the wind picked up.

As the sun breached the mountaintops, Molly knew the day would be one of promise. This was the type of excitement she thrived upon. The caravan had already crossed the open valley and was beginning its ascent upward toward the stark, leafless stands of maple and aspen. The mule train narrowed into a single-file procession traveling up an endless, ever winding path leading to a distant mountain pass.

As soon as things were back in control, the muleskinner was back at Molly's side telling her more about the countryside, the trees, the wildlife, and the climate. The trees were lodge poles, Ponderosa pine, Douglas fire, grand fir, spruce and hemlock. That was important to know, he explained, since the lumber industry brought in more money than the mining activities.

The deepening of the drifts happened almost unnoticed until Molly saw some drifts were now chest high on the lead animals. The caravan had to stop often to allow the mules to rest and to swap out the lead animals with other mules. Sometimes the drifts were so high the drivers had to shovel passage ways through. Adding to the growing problem were the dozens of individuals now blocking the trail as they tried to walk to Murray, their few belongings wrapped in burlap bags slung over their backs or on crude sleds.

"Why are these people walkin'?" Molly asked, concerned by their thin clothing and the rags covering their faces to keep out the bitter cold.

"They think gettin' to Murray early will give 'em a leg up come spring. Greedy fools. Half of 'em are gonna freeze 'cuz when they get where they're goin' there ain't gonna be no place to stay. All they got is what's in them bags on their backs but the thought of gold just keeps 'em goin'."

Spurring his horse, he rode off again. Molly was left watching the wretched souls pushing on to Murray, their feet freezing in their boots. Now and again she spotted snow-covered stick-and-pine bough shelters along the wayside. At least some of the walkers could find protection there from the wind.

"Get off the trail!" the skinners yelled.

Once the caravan passed by, some of the walkers scrambled onto the trail to take advantage of the packed down trail caused by the animals plowing through. For a mile or two, they were able to keep up but eventually tired and fell back to trudging along slowly, hoping to reach Murray before nightfall.

At the top of the pass, the mule train rested awhile, changing lead mules again. Molly dug a handful of oats from one of the saddlebags and offered it to Willow for strength. The little mare seemed grateful for the nourishment. They had thirteen more miles to go. Then a frigid breeze blew aside her neck scarf. She looked up to see a black sky descending at an intense speed.

"Check the tie downs," the muleskinners bellowed. "There's a bad one comin'. Everybody get set fer a blizzard."

Within minutes, a stinging ground blizzard hit the caravan with all the force Nature had to offer. Like a demonic banshee, the wind screamed in and out of the trees, wrapping icy fingers around everyone and everything while shoving the already-cold temperatures even farther below zero. Then came the snow blowing sideways then up, then down, sending stinging ice crystals into every part of exposed flesh. It took hold in the faces and tails of the animals, freezing on their lashes and ears.

"Git the dog," one driver yelled, noticing Nicky trying to leap through the drifts then dropping out of sight until jumping up again. He was exhausted.

Molly yanked on Willow's reins then whistled for Nicky to jump into her open arms. She tucked him into the leather pouch then fastened the strap so he was concealed inside. Then she nudged Willow forward again.

The caravan was delayed for nearly an hour while tarps and ropes were tightened down on the cargoes. The blizzard grew intense as it piled the drifts even deeper. The skinners struggled to walk alongside the animals so they could shovel ahead of each animal's footsteps. Once the animals passed by, the trail blew shut again. The shouting of the drivers was even drowned out by the unholy shrieking winds.

"Keep the mules and horses moving or they'll freeze in their tracks," one man yelled.

Molly worried about Willow. She was struggling, her breathing labored. Molly's face was almost completely wrapped in scarves but she could still feel the cold pushing through to her skin. From the corners of her eyes she could see the walkers desperately trying to find cover, some digging desperately with their bare hands into snow banks just to make some shelter while others crowded into abandoned huts or strung blankets between the trees where dozens of them could huddle together, their arms around each other to share body heat. Their faces reflected fear of dying.

Ahead, off to the side of the trail, Molly saw a snow mound that suddenly moved. She stared at it until she realized it was a woman kneeling in the snow, her arms wrapped around a child. They must have become exhausted and could go no further.

"Wait, stop the caravan," she shouted, reining Willow to a halt. Scrambling out of the saddle, she dropped into a four-feet deep snow bank. Plowing her way to the woman, she reached out and grabbed her arm. The woman looked up at her, her lashes coated in ice as she peeked out from beneath the scarves wrapped around and around her head.

"Git on m' horse," Molly shouted, yanking the woman to her feet. "What's this?" she asked, touching the hump on the woman's back.

"Baby," the woman whispered.

"A baby, too?" Molly gasped.

"What's goin' on here?" the muleskinner yelled, shoving his way through the snow to get to Molly.

"Get this woman onto m' horse then hand up the child," she ordered as she struggled back into the saddle, her clothes now caked in ice and snow.

Once the woman was on Willow with her, they sandwiched the child in between them.

"Move forward," Molly yelled.

"Yer horse'll falter under that load," the skinner warned but Molly knew she had no choice. She had to help.

"We're wastin' time! Git movin'," she repeated. She glared at the driver with eyes colder than the howling arctic wind. "At the next shelter, stop and we'll get off."

Progress was agonizingly slow. In the history books, the storm would become known as one of the worst in the history of the region.

Willow was laboring even more and Molly could feel it. She had to find shelter. At a small still-vacant stick shelter, the caravan stopped briefly while two men helped Molly and the little family off Willow's back. While the woman and children were pushed into the tiny shelter, Molly whistled for Willow to follow her off the trail so the caravan could move on. One of the men took Willow by the reins and led her to shelter behind a large drift beneath a pine tree. The drift broke the wind. He tied her there, patted her a couple times, then let Nicky out of the saddlebag and carried him back to Molly.

"Yer horse will be all right up there. Can't hardly feel the wind up there."

Molly smiled gratefully.

"Git as far into that shelter as ye can git," he insisted, helping Molly through the drifts. First she peeled off her fur coat, wrapped it around the woman and children then crawled in beside them. The driver hurriedly spread two wool blankets over them then covered the opening with pine boughs.

"Good luck," he shouted above the wind.

"We'll come on in tomorrow. How far is it?"

"Seven, maybe eight miles. Sure ya can make it?"

"We'll make it," she vowed.

Molly fidgeted in under the fur coat until she was squeezed tightly up against the woman who was struggling to remove the baby from the cradleboard on her back. Molly helped free the baby then pushed her into the mother's arms. The older child had a death grip around her mother's arm and was shivering uncontrollably. Molly pulled the coat tighter around them all then used the two blankets to block out drafts. The pine boughs were already collecting snow that would provide insulation to help keep out the cold. Confident they would be able to share their warmth and survive the night, Molly opened a corner of the shelter, whistled for Nicky, then allowed him to burrow in between her and the children. Nicky licked the children's faces then snuggled in between them.

The clattering of metal and leather trappings told them the mule train was moving on. After a while, an eerie silence settled over the tiny snow shelter but the shivering within grew less severe. To pass time, Molly sang lullabies she remembered from childhood. Once warm, the children fell asleep. Only Molly and the mother remained awake.

"Thank you, Molly," the woman whispered.

"You know m' name?" Molly gasped.

"I know you, Molly. It's me, Annie Blue."

Chapter 22

January 1883

20 January 1883

Dearest parents,
    An amazing thing has happened. I've found a place. It's as though I was destined to come here. People flock around me and call me a heroine for having saved a young mother and her children during a terrible blizzard. It is wonderful to be so admired.

Your daughter,
Maggie

W HEN MORNING CAME, MOLLY AND her friends rode slowly down out of the hills. The storm had raged on through the night leaving terrible conditions for Willow to plow through with such a heavy load so Molly let her set her own pace. Frequently, when Molly could feel her labored breathing, they stopped to allow her to rest. Behind them, walkers were emerging from their shelters, too. Surprisingly, all had survived. A few walkers were ahead of them breaking trail so that helped Willow, too.

    Breaking out of the timber, they saw Murray down below. Curls of smoke rose from the buildings and tents, much like welcoming signals. A crowd was gathered in the street.

"She's coming," someone shouted. "The angel of mercy's coming!"

Cheers of elation resonated through the crisp morning air as people rushed forward to greet Molly. They pushed to try and touch her legs or her horse as she rode past. There was laughing and shouting and cheering amongst the people. A real-life angel had arrived in Murray. Even Nicky poked his head and paws out of the saddlebag to bark excitedly.

Molly reined Willow to a stop in front of the courthouse. Like a queen looking down upon her subjects, she scanned the faces of the people, unable to know what to say. Finally she gave orders to the men crowded around.

"Find this woman and her children a warm cabin with plenty of food, then bring the bill t' me."

Three men rushed forward to take the baby from Annie then helped Annie and Dew off Willow's back. Annie's eyes locked with Molly's as they exchanged smiles. Then the little family was hurried off down the street.

Turning her attentions back to the crowd, Molly smiled brightly.

"What a fine welcome," she beamed. The crowd cheered.

"Ah, a livin' angel has come to us, and a blazin' beauty at that!" a ruddy young Irishman declared as he took hold of Willow's reins. He stood beside the horse staring up at Molly. "Do ye have a name, angel?" he grinned mischievously, winking at her.

"Aye, m' name is Molly Burdan." Her words heavily reflected her Irish heritage.

"Molly B'Damn? What kind of scandalous name might that be fer such a fine Irish girl?" he gasped in fake astonishment. "Well, Molly B'Damn, welcome to Murray, the town what loves everybody, especially angels!"

With that, he spun around, clapped his hands together, waved his arms in the air, and incited more cheering as he did a brief Irish jig for her enjoyment.

"Molly, Molly, Molly," the crowd chanted in a near-deafening roar.

Molly could not believe it. Could it be she had actually found a place where no one would care if she were a prostitute?

The handsome, red-headed Irishman bantered back and forth with Molly since he was a witty fellow full of fun and merriment. Never one to back down, Molly met his jibes with those of her own, their eyes sparkling at the fun of it all.

"Ye're a sassy wench," he teased. "Seems I've met m' match."

"That ye have, laddie," she laughed. "I can give as good as I git."

Phil O'Rourke was his name, she would learn later, and he was one of Murray's most colorful characters. He'd been in town more than two years so considered himself a native.

"And what might yer business be, Molly B'Damn?" he asked.

"I'll be movin' into Cabin One," she replied, her head turning toward the cabins lining Prichard Creek.

An audible sigh resonated through the crowd. Cabin One always went to the head madam of any red light district.

"Ah, I shoulda known. Darlin' Molly's a dove—our angel of mercy is a dove—the dove of Silver Valley. What say folks?" More cheers.

Leaning from the saddle, she did a controlled fall right into Phil's arms. He caught her easily, set her on her feet, and then barked out orders for people to find her belongings that had been set aside by the mule train.

"Take 'em to Cabin One," Phil ordered.

"Somebody better warn Broncho Liz[13] we're a comin' then," one man shouted. "She's gonna be madder than a grizzly."

Broncho Liz was a huge woman with a vile tongue and a surly disposition. No one wanted to be guilty of riling her up so they banded together for courage while letting Phil do the knocking on the door.

"What do ya want?" Broncho Liz bellowed from inside. "Ya know it's too darned early fer frolickin' so git away from my door and let me sleep." Everyone could hear her cursing.

[13.] Broncho Liz and the other prostitutes described herein are authentic and were associates of Molly's.

Phil rapped louder on the door then backed away. Broncho Liz, the woman who swore she was born riding a broncho, wasn't exactly the type of woman any man wanted to trifle with.

"This here's business, Liz," yelled Phil. "Open the bloody damn door!"

Inside the shabby, run-down cabin, Broncho Liz rose slowly from her bed, hiking up the drooping sleeve on her sheer nightgown as she shuffled barefoot over to the curtainless window. She could see the crowd outside clustered around a woman dressed in fur.

"What in tarnation is goin' on?" she snarled, whipping open the door. "What the hell do you want, Phil? I'm gonna make ya sorry fer wakin' me up!" She scowled at him then glared at the other miners.

"This here's Molly B'Damn. She's takin' over yer cabin," Phil stated bravely, a nervous grin flashing across his face. He had no love for Liz so was actually pleased to deliver such bad news.

Broncho Liz was one of those immensely colorful characters living in the tough mining camp of northern Idaho. She had proclaimed herself head of the red-lantern ladies and Queen of the Underworld long before Molly arrived on the scene. She flaunted her title mercilessly and demanded respect. Standing nearly six-feet tall and weighing well in excess of two-hundred pounds, she did bear a strong resemblance to the horse she swore she had descended from. Her brown hair hung stringy and straight, always greasy and hopelessly snarled. Though barely thirty years of age, her face was etched by years of wild living.

"Who says she's taking over?" Liz growled, her black eyes focusing on Molly.

"Says me," Molly replied, stepping past her. "Ye got a problem with that?" She beckoned for her bags to be brought in, which they were.

"Yeah, I got a problem with that," Liz growled, kicking at one of the bags.

"Well, git over it cuz I only work out of Cabin One, right boys?" The men all grinned and nodded.

"Do I got a say in this?" Liz snarled, scratching her butt. She wasn't exactly happy about giving up her status without a fight, yet there stood Molly, beautiful and self-confident with looks that easily trumped Liz's bovine appearance.

"Guess from the looks of ya, there ain't gonna be no contest 'tween us, is there?" she admitted. "I'll git my things but if ye're just passin' through then I ain't movin'. You fixin' to stay or not?"

"Don't know yet," Molly replied casually while looking around the filthy room. The cot's soiled bedding hung to the floor; a torn screen in one corner of the room was draped with Liz's clothes except for the gray woolen undergarments that lay loose on the floor and a wool cape slung across the back of the only chair in the room. Next to the chair was a cold, iron claw-foot stove. It would have provided heat had a fire been started.

"Ain't ye got no firewood?" Molly asked. "It's colder than a witch's nose in here!"

"Ain't no need fer heat when I'm sleepin', and don't need none when I'm workin' cuz I create all the heat I need," Liz laughed vulgarly, slapping a miner on the butt and winking at him.

"Phil, can ye start a fire? It was blood-freezin' cold on the trail last night," Molly asked sweetly, smiling at him and her adoring new fan base.

A nod from Phil sent men scurrying after wood and charcoal embers to start the fire. Two men grabbed buckets for water and headed to the creek to water for coffee and cleaning. One look at Molly and everyone knew she'd like a clean place. Phil swept his arm across the stove top, clearing it of a grimy fry pan, a teapot, and a couple tin cups. "Men, clean up this mess. Can't have our dove livin' in squalor."

"Hold on, ya fools. Ya can't just dump my belongings," Liz complained. "Who are ya anyhow? What'd ya say her name is?" She'd forgotten it already.

"Molly B'Damn's her name," Phil answered. "Now git yer things out of here. The lady's probably tired. She's been through an ordeal, ain't ya Molly?"

Liz grudgingly gathered her things, cursing under her breath all the while, then kicked aside what she didn't want before storming out the door still dressed in her flimsy nightgown.

"Liz, wait," Molly called out to her, motioning for the men to leave them in privacy. "How many gals live on the row?" She reached for Liz's cape and draped it across her shoulders.

"A dozen, I guess. Some been here awhile, others come and go. Belle's been here longest. Three years now. Came over from Virginia City when her man got mauled by a grizzly down by Bozeman. She didn't have no money, no place to go, so took up doin' men like the rest of us. Never found nothin' of her man 'cept a boot. Damn bear ate everything."

Molly frowned. She hadn't wanted to hear the gory details.

"And the other gals?" she asked, rubbing her cold hands before the now-roaring fire.

"Amber was here 'til last week but she done run off with a fella named Dalton. If he dumps her, she'll be back, or not. Ya never know with them pretty ones. They get work no matter where they go." Liz raised her eyebrows at Molly as though she was the subject of Liz's story, then continued.

"She was a tiny thing, barely fifteen years old, but tougher than nails. Men wanted her most 'cuz she looked so innocent. Heaven knows ain't none the rest of us got any innocence left. My men, they like being treated rough—and I don't hold back nothin'," she bragged. "They come back again and again, always beggin' fer more." Reaching for a tobacco pouch hung around her neck by a leather cord, Liz rolled herself a cigarette then took a sliver of burning wood from the stove to light it with. After inhaling deeply, she stared at Molly.

"Ya wanna know more?" she asked, pleased at being a fountain of information. Molly nodded.

"There's Jennie Rowl, a tiny little thing, thin as a willow and always happy. Loves growin' flowers in the summer. She's married but ol' Jack, he don't mind her capers since she brings in more gold than he does. She keeps him in whiskey and gamblin' money so he lets her do as she pleases. Jennie likes flaunting herself in satin and feathers. Men say she's a wildcat under the blankets."

Suddenly Broncho Liz stopped talking.

"Somethin' wrong?" Molly asked.

"You fixin' to skim off the best and richest fer yerself?" she asked suspiciously. "I got m' favorites, just so ya know, and I'll fight ya if ya try to take 'em."

"I'll decide later," Molly replied. "Fer now, git settled wherever ye plan to stay then gather the others together and bring 'em here so's we kin talk. And don't step on m' dog." She patted her thigh beckoning Nicky to her side.

Once Liz was gone, Molly studied the awfulness of the cabin. It was dark, filthy, and incredibly cold since the logs were so poorly chinked. Half of the smoke from the stove stayed in the room, the other half went up the chimney. The windows bore evidence to the smoke by the caked-on grime obliterating the light. A single kerosene lantern hung near the cot.

Phil had been waiting by the creek for Liz to leave. He hurried to the cabin to offer his help.

"Thought ye'd be wantin' t' clean up a bit," he surmised, snatching his hat off and tossing it onto the bed. "I'll help ye. M' thinks Liz was not only born from a horse but was raised with pigs."

"This is gonna take a lot of work," she muttered. "It ain't no Julia's Palace, that's fer sure."

Phil had no idea what Julia's Palace was.

By the time the other women started showing up, the room was somewhat more presentable. Phil had even taken soap and water to the windows so light could enter. Rags had been shoved into the widest cracks to hold out the cold. On the stove, a kettle of hot water was steaming.

"Git us some whiskey, would ya, Phil? And some cups."

Phil took his leave but not until Molly had favored him with one of her brilliant smiles. It was all the payment he wanted. Later, he would ask for more.

At first, the ladies seemed hesitant to enter but Molly beckoned them inside.

"I'm Molly. Just so's ye can git to know me, I'm Irish born, came to America ten years ago, lived awhile in Boston 'til m' scoundrel husband sold me into prostitution. Walked out on him and came west. Now, tell me about yerselves."

"Never knowed a madam wantin' to know nothing about us," Belle chimed in. She was every bit as pretty as Broncho Liz had suggested, with hair the color of the setting sun and hazel-green eyes heavily lined in kohl. Unlike most of the others, Belle was sparkling clean.

Several of the women, she learned, bunked together, partly for convenience but mostly for security. Liquored-up miners could get real mean at times so having a housemate often seemed practical.

When the last girl finished telling her story, Molly explained what her role as head madam would be. She would become their business manager and, as such, would be paid one-tenth of their earnings.

Outraged, the women began to protest. None of them wanted to share their earnings. By rights, they deserved every cent they earned.

"Calm down," Molly replied when the furor calmed down. "I been lots of places, seen plenty of brothels, most of them high-class, and I seen how doves of every type live. I also know the differences in their earnings. Here in Murray, we're goin' high class, and we're gonna be earnin' more gold than ye can imagine. I'm gonna help ye save, too, for them cold, dark days when ye can't attract men anymore, least wise not the way ye did when ye were young. Pay me what I say and I promise not to compete fer yer customers. Ye know if I wanted to I could take most of yer fellas away from ye."

The women whispered among themselves. She was probably right.

"Truth is, whorin' was never m' choice in life but I'm a fine business woman. Learned from the best in Dodge City and Denver. Now, if ye're wonderin' what the money will be used fer, here's the way it will be. I'll help ye earn more, ye'll share with me, then I'll help ye fix yer cabins, buy nice clothes, order in fancy furnishings. Whatever ye want, I'll pay fer it. Understand?"

She waited for her words to sink in while the women whispered among themselves.

"I like the idea," Jennie declared at last. "I been a-wantin' a change in lifestyle." She glanced at the other women and soon they all agreed.

"Good, but I ain't done yet," Molly continued. "Ye need to start bathin' every day."

"Bathe? In the dead of winter?" Broncho Liz gasped. "Ya want us dippin in that ice-covered creek when it's twenty-below-zero? Ye're plumb crazy if ya think I'm gonna do that!" She grinned lopsidedly.

"The men will gladly haul water fer ye if ye offer to let 'em watch ye splashin' around a bit. Fer a coin or two, they kin scrub yer backs, too. If ye pleasure them, they'll pleasure ye with more gold. That's when ye tell them they're gonna need bathing, too, before they kin romp with ye." Molly beamed. She knew exactly what she was talking about.

Liz snorted while the other women snickered.

"Ain't none of my men what take baths more than once a year," Jenny chortled. "Don't know what it'd be like to bed a clean fellow."

"Men anxious fer a tumble with a sweet smellin' lady will take to bathin'," Molly promised. "Fer an extra coin or two, ye can offer to scrub their backs, too, and trim the burrs from their hair and beards. They'll git to likin' it, I promise, and yer fees will move up faster than a jackrabbit on the run. And while ye're washin' yerself, wash yer clothes and beddin'. Chiggers ain't no fun to sleep with."

"Them fellas are gonna get real mad when they find out they gotta bathe in that icy creek," Liz declared, her thoughts on her favorite, Old Lightning.

"I thought ye liked tough guys," Molly teased.

Liz sputtered then a smug grin crept across her face. "I'll go fer it but just know, if ya hear hollerin' and stuff being broke up, it's Lightnin'. He ain't gonna be happy about this. I'll have to offer him lots of warmin' up time if he's gonna go fer it—and free whiskey." She tossed her head back and laughed wickedly.

Phil arrived with the whiskey then quickly disappeared back outside when the women yelled at him to get out 'cuz women's business was going on.

Molly talked of fumigating the cabins spring and fall, hanging curtains on the windows and putting rugs on the splintery floors. Better chinking would keep out the cold, and patched roofs would keep out the rain. Any girl wanting a bigger cabin could come to

Molly and she'd be certain to build another cabin or enlarge the current one. Last of all, if they couldn't read, they should learn. Wealthy businessmen always pay more to bed educated ladies.

By the time the doves left Molly's cabin, they were buzzing with new ideas. Meanwhile, outside Cabin One, long lines of miners and cowboys were lining up hoping for a tumble with Molly herself. She begged out with the excuse it had been a long and tiresome day. What she needed now was food and sleep. Almost before the words were spoken, the miners were scrambling to fetch food and clean bedding. Phil was the last to leave her cabin.

Chapter 23

April 1883

15 March 1883

Dearest Parents,
    Murray is wonderful. Because I help people, the town calls me an angel from heaven. Life here is exciting and challenging, each day an adventure. Soon we'll make plans for your visit.

Lovingly,
Maggie

As predicted, the men were receptive to preparing baths for the doves but not at all happy to bathe themselves in the icy waters of Prichard Creek. It was only after learning they could watch the women bathe that their attitudes changed. Lightning did not come around that easily, however. He ranted and raved, smashed things, yelled and stomped from one end of town to the other voicing his annoyances with the red lantern ladies. Finally, Liz turned on the charm and gave him exclusive rights to her cabin while she bathed in frothy, sweet-smelling bubbles—then offered to let him share the bath. That offer was too good to pass up so Lightning thereafter was an ardent supporter of the new rules.

Unlike many of the west's gold towns, Chinese workers in Murray were accepted, particularly in the winter when they willingly did work no one else wanted to do. They agreed to do the women's laundering no matter how cold were the days. Undaunted by sub-zero temperatures, they scurried back and forth between the cabins, creeks, and their own little shanties carrying buckets of water that sloshed as they ran. Laundered clothes were freeze-dried then flat ironed, with Molly picking up the cost.

Newcomers to Murray were notified first thing that if they had plans to frequent the fairy belles, they'd best learn to bathe in the creek. The rules were set in stone, they were informed, since the miners themselves enforced the rules just as if they were self-appointed vigilantes. Those refusing to cooperate were sent to Broncho Liz who had her own unique style of manhandling. The up side was in learning the whores of Murray were not only clean but their beds were free of bedbugs and chiggers.

It didn't take long for the ladies of the line to come up with other ideas on how to generate higher pay from their customers. Some had fine pastries and wine waiting, some provided imported cigars, and some were treated to music and dancing. It was heartening to Molly to see the line changing almost before her eyes. While the cabins were not yet classy bordellos, they were moving in that direction. And true to her word, Molly entertained only a select few individuals, with Phil O'Rourke taking first honors. Within weeks, however, her income was such that she gave up doing men altogether. Part of it was due to the memory of Sam Maddison and his promise that he would come to her in the fall, the other was because she hated being a whore.

By spring, Sam hadn't shown up but she kept hoping he would find her. To maintain her position on the line, she occasionally performed baudy performances to standing-room-only crowds, stripping down to where only her long, blonde hair provided any modesty at all. Such performances maintained her reputation among the other prostitutes as well.

She christened her cabin The House of Pink. Miners and carpenters did extensive renovations including adding a second floor where her parents could stay when she sent for them. The lower level was used for parties and entertaining.

When her doors opened for celebrations, as they often did, there was always the finest food and champagne for everyone, with brass bands performing as well. She had learned from the best how to throw a party.

Molly was anxious to experience spring in the Coeur d'Alenes by exploring the thick forests and seeking out flowers peeking up through the fast-melting snow. After mentioning wanting to ride into the countryside, Phil showed up on his horse one morning with Willow in tow, all saddled and ready to ride. In his saddlebag were cheeses, a loaf of bread, and a bottle of wine.

"Ye ready fer a history lesson?" he asked brightly. "This country's got more character than all the rest of the west lumped together."

Molly was delighted and nearly beat him to the horses. Nicky, too, was jumping around with excitement. He chased his tail in circles, barking.

Casually they rode through the meadows and open flats, often pausing to enjoy the bluebells and buttercups. Songbirds dipped and dived through the air chasing bugs while coyotes loped through the meadows looking for squirrels and rabbits.

"Been t' Eagle City yet?" Phil asked. She shook her head so he headed out in that direction.

"Eagle was the first settlement in this area. Started with a dozen people then grew t' more than ten thousand in a year's time. Lumberjacks tried to clear off all the timber just to keep up with buildin' shelters and shops so ye can still see stumps everywhere. The trees will come back. We git lots o' rain."

Eagle City was bustling with activity when they rode into town even though it was not yet midday. Phil was greeted by a lot of people he knew and listened attentively as they told how fast miners were leaving the area. Too expensive to work claims needing large equipment and hydraulics for water mining. Many of the miners were dead broke so were packing up to move elsewhere, mostly to Murray. Phil aloud wondered why so much building was going on if everybody was moving out.

They didn't stay long in town but rode out toward an outcropping of granite cliffs looking down over the valley. After tethering the horses next to a stand of willows, they found some boulders to perch on while they enjoyed their food.

"The East Fork and West Fork of Prichard Creek come together here," Phil had explained as they rode past the junction of the creeks. "Prichard Creek rolls on through the valley all the way to Murray. Folks say there's so much gold in this valley it gets caught up in the grass roots."

"That's what Calamity told me," Molly smiled.

"Ye met Calamity?" he asked since Calamity hadn't been to Murray in a while. "She don't stay long. Just drinks, gambles, then goes again." Phil pulled up a fistful of grass, looked it over then dropped it back to the ground. "Ain't no gold in there," he grinned. "Wish there was 'cuz I'd stake a claim right here and now. I'd name it The Silver Dove." He winked at Molly.

"Truth be known," he went on, "the gold rush started right here. Old man Prichard[14] found it when him and his friends was lookin' fer a place to start a religious colony. The gold changed their plans once and fer all. When Prichard saw that gold sparklin' in the creek, he took to whoopin' and hollerin' like a drunken fool then stuck his claim right into the ground, claiming it all fer his own self."

"He claimed it all?"

"Well, most of it 'round here. Boasted nuggets as big as yer fist. Once he and his friends got their senses back, they decided to keep the gold's location secret so sneaked into Spokane Falls to have the gold assessed. Might have worked if they'd kept their flappin' mouths shut but they couldn't help braggin' about it to all their friends. Caused all hell to break loose. Like termites out of a rotten log, gold-hungry folks swarmed 'em demandin' to know where the gold was. Prichard tried to put 'em off 'til spring but they weren't in no mood to listen. They tried to hang him, even had the rope knotted and hangin' over a branch before Bill Osburn was able to talk 'em out of it. Said nobody could git into Murray 'til the snow melted anyhow, so the mob backed down."

[14.] In 1882, A. J. Prichard and four companions found 2 oz. of gold in a creek later named after him.

"It was Prichard what started all this?" Molly asked, fascinated by the story.

"Yup, he done it. That winter was freezin' cold but five-thousand idiots took to the trails anyhow. When gold fever strikes, ain't nobody got any good sense, me included. Them fools plowed through twelve-foot drifts just to git here. They bought up every inch of land, sometimes paying two-thousand dollars just fer places to set their tents on. Log shelters were built without windows even. All them folks cared about was havin' shelter from the snow and wind. Still, people froze in their beds. Them flimsy tents only had pot-belly lamps for heat and that didn't work so well. If there weren't lamps, candles were used until the stores run out of candles. Temperatures kept droppin' so desperate people kept each other awake all night, stampin' their feet and dancin' 'cuz if they laid down to sleep, they froze. Lost toes and fingers anyhow.

Molly's horrified expression caused Phil to burst out laughing.

"I swear, it's God's truth. Them fools risked freezin' just to get a jump on finding gold come springtime. Those what had money gambled all night, drinking whiskey to keep their juices flowin'. If that didn't work, they picked fights, sometimes shootin' each other out of pure meanness. Fact is, they killed off everybody in town that winter. Not a soul was left breathin'."

"What?" Molly gasped. "They all died?"

Phil couldn't stand it. He burst out laughing so hard he nearly fell off his boulder. It was a joke and Molly had fallen for it.

"Darlin', I live to tell that tale," he grinned, his eyes twinkling.

"Oh, ye ornery scoundrel, Phil O'Rourke," she quipped. "Ye lied t' me. I'll never believe ye again."

"Oh, Lassie, 'twas just a tale to tweak yer imagination. Story tellin's one of m' deadly sins. Truth is, most of what I told ye is God's truth. Ye saw Eagle City and all its law offices and banks and boarding houses. There's plenty of saloons. Sad thing is the town's gonna fizzle if the gold dries up."

"Are ye lyin' again, tellin' me the gold's runnin' out? Where's the people gonna go?"

"To Murray. Ain't ye seen all the prospectors wanderin' in? Did I tell ye George Murray got credit fer the name but Prichard shoulda had it. He's the one what settled the town."

Molly and Phil mounted their horses and continued their ride through the valley with Phil pointing out landmarks.

"There's some juicy scandal about ol' Prichard," Phil whispered as he pulled his horse up close to hers. "He always said he claimed his gold fer a three-hundred-pound widow lady from Illinois. Mary Lane was her name. 'Cuz of her size she couldn't travel on boats or trains so she bankrolled Prichard's wanderings. He owed her big time so he called one of his biggest discoveries the Widow's Claim. Well, there's this ugly woman named Eddington who wanted the claim fer herself and challenged him for it in court. She lost so she decided to marry Prichard to get the claim. Prichard was mortified. No way he wanted hitched to that awful woman so he beat it out of town fer a while." Phil laughed so hard he had to hold his sides.

"Wyatt Earp tried to jump Prichard's claims, did ye know that?" Phil said.

That surprised Molly. She reined Willow to a stop and stared at Phil.

"Ye're lying, ain't ye? Wyatt wouldn't do that."

"Oh, so ye know Wyatt, too, do ye?"

"He's a dear friend," she replied. "Now, is it true or not, what ye're sayin'?"

"It's true, I swear. Prichard's a cagey fellow. Claimed nearly everything he stepped on. Earp called him out on it saying it's illegal to file by proxy since US law only allows twenty acres to a placer claim if the person filing on it works it every year. Prichard fought Earp in court and won but Earp took him to court again and won the second time around. Trouble is, he couldn't pay the $8.67 taxes due on the claim so got run out of town fer a while."

Molly laughed out loud. Now that was the Wyatt she knew!

"Is Wyatt around here now? I'm surprised I've not seen him. He's so fond of faro I can't imagine him wantin' t' pan fer gold."

"Last month them Earp brothers invested a lot in Eagle 'cuz they figured the economy would rebound. The White Elephant

Saloon's theirs, did ye know that? That little songbird lady friend of his sets up performances there but she don't never let him out of her sight. He's got a keen eye fer the ladies."

"Wyatt's in this valley?" Molly couldn't believe her good fortune. She would love to see him again.

"Last I heard he was. He and his friends are pushing t' connect Eagle and Murray so the trails between the two and over t' Kingston and Osburn git better. They're wantin' good supply roads so they kin keep their businesses growin'."

"What does Coeur d'Alene mean?" Molly asked, changing the subject.

"It's Indian, far as I know. Has t' do with how Indians work the animal hides. General Sherman built the fort so us ruffians could be exposed to law and order." Phil chuckled. "'Course, we like makin' our own laws." He spanked the scabbard holding his rifle. "M' rifle's a good equalizer."

"Ye ever shot a man?" she asked, knowing full well he would probably never do such a thing.

"Never needed to. Ye know I'm a lover more than a fighter. Just ask the girls." He grinned at Molly, raising his brows in invitation but she just shook her head and smiled back. "Folks what know me quake in fear of m' prowess. Even bears turn tail and run when they see me a'comin'," he insisted.

"Ye bed the bears, too?" she asked, laughing out loud. Phil didn't find that too amusing.

"Now, darlin', let me ask ye a question," he said after a bit of silence. "We're all hopin' ye'll stay awhile in Murray. Are ye or not?"

"I ain't leavin' any time soon, if that's what ye're askin'. Truth is, m' life swings like a pendulum. When the clock strikes the right number, I move on. Fer now, though, I'm stayin'—if only people will stop callin' me a silver dove. I'm a soiled dove and there ain't no silver on m' wings." She raised her arms and shook them.

Phil didn't say much after that. Molly rode behind him wondering what was bothering him. She could have told him the truth, that she wasn't even considering leaving Murray what with all its excitement and the way the people felt about her. She liked that businesses were growing and entertainment was even coming to town now. Lurline Monte Verde was bringing in stage shows with stunts, music and dancing.

The churches even welcomed everyone, saints and sinners alike. She heard funerals united people in all the different churches where all ministers worked together to uplift the grieving and give due respect to everyone. Murray, Phil reminded her, had never held a pauper's funeral. Those words were priceless in her ears.

They rode back into town at sundown. Before them she saw a growing city of tents, shacks, and new buildings all wedged together in every direction. Gold Street, the place where Murray's nightlife flourished, was impossible to see from Main Street but the glow from the lanterns in the windows on Pleasure Alley was already visible. Tinny music from calliopes was resonating through the air calling town residents into the streets and saloons. Gamblers were taking their seats at the poker tables ready to bet anything and everything, including their gold and the horses tied to the watering troughs, if they felt their hands were good enough. High-stepping hurdy-gurdy girls hired to work the tables to keep beer and whiskey flowing were even out on the boardwalks.

"Phil, I'll not be goin' anywhere fer a while," Molly confessed. "This place is feelin' more and more like home."

Phil's face lit up. He was hoping she'd stick around since he was growing increasingly fond of her.

At the livery stable, he helped Molly off Willow, intentionally holding her longer than intended. Sweetly, Molly pushed him away but not before kissing him on the cheek.

"Kin we go fer another ride someday?" she asked sweetly. "It's been a wonderful day." He nodded.

With that, she clucked to Nicky then hurried past Phil toward Gold Street leaving him lamenting over whether or not he would ever be able to lay claim to Molly's heart.

Chapter 24

May 1883

21 May 1883

Dearest Mum and Da,
    I'm so happy. People love me and beg me to stay. Here gold flows through people's hands like water. You'd be surprised how much gold there is. A goldsmith would do well here.

Lovingly,
Maggie

An early morning knock on the door surprised Molly. Nicky, always ready to protect, didn't even growl but instead ran to the door, his tail wagging like crazy. He looked back at Molly and barked then ran around in a tight little circle before barking again.

"What's gotten into ye, small one?" she said.

Outside stood Annie Blue with her two young daughters. Even before she could invite them in, Daisy was in Molly's open arms, chortling as she was lifted up then hugged. She giggled when Molly tickled her.

"Ah, how big ye are," Molly exclaimed.

After setting her to the floor, she kneeled in front of Dew who timidly stepped back behind her mother. "Dew, ye are so beautiful," Molly smiled, holding out her hand and drawing Dew into a shy embrace.

"Come inside," she urged them all, standing up and taking Annie by the hand.

Nicky immediately captured the attention of the children, barking and licking their faces before chasing his tail and running around in circles. The girls were soon romping on the floor with him.

"I bring gift from husband to Angel who saved his family," Annie explained, holding out a fabric-wrapped parcel.

"A gift?"

"Yes, a gift from husband."

Molly accepted the heavy bundle, carrying it to the table where she quickly untied the bindings. Inside was a magnificent white buffalo hide large enough to cover her entire bed.

"This is magnificent," Molly exclaimed, holding it up. It extended clear to the floor. Tears welled up in her eyes as she touched its softness to her cheek.

"White buffalo sacred," Annie explained. "Legend says Great Spirit brought peace pipe to our people as young woman wearing white buckskin dress and moccasins. She left as white bison calf. Years ago, hunter killed sacred white buffalo. Tribe was very sad. A white man found hunter, took back hide and returned it to my people. Tribe name him Snow Buffalo in honor. He stayed to help tribe survive the hard winter. When he leave, chief gives him daughter as wife and bison hide as gift. Annie is wife. Now husband gives robe to Angel who saved his family."

"Snow Buffalo is an Indian name? What is his white name?" Molly asked.

"Joseph Maddison," she answered.

"Maddison?" Molly exclaimed. Could he be Sam's father?

"Annie, why were ye on that trail through the mountains? Is yer husband in Murray?"

"It was mistake. No caravans go to Coeur d'Alene and I not know the way so we follow others to Murray. People say it not far. Husband did not know where we were. After snowstorm mule team take us to Fort to husband. Now I come to Murray with gift for Molly."

When Annie and the girls left, it was to return to Snow Buffalo. Molly bid them well, holding the girls close one more time. They were now emotionally bound and that would never change. Alone again, Molly wrapped herself in the warm buffalo hide and lay down on the bed. Nicky leaped up beside her to nuzzle his face in beneath her chin.

"Life is good for us here, Nicky," Molly whispered. "It's like Julia said. There's a place fer everyone. I think this is our place."

Chapter 25

July 1883

22 June 1883

Dearest Mum and Da,
    I'm fixing a place for you. Begin to make plans. Maybe I can convince you to stay in America after our visit. I miss you both.

Lovingly,
Maggie

Dearest Charlie,
    I've not heard from you in a while. Please tell me you are well. Is Becca all right? She must be growing up by now. Please tell those wonderful scoundrels in the pub that I miss them all, especially Simon.

Adoringly,
Maggie

T HE RED LANTERN DISTRICT WAS flourishing. Molly devoted her days to promoting the ladies of the line, calling herself an entrepreneur. The women were happily enlarging their parlors and furnishing them with goods brought into town by the mule teams.

Knowing they also had nest eggs securely banked did a lot for the doves' self-esteem issues as well.

The House of Pink was white washed then trimmed in hot pink. A large slate stone was etched with the name and placed alongside a ten-foot tall alabaster statue of Venus, the goddess of love. The inner furnishings of the house were copy-cats of styles she had most admired in the bordellos of Mattie Silks and Julia Bulette. Colored glass windows, blood red or emerald green tapestries and rugs, ornate tables, and floor-to-ceiling bookshelves adorned the main rooms. The dinnerware set out for parties featured gold edging that matched the silverware. Molly insisted the kitchen be spacious and well suited for her to do her own cooking if she felt the urge. She was, after all, her mother's daughter—plus, her mother would be coming and would want a fine kitchen to cook in.

Molly's nightly ritual was precise. At ten o'clock, rain or shine, she left her house adorned in one of her many fancy gowns to visit one of the many saloons. She was always stunning in dresses seemingly molded to her curvaceous body. Her favorite colors were royal blue or midnight black with diamond-studded wristlets to hold up her trains. Rouge colored her cheeks and lips while her golden curls were tied up but not tight enough to keep them from tumbling casually around her bare shoulders. If she wore jewels, they were usually pearls or sapphires.

"Anyone here wantin' to party?" she would ask sweetly as she stepped through the doors causing everyone to turn and admire her. She loved making grand entrances.

"Molly," asked Amy, one of the doves, "should we be changin' our styles to match those of the cities? You know, them white eyelet dresses with puffy mutton sleeves?"

Molly's robust laughter gave her her answer.

"Darlin', Murray's finest want their women dressed in bright, daring colors that make them think of fire and romance, not purity and innocence. They don't pay us to be pure! They want naughty!"

When Molly learned the White Elephant Saloon had closed in Eagle and re-opened in an already existing saloon in Murray, Molly knew Wyatt must be in town. She hadn't seen him since Dodge City so couldn't wait to get to their new saloon.

Wyatt was playing faro at one of the tables when she walked in. Everyone stopped playing so he turned to see what the distraction was. And there stood Molly, every bit as beautiful as she had been the last time he saw her in Dodge City. He gasped in surprise, stunned by her appearance. Leaping to his feet, he rushed to her side, his spurs jingling. Raising her fingers to his lips, he kissed them gently them smiled that roguish smile of his.

"Dear Lord, Molly, could you be more beautiful? I kin hardly believe my eyes." Molly was delighted.

He escorted her to the faro table where Josie, his companion, was seated.

"Ah, the scoundrel found a new lover, I see," Molly teased, checking Josie out from head to toe.

Josie was a pretty woman, not exactly beautiful but not unattractive either. Her hair and eyes were brown, and her smile showed a distinct gentleness.

"Wyatt told me about you, Molly," she said in a soft voice. "I'm not certain but I think he loves you more than he does me."

Molly flashed a dazzling smile at Wyatt then sat down beside Josie. She liked this woman already.

"Wyatt and I shared a difficult time in Dodge when a dear friend was needlessly murdered. It is that which binds us together, not romance. Wyatt is one of the few treasured people in m' life. Actually, he tops the list." She ordered an Irish whiskey then downed it in one swallow.

"Do you always make entrances like that?" Wyatt asked, unable to take his eyes off Molly.

Molly winked at him then looked around the room, smiling at each man whose eyes she caught. "It's what I do, Wyatt, ye know that. Now, what's a girl gotta do to keep the whiskey comin'?" Her eyes were bright but sultry.

Wyatt headed off to get a full bottle of her favorite whiskey. That left Molly alone with Josie.

"I'm happy Wyatt found ye," she confided. "He's been such a lost soul. I see from his face he's happy now."

Josie agreed. "We've a special connection. I feel fortunate he lets me be part of his life."

Wyatt returned with the bottle, waiting while Molly took another drink. He remembered how much she enjoyed her Irish whiskey.

"You're good for business," he exclaimed. "The men adore you. How come I didn't know you were in Murray?" he asked.

"Like I said, it's m' business, cowboy," she teased. "And ye wouldn't have it any other way, now would ye?" She slowly drew her finger down his cheek, then toyed with his handlebar moustache.

Josie simply smiled. She knew Molly was teasing, and she knew what was between Molly and Wyatt in no way threatened the love she shared with him.

"You want to be careful not to rile this lady," Wyatt warned Josie. "She's got a hot temper. God help the man who mistreats somebody while she's around. She's likely to shoot the perpetrator right between the eyes." He shook his head solemnly, emphasizing his words.

"Now, Wyatt, ye exaggerate," Molly purred, toying with the empty whiskey glass, then motioning for another refill.

Wyatt snorted. "Like when you sent trays of food flying across the room and bottles of whiskey crashing to the floor 'cuz some starvin' fellow got refused a meal. I've seen you fling entire pokes of gold onto the floor for everybody to claim while you stood spraddle-legged over the gold, guarding it with your pistol drawn in case anybody dared interfere with your brand of justice. "Leave it be," she yelled at the target of her anger, "or I'll shoot ye dead. Ye ought not to take advantage of them what's got nothing.""

"It wasn't exactly like that," Molly argued. "Ye forgot to mention I was on m' horse at the time." Wyatt burst out laughing.

"You're right. I forgot about that. She rode into the saloon dressed only in furs once. Her bare legs were showin' clear to her thighs. She was so riled she snapped whiskey bottles off the shelf with a whip then rode her horse right to the counter demanding food and drink for every beggar in the place. "Belly up to the bar, boys, drinks are on the house," she yelled, snapping that whip like an avenging angel."

"Wyatt, you're embarrassing me," Molly told him, pulling on his arm so he would sit down and stop talking about her as though she was yesterday's headline in the newspaper.

"Ah, Molly, I'm just teasing. Truth is, Josie, this woman has the heart of a warrior."

"Wyatt, I swear, keep this up and I'll go visitin' a different saloon." It was not her intention to leave but she was growing uncomfortable listening to Wyatt tell of her escapades, even if they were true.

She stayed with them for most of the night, enjoying herself more than she had in months.

A few weeks later, the White Elephant became a target for one of Molly's wild rides of vengeance. A one-armed cowboy rode into town down on his luck and unable to find work so he could buy some grub. Never one to be surprised by Molly's actions, Wyatt just stood back and let her vent her rage. The Gold Strike Saloon was frequented a few nights later.

"Just be glad she's only giving away whiskey," Wyatt advised his barkeep. "I remember the time she rode into a saloon with a hammer in her hands because the owner turned away hungry wanderers. When she got done, there was nothing left but splinters and broken glass."

"Why do ya put up with that?" the man asked.

"Try turning some starving fellow away and you'll see why. She's so adored around here that if she say's she'll shut a place down, she'll shut it down and nobody will walk through them doors again. She's got more clout than the mayor himself. And when she leaves the place, she'll demand ya give the beggar a job, too. Even I won't cross Molly B'Damn!" He slapped his gloved hand down on the bar then turned and walked off.

In truth, Molly never expressed remorse for her violent tirades either. If she vented for some misdeed, then the perpetrator most likely deserved it. In her mind, she was honoring Julia's memory by helping the down and out. Still, on Sunday mornings she was always seated amongst the congregation at one of Murray's many Protestant churches. After waiting until the service began, she would slip into the chapel to sit at the back corner near the door, unnoticed. She always listened reverently to the sermons before generously donating to the collection baskets. Never, though, would she attend a Catholic service held by traveling priests of Cataldo Mission who often crossed the mountains to preach in Murray. Once Phil made the mistake of coaxing her to attend a Catholic service but he got such a tongue lashing that he never asked again.

Chapter 26

September 1883

22 September 1883

Dear Mum and Da,
    Autumn is back. I met an old friend, too. Wyatt Earp is a legendary lawman in the west. When you come, I promise to introduce you. Have you heard from Charlie lately? And how Is Nicholas?

Lovingly,
Maggie

CALAMITY JANE WAS A WOMAN always on the move and, like Molly, was always looking for adventure. She traveled the west searching for action. Her shooting skills were legendary, her tall tales outrageous, and her followers unlimited. Whenever she made it as far as Spokane Falls, she always crossed over the mountains to visit Eagle City and Murray. Even when the passes were closed by heavy snow, which was often, she managed to make it through. She once told of her horse breaking its leg and having to be shot on the far side of the pass. Customers in the saloons always grew silent when she told this particular story of her struggle to survive.

"The snow was blindin' me. I couldn't see m' nose on m' face," she explained. "There wasn't no landmarks fer me to follow, no trail, no other riders to help me out. All there was was that cussed blizzard swirling around me."

She told the spellbound audiences how she gutted out the horse then crawled into its body cavity, pulling in pine boughs behind her and huddling in a single blanket to keep warm. For three days she slept while the storm raged on. When she emerged, she came face to face with a lone wolf feeding on the horse's entrails. It looked her in the eyes, snarled a few times, then went back to eating. She just lay there and watched until he was done. After licking his chops and cleaning off his paws, he gave Calamity a parting glance, leaped to his feet, then took off on a slow lope up the mountainside. Every so often he would stop and look back as though urging her to follow. When she realized he was going to be her deliverer, she scrambled out of the cavity and hurried to keep up with him. Finally, exhausted and unable to plow through any more drifts, she dropped to her knees in a snow bank and just sat there. The wolf came back and waited, growling low in his throat. Summoning up her remaining strength, she pushed herself up and continued following him until he stopped on a ridge overlooking a valley below. There was the town of Murray.

"I couldn't believe what I was a seein," she proclaimed. "That gol-darn wolf saved me. When I looked around fer him, he was gone. Vanished. He musta wanted to pay me back fer givin' him such a good meal."

No one ever knew if she was lying or not. Even a free bottle of whiskey couldn't make her denounce the story. All anyone knew for certain was she had stumbled into Murray on foot one winter, nearly frozen, and from that day on no amount of coaxing could make her shoot a wolf.

Calamity enlisted a troupe of dancing girls to travel to Eagle this particular fall. Inside an enormous canvas tent, she took to the stage like a seasoned performer entertaining the men with hilarious monologues and shooting demonstrations. Afterward she introduced the dancing girls who performed a bit then went into the crowd offering dances to the men. Only one dance per person, she insisted, since there were too many people to get to in the time they would be there. The men were delighted to have even one dance with a pretty girl and to inhale the deep heavy perfumes each girl wore. When fights broke out, they were settled by Calamity's' blazing six shooters.

News of the highly-successful performance quickly reached Murray, causing quite a stir. The businessmen hired Calamity to bring the act to their town, which she did.

Calamity never sought Molly out when they were in the same town but they still encountered one another now and again. Their greetings were cordial. Nothing more, nothing less.

As the seasons changed and the nights grew colder, sickness came to Murray. Molly hated hearing that some of the miners were sick, suffering all by themselves up the many different canyons. Sometimes she would discreetly order packhorses loaded up with supplies to personally take to the ailing individuals. That prompted Phil to dub her "the valiant warrior," a name that stuck but not as firmly as "angel of mercy."

"Phil," she often chastised him, "either git on yer horse and ride with me to deliver these here supplies or shut yer mouth and git out of m' way. I ain't got time fer worthless patronizin'."

"Ye know I'll ride with ye anytime, Molly," he replied. "Somebody's gotta keep ye safe." He chortled to himself.

"There ye go, thinkin' I cain't take care of m'self. Do ye really think me to be such a weaklin'? Maybe we ought to punch it out, ye and me, and see who's the puniest." She loved prodding Phil.

"Ye probably could whip a she-bear," he conceded one day, spurring his horse to keep up with her on a mission to help a miner who had fallen off an outcrop and broken his leg. "Truth is, I'm needin' a ride in the autumn air so as to clear m' brain. I ain't goin' just to witness yer acts of charity in case that's what ye're thinkin." His high-pitched laughter always made Molly smile. Phil was always such a delight to be around.

"If ye think I'm needin' a man to help me out, ye'd best turn back now 'cuz I ain't needin' nobody, certainly not some cocky little Irishman."

"Admit it, ye need m' handsome face to keep yer spirits up. Ladies love havin' m' good looks close at hand so they kin feast on 'em whenever they're wantin' a treat."

"Aye, ye are a joy," she admitted. "I enjoy yer company even if ye're the devil's keenest liar."

Phil gasped as though shocked by her words. "Molly, what ye sayin?"

For several days, Molly attended to the ailing miner while Phil cared for the livestock and chopped wood for the fire. He even fashioned a sturdy crutch from a downed aspen to enable the miner to at least hobble around while his leg healed. Molly cleaned the cabin, baked bread, and prepared venison stew over the fire. Commodities were stocked onto the shelves to help him fend for himself once she and Phil left. Only when she was satisfied the miner could get by did she agree to return to Murray.

They had been gone a few days. When they reached town, crowds were already gathered all along Gold Street. Mischief had been afoot while they were away, and it came wearing the name of Broncho Liz.

From out of an alley she galloped onto Main Street astride her brutish buckskin stallion. She wore nothing more than a transparent shift that billowed out around her like a giant balloon, leaving nothing to the imagination. Her waist-long hair flared around her like a cloud but scarcely covered her nakedness. Gleefully waving her arms in the air, her knees locked against the horse's bare back, she threw a mocking grin to Molly. She never stopped trying to regain her queen status from Molly.

Phil gasped and glanced at Molly whose eyes had turned as black as night. Molly was hardly amused.

Without a word, Molly yanked Willow's head around and headed straight to the livery stable. After snapping out instructions for Phil to take care of the horses, she told him to pass the word around that she would be bathing at twilight in front of The House of Pink.

"In front of?" he gulped, his mouth dropping open.

Molly chucked him playfully under the chin.

"Ye heard me right. Bathing. And don't ye be late if ye want a good view."

He couldn't wait to tell everyone, and the word spread like wildfire.

By twilight, when Molly's door opened, thousands were already gathered to watch. Lanterns on the row glowed red inviting gentlemen callers but the men of Murray only wanted Molly.

She stepped outside like an angel descending from the heavens, her feet bare, her body covered in a translucent black silk robe edged in white rabbit fur. Golden curls straggled loose around her face accentuating her long, soft neck. She moved slowly, without rush, smiling as a slight breeze teased her robe to expose its blood-red edging. Behind her, she dragged a shiny, ornate copper bathtub embellished with golden butterflies and nymphs in flight.

Molly was a seasoned performer who knew full well how to heighten an experience. Now and then she paused to examine a flower or touch a pretty stone with her toe, exposing her bare leg, as she moved toward the bridge, then across and down the flagstone path toward Gold Street. She paused at the statue of Venus to let her fingers slide slowly down its smooth curves, smiling sweetly at her audience. As she drew near the crowd, it parted like the Red Sea just to let her pass. Everyone was enthralled, and Molly knew it. Not only was she breathtakingly beautiful but at this moment she also appeared fragile and innocent.

When she reached Gold Street, she looked all around for a place to set her tub where everyone could see. Once it was down, she yawned and stretched out her arms like a sleepy kitten. She extended one hand to Phil for steadiness while she looked down into the empty tub.

"Do ye need us to fetch water?" he whispered.

She shook her head then allowed a pout to creep across her face.

"It does look cold in there," she admitted.

Confused, Phil just stood there not knowing what she wanted from him.

"Maybe ye could let m' hair down?"

Ten men fought for that honor but Phil elbowed them back, cursing loudly. He intended to be the only man assisting Molly. Others in the crowd grumbled and protested but his eyes warned them to stay back. With clumsy fingers, he released the ribbons and stared as the rest of her golden curls tumbled down over her shoulders. One tie got knotted which caused much frustration on his part but not on hers. She was on stage and playing her part to the hilt. By the time the knot came free, Phil was sweating like a hard-run race horse.

Molly kissed him sweetly on the cheek causing his knees nearly to buckle.

"Lord love ye," he muttered huskily, stepping backward and nearly falling to the ground.

A reverent silence settled over the crowd as they waited. Even the girls from the line had shown up. Liz's mouth was agape as she watched the master at work.

"Well, boys," Molly drawled in a deep, raspy voice, "ye ready fer a show?"

The roar of the crowd was deafening as the mob pushed forward causing the men in front to muscle people back so she had room to work. The explosive crack of a pistol startled everyone, even Molly. Phil stood beside Molly, his pistol smoking and his legs braced for battle.

"Calm yerselves, fools, and back up so's the lady can take her bath!"

"Y' all ain't expecting me to sit in a cold tub, are ye?" Molly whimpered, peering into the empty tub. "Anybody got some gold to put in there to keep m' bottom warm?" She wiggled her hips suggestively causing a crush of miners to break rank, shoving past Phil to empty their pokes into the tub.

"Here's gold fer ya, Molly," Lightning bellowed. "We don't want ya catchin' cold, no ma'am." He snuffled loudly then chortled like he had hiccups before looking back at the delighted onlookers, motioning for them to step up, too.

"Thank ye, Lightning," she smiled, "and since ye were so quick to help, can ye hold m' hand so I don't slip?"

Lightning was there in an instant, his beefy hand outstretched.

"It still looks cold, don't it?" she frowned. "Ain't nobody else got somethin' to warm me up? Casper, ye got anything in that poke of yers so I kin get t' bathin' m'self? I came to bathe in gold, not sit in an empty unfriendly ol' tub." With a heavy sigh, she stuck out her lip then toyed with it with one finger.

Phil was beside himself. "Ye heard the lady," he yelled. "Warm up that tub! I'm gittin' anxious to see the rest of the show." He dumped the rest of his pouch into the tub with one hand while waving to the others to follow suit, which they did.

As the level of gold grew deeper, Molly heaved a grateful sigh. Daintily, she steadied herself on Lightning's strong arm then stepped into the tub, the robe parting to expose her slender bare legs.

"Lightning, will ye loosen m' robe?"

Lightning could hardly believe his good fortune. With awkward fingers he yanked at the ties, proud when they fell free and the robe slipped down over Molly's bare shoulders. He caught the robe before it hit the ground, clutching it to his chest like a prize won. Molly stood before the crowd dressed only in her birthday suit. An audible sigh of admiration swept through the crowd while skirmishes started up amongst those unable to see what was happening. Some of the onlookers began scrambling onto roofs or hiking themselves up onto the shoulders of their friends so they could see.

Jealous of Lightning's good fortune, Phil held out his hand to also help Molly lower herself into the tub. She winked at him then smiled and addressed the crowd. "All right, boys, cover me with gold," she laughed, her arms crossed over her chest as she pretended to shiver. "I'm freezin' cold, can't y' see?"

"Yeah, Molly's freezin'. Git up here men," someone hollered. A hundred cheering onlookers crushed forward holding forth their pokes in their outstretched arms. Each man with gold got to come to the front to pour the gold over Molly. They emptied gold dust and nuggets from saddlebags, pouches, boots, hats, and pockets. Nuggets of silver sparkled there, too. For nearly an hour, gold was added to the tub as it piled every deeper over Molly's bare body. With well-timed, provocative wiggling, she kept nestling herself ever deeper, purring like a kitten as she scooped gold dust up to trickle down into her hair and across her shoulders.

That breathtaking bathing performance[15] by the Silver Dove of the Coeur d'Alenes would become legendary in time but, for now, Molly was rolling the boys with all the skill and polish of a professional. She knew exactly when there was gold in the miners' pokes, and she knew exactly how to get them to give it up.

Time moved slowly as Molly proceeded to wash with gold dust, scrubbing her neck, her face, and her arms, all the while humming softly and smiling at her hypnotized audience. She invited men to come help her wash or perhaps to lift up her hair as her body took on an ethereal glow.

"Who's got the biggest gold nugget in town?" she asked Phil, who stood over her like a stellar guardian. "Maybe he could wash m' toes?" She wiggled her feet up to the tub's rim then waited.

Wyatt stepped forward holding out a dozen large nuggets. "I'll be doing the whole leg, not just the toes," he laughed as he perched himself on the edge of the tub. Molly couldn't have been happier. With a teasing smile she raised one foot to his lap and allowed him to tickle her toes with gold dust, then the other foot came up. When she was satisfied with a job well done, Wyatt grinned and shook his head.

"Fer all that, I get a kiss, too," he told her. She accepted the kiss willingly then seductively whispered so only he could hear.

"It's what I do," she repeated.

"And you do it so well," he grinned.

Innocently, she nodded then turned her attentions back to the crowd while Wyatt kept his seat alongside her.

After another hour, and with the crowd's excitement still at fever pitch, the sound of harmonica music began to filter through the night air. Soon there was fiddle music and men began dancing with one another or fighting over the hurdy-gurdy dancers. The men hopped about like clumsy leprechauns, leaping in their heavy boots and singing aloud whether in tune or not with the music.

Wyatt, always alert to an opportunity, ordered tables set up in the streets and food brought out to feed the hoards. Whiskey flowed like water as the night became an endless celebration of unprece-

---

[15.] This event actually happened and made headlines in the local papers.

dented merriment heretofore unmatched in all the tales of the west. And not a single person got shot.

As the novelty wore thin, Molly asked Phil and Lightning to help her out of the tub. Happily they helped brush away the clinging gold dust then held out her robe.

"It's a mite uncomfortable sittin' on nuggets," she confided, causing them both to laugh.

With the robe cinched in place, she went looking for the fiddler. "Lend me yer fiddle?" she asked the man. He couldn't have been happier to handle the fiddle to her. Once she had fiddle in hand, the second part of her performance began.

No one had known before that night that Molly could fiddle, much less dance—and it was a sight to behold. She hadn't touched her fiddle since arriving in Murray but now she was ready to play—and play she did. Her fingers expertly released tunes she'd known since childhood. Her dancing was light and graceful as she lost herself in the joy of music. When she finally surrendered the fiddle back to its owner, Phil handed her some slippers so she could dance with the miners. He also poured her a glass of Irish whiskey that was instantly downed and held out for a refill over and over again.

Editor Adam Auhlbach[16] printed in Murray's newspaper's head-lines that week about "Molly B'Damn, the woman who rolls boys and bones." He had been in the audience that night and knew the story would boost his readership throughout the Silver Valley. What he didn't report was that Molly's take that night was more than for-ty-thousand dollars' worth of nuggets and gold dust.

Molly woke up in her bed the next morning with a pounding hangover and Nicky licking her face. "Ah, little one, can't ye let a lady sleep?"

He barked playfully, tugging at the covers with his teeth. She ruffled his fur, amused by his energy and luxuriating in a warm gid-diness she felt when recalling the success of the previous night. Her

---

[16.] Adam Auhlbach was editor of the Coeur d'Alene Sun in Murray and a friend to Molly. He died in Murray in 1933 at the age of eighty-seven.

feet were sore and bruised by the boots of the high-stepping miners but she couldn't recall how she got home. Probably Phil, she thought.

On the main room's table and all around on the floor were stacked bags bulging with gold, all waiting to be hauled to the bank.

"Oh, my," she exclaimed, "we did do well, didn't we?" Nicky barked then jumped onto the settee near one of the tables and watched as Molly counted some of the gold.

"This is more gold than I've ever seen," she told herself. Scandalous behavior paid well, no question about that.

Suddenly, Julia's face flashed before her eyes. Julia had been a wealthy woman, too, but someone murdered her to get to what she had. A chill coursed down Molly's spine. Everyone in town knew by now what had taken place last night. She could easily become a target just like Julia was.

"Nicky, we gotta git this gold t' the bank," she declared, scrambling to locate her pistol. "Stay close by or we could end up like Julia, dead and buried in Pauper's Field."

Within minutes, she was dressed and carrying bags of gold toward the bank. She made trip after trip until, breathing a sigh, the last deposit had been made in the name of Maggie Hall.

As she left the bank, she decided to eat breakfast at the Gold Strike Saloon. As she stepped onto the boardwalk headed that way, a familiar voice called her name. Whirling around, she saw Sam Maddison standing behind her.

"I wondered when you'd show up," he drawled.

Molly leaped into Sam's open arms, hugging him tightly. "Where did ye come from?" she laughed.

"Oh, I've been sitting outside this here saloon waiting for you to wake up. I figured you must have been exhausted." His eyebrows raised up as he watched her expression.

"You were there?" she asked, dropping the Irish accent.

"Ah yes, I was there, and I realize now that you were right. There's more to you, Girl, than I realized." He pursed his lips, watching her from dark, scowling eyes, then grinned, his blue eyes twinkling. "You're a celebrity. Maybe I've been away too long."

Possessively and with a grin as broad as all outdoors, Molly linked her arm with his, winked at him, then led him toward the saloon. "I'm starved," was all she said.

After the meal, she ordered a shot of whiskey for herself and one for Sam.

"Here's to entertainment," she declared, raising the glass.

Chapter 27

September 1883

> 30 September 1883
>
> Dear Mum and Da,
>   Life is wonderful. Samuel found me again and I am happy. I didn't realize how much I missed him. I want you to meet him.
>
> Your daughter,
> Maggie

PHIL O'ROURKE ENTERED THE SALOON while Molly was sitting with Sam. The stranger's face seemed vaguely familiar but he couldn't recall why. What he did notice was the way Molly looked at him.

"Molly, how be ye this morning?" he asked cheerily, his eyes focused more on Sam than on Molly.

"Life is wonderful," she replied, briefly glancing up at him before returning her attentions to Sam. "My feet are bruised but I'm happy as can be. This is my dear friend, Samuel Maddison. He's the one what found Willow for me." She reached out and covered Sam's hand with her own.

Phil's heart wrenched. Sam was obviously more than just a friend. He tried to shrug off the pangs of jealousy but he couldn't do it so, with a heavy heart he bid them good day and left the saloon for the White Elephant where he intended to drink himself into a stupor.

"You didn't say you were an actress," Sam told her. "Bathing in gold is an act I've never heard of, much less been witness to. It was quite entertaining."

"Sometimes life in Murray gets boring and needs spicing up," Molly replied, coyly dropping her eyes. "If I'd known you were in the audience, I'd have asked you to help me out."

"Couldn't get through the crowd," he replied. "I tried, believe me I tried. Somehow I doubt if life ever gets boring with you around. Are there other talents I should know about?"

"None I can think of," she laughed, her heart beating like an infatuated school girl's. "How did you find me? I didn't stay long in Virginia City."

"I just kept asking if anyone had seen the prettiest girl in the west and everybody knew exactly who I was looking for. Since I'm looking for my father, too, the quest for you both led me right to north Idaho."

"Where is your father?"

"I'm not certain but I think he's in Fort Coeur d'Alene or working the timbers near there. I have to find him soon. My mother is dying and wants to make peace with him. I told her I'd take care of things but she wants to see him. I think they still love each other. At any rate, when I find him we'll ride back to Utah together or get onto a train in Montana to save time." Sam's expression reflected his concern.

Molly and Sam soon left the saloon and went right to Molly's place. "What do you think of my house?" she asked.

"It's very impressive, Girl," he exclaimed. He actually felt a little uncomfortable there so avoided the subject of her business. "It was dark last night so I didn't see much of the place."

"You were here?" she exclaimed, staring at him.

"How do you think you got home with all that gold? I couldn't imagine you wanting to lose what you worked so hard for." He laughed, his blue eyes bright and challenging.

"We should talk about last night," Molly started to explain.

"No need," he interrupted. "I know what you do."

"It's time I tell you about myself." She motioned him into a chair near the window then sat down beside him. "When I was in Boston, I married a fellow. He was rich and handsome and swept me off my feet. I was very young and thought I loved David more than anything. Unfortunately, his father disowned him because of me. They didn't want a lowly Irish girl defiling their uppity family. After being disowned, David became desperate for money but he didn't want to work. Finally, in desperation, he begged me to prostitute myself so he wouldn't go to debtors' prison. He was so depressed and sad that I gave in thinking it would only be once. Instead, it became a frequent occurrence and I found myself trapped in a situation I couldn't control. As the money rolled in, he became greedy and controlling. When I couldn't stand it anymore, I left him and came west. The only good thing from my time with David was finding Nicky." She bent down and scratched the little dog's ears.

"Is that how you afford all this, through prostitution?" Sam asked, looking around the room.

"It used to be how I earned my way. Not anymore. Now I am a business manager for the other prostitutes. They're vulnerable and used to living only for each day. Now I take a percentage of what they earn and set some aside for me and some for them for when they are sick or in need of special things. There will come days when they can't work anymore. The earnings I set aside will help them live in hard times. And that's how I can afford this house."

"I've seen cribs of slave prostitutes in Salt Lake City but they're a far cry from anything like this. You do have good taste, Girl. Brother Brigham's house is the only one I've seen fancier than this."

"Sam, did you hear what I said. I used to be a madam but I'm not one anymore. You gave me the desire to stop whoring. I don't want you disappointed in me." A hopeful smile flashed across her face.

"It never occurred to me to be disappointed in you. I did feel like a fool when I realized just how popular you are but I never thought you lied to me."

He stood up and wandered around the room touching things, taking it all in with his eyes. He opened the Bible with her name engraved on the front and read of Molly's marriage before closing it again.

"How often do you bathe in public?" he asked, raising his brows as he looked back at her. "I'd not like my wife to do that very often."

"Last night was a first," she giggled, "and we're not married so it shouldn't matter anyway."

Sam sat down and beckoned Molly to his lap.

"Phil helped me carry your gold here while you were still dancing in the streets. Getting you home once you'd had your fill of whiskey was a task in itself. Phil was so drunk he could hardly stand up but I needed help finding out where you lived so he led the way. Hell, I had no idea you lived like this."

"Phil is a dear friend. I don't know what I'd do without him," Molly replied. She pushed back on errant curl on Sam's head.

"What about us, Molly? You say we aren't married, and that's right, but I want to change that. Will you marry me?"

Molly's heart skipped a beat. She stood up and began to pace. This conversation was going down a road she still wasn't ready to travel.

"Sam, I'm afraid of what you're asking."

"And what is that?"

"I'm afraid of being hurt again. I don't trust men, not even you. I've learned the hard way," she whispered lamely.

"You think I'd hurt you or let you down?" he asked. "Is it your intention to stay here in Murray managing prostitutes the rest of your life?" he asked, his eyes boring into her soul.

"For now I'll stay. When I tire of this place, I'll probably move on again." She tried avoiding his stare.

"Girl, I'm gonna say this plain and simple. Come back here and look at me." His fingers lifted her chin and brought her face to where she had to look him in the eyes. "Since the day you stepped off that stagecoach in Eagle Rock, you're all I've wanted. Why I ever let you ride out of my life, I can't figure, but now that I've found you again, I don't want to lose you again."

"Sam, I've tried to tell you before. You don't know anything about me. My past is dark and sinful. Why would you want me to be your wife? Men don't marry whores, you should know that."

"Some men do, and I'll gladly add my name to that list if you'll let me."

She pushed away from him again, pacing around the room. "The first man I ever loved betrayed me for money. He swore he loved me but he loved money more. Since then I've been used and abused by hundreds of men whose names I don't even remember. I've a dark side, my temper is volatile, and I have an insatiable need to keep moving. I'm not the kind of woman you should even want to marry. To see my past is to see my future. God says I'll go to Hell for what I've done."

"Did you kill someone?" he asked.

"No, I didn't kill anyone," she snapped. "I'm not that deranged!"

"Have you done anything good in your life?"

"Of course I have," she replied, calming down.

"Are you afraid of me?" he asked. "Afraid I'll be like your husband?"

"Yes, I'm afraid you'll betray me. Men always betray the women they love." Molly was shaking now and starting to cry.

"Then you really don't know me either," he replied, now standing behind her. "I intend to marry only once in my lifetime. Only once. And when I marry, I want children. Do you want children or is that another thing you are running away from?" His words took on a sarcastic tone.

"I wanted children once but David killed that dream, too. I'd never want a child born from prostitution."

"I'd never hurt you," he said quietly, taking hold of her shoulders and turning her around so she faced him.

"That's what David said," she replied, looking him directly in the eyes.

"Do you love me, Molly?" he asked.

Molly just stared at him, unable to say the words.

"Is there someone else? Phil maybe? It's obvious how he feels about you."

"Phil is a friend. I have lots of male friends."

"Molly, when I ride out of here today, will you even care that I've gone?" he asked. He wore a scowl that showed how unhappy he was with this conversation.

"I'll be sad," she whispered, "but I'll survive." She walked to the window and stared out into the waning daylight. "Can't we just be friends, Sam?"

"Girl, I'm a religious man, straight and simple. I believe we are born to fulfill a greater destiny. We chose the types of trials we'd be willing to take on in life, and we chose the people we would share our lives with. It was pre-ordained that you and I would find each other, I believe that. I can't just walk away because you're uncomfortable with the idea of marriage."

"Believe as you will, Sam, but God abandoned me long ago," Molly argued. "My soul is doomed. Why would you want to be with me knowing where I'm headed when this life is over?" Molly began to cry.

"Because that's not the kind of God I believe in. My God forgives people, no matter what. He knows what's in our hearts and the kind of people we really are. We may not be perfect but that's true of everyone. He knows that and simply hopes we'll do our best in life."

"I'd like to meet your God," Molly sighed. "He's not at all like the God I've worshiped."

"Molly, marry me," Sam said. "We'll start a new life together."

Sam waited for her to speak but she didn't. With a heavy sigh, he reached for his hat and headed for the door. Perhaps he had made a grave mistake in thinking she loved him as much as he loved her.

"I'm going after my father," he stated simply. "Once things with him and mother are settled, I'll come back one last time. When I do, I'll expect an answer to my proposal." He wiped away her tears with his fingers then kissed her lightly on the cheek. "Don't leave here until I come back, okay?"

She nodded.

"All right, then I'm headed on to the Fort."

"Wait, I have something to tell you," Molly declared, wiping away her tears. "I think our newspaper editor can help you find your father."

"I'd appreciate the help. Dad's probably cutting trees somewhere around here."

"I know his family, that's what I need to tell you," she laughed, running into the bedroom and returning with the white buffalo robe.

"What's this?" he asked, holding up the hide.

"This is what got him the name Snow Buffalo. His wife gave the robe to me just weeks ago."

Sam was astonished. "You know my father?"

"No, just his wife Annie Blue and the girls."

"There's a story here, isn't there?" he surmised, running his fingers through the soft fur. "Maybe when I come back, you can tell me about it."

"Annie says they live in the mountains near the Fort. When he traps in the winter, she and the girls live in the Salmon River range with her people. Let's go ask Adam for help."

They hurried down Main Street to the news office of the Coeur d'Alene Sun. A gold bell over the door announced their arrival causing Rose, the petite fiancée of the owner, Adam Aulbach, to look up from her typesetting. Adam was sitting next to her on a stool, humming off key.

"Good afternoon, Adam," Molly purred, stepping around the counter to kiss her fingertips and touch them suggestively to Adam's cheek.

Adam shrieked, embarrassed by her brazenness, then leaped off his stool sending type flying everywhere. He glared at Molly, his dark eyes angry as they darted back and forth between Rose and Molly. Molly could get under his skin faster than any person in town.

Rose and Molly were actually good friends so Rose found no threat in Molly's actions. As Adam hopped around the room on his tiptoes, as he always did when he was angry, he pointed his fingers right in Molly's face.

"You are not allowed behind this counter, Ms. Molly," he bellowed, completely out of control, his cheeks flaming red. "We've talked about this before!"

Rose, amused by Adam's high-strung reaction, just smiled, her brows raised in mock surprise. Molly tossed a playful wink her way. Adam was so stodgy it gave Molly a treat just to get a rise out of him.

"Calm down, sweet man," Molly said quietly, her eyes sultry and inviting. "Rose might think you have secrets." She laughed then winked again at Rose. "Besides, I need to check on my invitations. Did you remember to edge them in gold dust for my party Friday? I expect to see you both there."

"Of course we're coming," Rose replied before Adam could say no.

"Molly," Adam kept shrieking, "it is inappropriate for you to come back here. Do not ever step behind the counter again, do you hear me?"

"Oh, Adam," Rose declared, "the entire town can hear you. Settle down. You're face is so red I'm beginning to think there's a reason Molly excites you so." Her teasing only annoyed Adam more. "She's our best customer so she deserves special considerations."

Adam was so upset he still couldn't even speak.

"Molly, don't pay attention to Adam. He's easily excitable, aren't you dear?"

Adam was so worked up all he could do was push Molly back out from behind the counter, his hands fluttering like a butterfly.

"My friend needs help," Molly explained after stepping out from behind the counter. "He's looking for his father, Joseph Maddison. Shoshones call him Snow Buffalo. Do you know him?"

"Of course I know him. Everybody knows him," Adam snapped, his ego still smarting. "I saw him in Wallace last week working a timber crew. He said he would be in Kingston all this week."

"Is Kingston far?" Sam asked. "Can I make it there in a day's time?"

"Heavens yes, it's just over the mountain. Joe rides a big chestnut stallion, biggest I've ever seen. It's got stocking feet and a half-blaze on the forehead. Chances are Joe's squaw and girls are nearby. She rides a black paint. Never walks like other squaws."

"That information is helpful," Sam grinned, shaking Adam's hand.

"You're his son?"

"Yes, from his first family in Utah."

"Joe's a polygamist? Well now, that's a story. You're the son Joe's always talking about. He says you're a keen horse trader." Adam had calmed down by now and was looking for another news story.

"Mother's dying so I'm here to fetch him home before she passes," Sam explained. "I have to get him in and out of Salt Lake City before the authorities know he's there."

"If you start now and ride fast, you can cross the pass before dark, then turn due west. Ask around. Everybody knows him. He's a fine man," Adam assured Sam.

Once outside, Sam went right for his horse. "I'd best be going," he told Molly. For a moment, he paused to look deep into her eyes.

"You may try to fool yourself into believing you're not in love with me, Girl, but I've looked into your eyes. I've seen how you really feel so don't you be going anywhere 'til I return. It might be a few weeks but I'll be back."

Molly raised her face to Sam so he could kiss her good-bye. Minutes later, he was in the saddle galloping out of town.

Molly felt deeply saddened when he left. Despite her arguments to the contrary, she did have deep feelings for him. Even Nicky was droopy when Sam left.

Inside the printing office, Rose was watching.

"Adam, I think Molly's in love."

"Molly, in love? Prostitutes don't fall in love," he snickered unkindly.

"Oh, Adam, don't be silly. Prostitutes have feelings just like everyone else. Just because their jobs are unusual, it doesn't mean they can't fall in love. This fellow is different. You can see in their eyes they're in love."

She reached for Adam's hand and squeezed it gently. Adam himself was an odd fellow but she loved him as much as Molly must love Sam Maddison.

Adam stared at Rose for a minute then looked out at Molly. She was still standing in the street watching Sam ride off up the mountain.

Chapter 28

October 1883

6 October 1883

Dearest parents,
    Winter is here already. Thousands of people are flocking into town buying supplies and looking for shelter from the terrible winters. Sometimes the shelters are no more than flimsy pieces of canvas. It's very frightening. I worry about them.

Your daughter,
Maggie

LIGHTNING[17] WAS A GRUFF OLD miner, not exactly old in years but old in life's experiences. He led a lonely existence as a gold panning miner. Many miners used hydraulic dredging but he detested the way the hydraulics raped the hillsides and stripped them of their vegetation. Most of the time Lightning stayed at his claim living in a cabin with his partner, Zach. Now and again he rode down out of the hills to replenish their supplies of food, equipment and, most importantly, whiskey. While in town, he got his fill of wild woman, particularly Broncho Liz who always gave him his money's worth.

---

17. Lightning was a true figure in Molly's life. The narrative about him is authentic. Some say he left her a fortune when he died.

He was a big man, gentle in heart, but when he drank too much, he turned mean. Liz was the only one who could control him since she matched him in size as well as temperament.

Lightning rode into town that fall on his skinny-but-reliable little mule, Jessie. In the saddlebag was a pouch heavy with enough gold to buy supplies to last the entire winter. After tying Jessie to the hitching post in front of the White Elephant Saloon, he strode inside, bought a bottle of whiskey, drank it down, then bought another. He was mighty thirsty. Before long, he was stupid drunk and growing increasingly obnoxious, shouting at everyone but no one in particular as he staggered toward Paradise Alley. He started out at Broncho Liz's place, bellowing angrily when she insisted he take a bath. Later, with bottle in hand, he visited more red light houses before finally passing out in one of them sometime before dawn.

It was midday when he awoke to not only find the cabin empty but his poke of gold was gone, too.

"M' poke's gone," he roared, storming half naked out of the cabin like an enraged bull. He kicked the door off its hinges as he stomped outside yelling for the whore who stole his gold to bring it back before he rung her scrawny neck. All down the line the ladies went into hiding, terrified for their lives. Lightning was big and mean enough to kill every one of them if he chose.

"Your thievin' whores done stole my poke," he raged, crashing through Molly's front door. He was so upset he was nearly in tears. "Where is it, Molly? Ya best tell me or I'll choke it out of ya," he snarled, grabbing her by the neck

"I never took yer poke," Molly answered calmly, her hands gently covering his. "I don't know nothin' about it. What I do remember is trying to send ye back onto Main Street last night but ye shoved me aside. Ye wouldn't take m' advice."

"Ye're lying, ya thief. Ya got my poke, I know ya do!" He released his hold on her, shoved her to the side then stormed around the house breaking everything in sight.

"I ain't lyin'. I don't know where yer poke is. Now git out of here, Lightnin'. Ye knew this kin happen when ye drink too much."

"I ain't goin' 'til I get my poke back. If ya don't got it yerself, then ya better find it." With one hand, he swept one of the tables clean then smashed an unlit coal-oil lamp.

"Lightnin'," she reasoned, "I got no control over them gals when ye're alone with 'em, ye know that! If ye can't control yer drinkin', ye're askin' t' be rolled. Ye were with every whore on the strip last night. How could I possibly know who rolled ye?"

Slowly his anger faded. He slumped down in a chair, dropped his big head down between his hands and tried to calm the pounding in his brain. She was right. It wasn't her fault.

"It's a whole year's work, Molly," he whimpered, looking up at her with big, sad eyes. "Now I ain't got enough to even buy a meal, much less stock up fer winter. What am I gonna do?" He began to sob, deep heart-wrenching sobs, rubbing his eyes with his meaty fists then running his fingers through his hair. "What'll I do? How we gonna make it through the winter?"

Molly just shook her head. For all his bluster, he was a good man and she felt sorry for him.

"I'll loan ye a grubstake," she decided, handing him a bag of gold. "Now go git some food in yer belly then git yer supplies."

"I ain't taking yer charity," he exploded, knocking over the chair as he stood up. He slapped away her outstretched hand holding the pouch of gold.

"It's a loan, ye old bear, not a gift," she snapped back as she grabbed his fist and shoved the pouch into it. "Are ye gonna deny me a chance to help a friend in need? Ye'd help me if I needed it, wouldn't ye?"

Slowly he nodded. He adored Molly.

"Like I said, it's a loan, not a handout, so I'll expect ye to pay me back when ye strike it rich!" She touched his face with her soft hands. "Take it, Lightnin'. Let me help ye, Old Bear." Her eyes were soft and pleading.

Lightning's expression softened as he reached for Molly then hugged her so tight she could hardly breathe. "Molly, ye're God's livin' angel, just like people say ya are. I'd give ya anything ya needed.

'Course, there ain't so much to give ya right now. It's all gone." He tried to laugh but couldn't.

"I know ye would help me, Lightnin'. Now, go find yer clothes then git over to the saloon fer some food so ye can calm that headache that's probably rattlin' yer brain. Git yer supplies before ye hook onto another bottle of whiskey, ye hear?"

He nodded then walked to the door. "Sorry about the door. I'll come back and fix it fer ya," he promised.

"I'll get Phil to take care of it. Ye need to get yer supplies before ye run into Liz again."

Lightning laughed then walked away.

Molly heard that Lightning had, indeed, bought himself a meal and some winter provisions before buying more whiskey and riding out of town.

The autumn season soon surrendered to the early snows of winter. Storms began blocking the mountain passes. Molly didn't hear anymore about Lightning for several weeks, not until his partner Zach came riding into town. He went straight to the Dutch Jake Saloon where he ordered up one drink and then another. His face was pale and somber when he announced Lightning was back at the cabin dying of mountain fever.

Phil ran to tell Molly.

Within minutes, Molly was at Zach's side. "Is it true, Lightnin's sick?" she demanded, grabbing hold of his shirt sleeve. Zach just scowled at her then yanked his arm away. "Answer me, ye stubborn cuss, or I'll blow yer head clean off yer shoulders!"

Zach was a short, stout fellow with a sour disposition even on his good days. His matted gray beard hung nearly to his belt and his clothes reeked of sweat and grime. He spat past Molly into the spittoon before giving her a look of sheer contempt.

"Ye're gonna take me to him, do ye hear?" she ordered, her eyes as black as thunder clouds. "I'll be back in fifteen minutes and ye're gonna lead the way."

Zach kept scowling.

"Ye gone deaf?" she growled. "Ye know ye're stone broke. How ye planning to buy medicine fer Lightning when ye got no gold?"

"What do you care?" Zach snapped. "Twas yer whores what stole our gold in the first place, and you let 'em do it. Them whores ain't nothin' but thieves, the whole lot of 'em. It ain't right, stealin' a man's hard work, it just ain't right."

"All the more reason fer ye to take me to Lightnin'," she insisted.

Zach studied her for a minute then shrugged. "All right, all right, git yer things. Lightning ain't long for this world. Might already be dead."

"Just don't be tellin' no one where we're goin' or why, do ye hear?" she ordered. "I'll git the food and medicine we need."

Hoisting up her satin skirts, she spun around and ran from the saloon with Phil close behind. A short time later, they were at the livery stable where Willow was already saddled and waiting alongside two mules loaded down with food, medicine, and other supplies. Zach was sitting on Jessie, waiting.

"Let me go with ye," Phil suggested.

"Ye don't need to ride with me. Zach's here. I can't have this fairy-tale about m' being a angel of mercy getting' any bigger," she confided. "Don't be tellin' people, Phil."

Reluctantly, he agreed.

"Ye're the gol-dangest woman I ever met," Zach admitted, spitting into the snow. "Why ye're doing this, I got no idea, but here ya are doing it anyhow. Can't figure ya out."

"Ain't no need to figure out nothin'. Lightnin's m' friend and that's the size of it," she replied.

It took four long hours for them to cross the valley of Prichard Creek then head into the mountains beyond the south fork up a steep, winding trail. The aspen stands were like pockets of gray shadows harboring herds of whitetail deer already banded up for winter. A solitary coyote fell in behind them to follow awhile, yipping at Nicky.

They reached the cabin at the head of Viper Creek just before nightfall. Evidence of panning activities were still visible along the water's edge.

"This yer cabin?" Molly asked.

Zach nodded.

The primitive little cabin stood at the edge of a thick stand of conifers not far from the creek. To one side was a lean-to shelter for the two donkeys, one being Jessie, the other a droopy little animal tied to a tether just long enough to allow him to reach the creek for water. Both animals were very thin.

Molly swung from the saddle and marched straight to the cabin barking out orders to Zach.

"Next time I see them poor animals, they better be eatin' somethin'. You tryin' to starve yer beasts?" she snapped, pointing to the donkeys. "Cain't ye see they're hungry, ya lazy scoundrel. Ye get no food 'til yer animals are fed."

Opening the cabin door, she stepped inside and saw only darkness. Once her eyes adjusted, she saw Lightning lying on a crude bed near the far wall. The room was freezing cold. She held her breath as she approached him, hoping he was still alive. When he took a deep gasp, she sighed in relief. Thank God they weren't too late. Dropping to her knees beside him, she called his name while raising the threadbare blankets off the floor to tuck in around him. He didn't respond.

"Partner, git in here," she shouted to Zach. "Stoke up a fire and git me some light. Lightning's burnin' up and shiverin' all at once. And git them supplies unloaded. What in the devil's keepin' ya?"

Zach scurried around attending to her orders, first building up a blazing fire then lighting a lantern so she could see. The medical supplies were piled on the table close enough for Molly to reach.

"When's the last time he ate?" Molly asked. "He's so thin."

"It's been a week now. He took some water but said it hurt too much to swallow. I couldn't stand watchin' him suffer so I left. He's been a good partner," Zach whimpered. "I hate t' see him die."

"Stop talking like he's a dead man or I'll shoot ye," she growled. "He ain't gonna die 'cuz I ain't gonna let him. Did ye take care of the animals? Willow needs fed, too." Zach hurried back outside.

Gently Molly placed her hand on Lightning's brow then pulled it back. He was burning up. She called for a bucket of water and some rags then demanded blankets be heated on the stove and brought to her. One limb at a time, she swabbed Lightning down to cool the raging fever. Each time she finished washing an arm or leg, she covered it with a warm blanket before moving to another limb. Last of all, she washed his trunk, neck, and face then covered him with hot blankets.

Every few minutes she drizzled drops of water into his mouth, raising his head slightly so he wouldn't choke. Despite his difficulty in swallowing, the soothing water seemed to offer relief.

"Lightnin'," she kept whispering in his ear, "ye owe me money and ye ain't gittin' out of payin' me back by dyin' so ye best keep on a drinkin'."

Every hour all through the night she repeated the bathing ritual until finally he grew quieter and slept peacefully. Satisfied that she had a few minutes to spare, she rose to her feet, stretched, removed her cloak, then set a pot of water on to boil. She filled a metal mug full of water, herbs, and honey to soothe his throat then put another pot on the stove for soup fixings made from chicken bones and onions.

Returning to Lightning's side, she tenderly applied bacon grease to his sore, chapped lips.

"Partner, we need a potion," she told Zack. "This fever's gotta come down."

With Zach's help, Molly mixed quinine and whiskey together then dribbled it into Lightnin's mouth. Each time he swallowed, she lavished him with praise. At times, he shook violently but at other times, he cooperated.

Zach was sent to the creek for rocks to heat on the stove. Once warmed, they were wrapped in rags and slipped in beside Lightning's cold feet.

Hours went by as Molly labored over the ailing man. The routines were repeated over and over again. Wash downs, warm blankets, herbal tea, the potion.

Zach did everything Molly asked of him but mostly he just sat in a corner dozing. Once during the night, he woke up to see Molly still at the ailing man's side, crooning to him and willing him to live.

"He ain't gonna make it, is he?" Zach declared sadly, peering over Molly's shoulder.

In a fit of frustration, Molly squared her back and glared up at Zach like an angry she-bear protecting her cub.

"Git out of here," Molly yelled. "I don't need ya talkin' that way. Git out! Git out!"

Zach shuffled back to his corner.

The sun rose then set again as Molly fought for Lightning's life. Sometimes she would doze off only to rouse herself minutes later to resume nursing him. Other times, she just held his hand and hummed Irish melodies to pass the time. The soup broth was drizzled a few drops at a time down his throat along with the potion.

On the third day, Zach brought her a mug of coffee and a biscuit. "Molly, ya got to eat somethin'," he insisted. "Ya can't let yerself get worn down, too."

Exhausted, Molly accepted the nourishment, eating the bread slowly while savoring the hot coffee. Just for a moment, she leaned against the cot and closed her eyes.

"By gosh, he looks a mite better," Zach said.

"Thank ye, Partner," she replied without even opening her eyes. "Ye're right, I think he's gonna make it. The fever broke last night."

Later that day, Lightning opened his eyes. He was surprised to see Molly watching over him.

"What ya doing here, Molly?" he whispered in a gravely voice. "Am I dead?"

"Nah, ye ain't dead but ye tried real hard," Molly smiled. "I heard ye was ailing so I came to help. Brought ye a surprise, too." From beneath the bed, she withdrew the stolen poke and set it down beside him on the cot. "Just had to ask the girls then darned if it didn't show up at m' cabin door. Don't know who took it and don't rightly care. It's back and that's what matters."

Lightning smiled weakly, squeezed her hand, then closed his eyes and slept.

Confident now that Lightning would recover, Molly turned her attentions to the cabin. She washed windows, dishes, and clothes. The clothes were hung outside on tree limbs to dry. Blankets were hung outside, too, to air out. Zach chopped wood for the winter fires and harvested willows and exposed grasses to feed the animals. A whitetail yearling wandered into the clearing and was quickly shot, dressed out, and butchered to give meat to the miners for the winter.

A chunk of venison was cut into chunks and dropped into a stew filled with mushrooms, carrots, beets and onions that hung over the fire.

"I got us a couple grouse," Zach grinned proudly the next morning, holding up the birds he had seen fly into a pine tree.

Molly was delighted and heaped praises onto Zach. Not only would they provide the kind of nourishment Lightning needed right now but they would provide plenty of tasty drippings to make gravy from to pour over their bread.

"Ye make sure Lightnin' gits a piece or two of this here grouse," she insisted to Zach. "Don't ye be hoggin' it all fer yerself. I can't keep comin' up here to feed ya so unless ye're gonna bring in a maid, ye better start keepin' this place clean or ye'll both be sick. Can't neither of ya cook?"

Zach just grinned foolishly.

More than a week passed before Molly decided Lightning would survive without her. Already he had regained enough strength to stand, albeit on very wobbly legs. He told her he felt like a new-born colt trying to stand for the first time.

"Ah, ye weaklin', ye're just wantin' to be waited on hand 'n foot," she teased.

Lightning snorted. "It's you what's making me that way but I kinda like it."

After laying in a substantial amount of baked foods, including a chocolate cake that brought exclamations of happiness from both men, Molly declared she was heading back to Murray.

The next morning she unceremoniously gathered her things together, climbed onto Willow, whistled for Nicky, and bid the two miners good-bye.

"Bring them extra mules back into town when ye're feelin' stronger and load them up with oats and feed fer your donkeys so they kin git through the winter. 'Til then, Zack, ye need to fix 'em a better shelter. It ain't humane to keep 'em tied up with no place to exercise or hide from the wind. Next time I see Jessie, she better be fatter." She shook her finger at Zack. "Don't make me come back up here to check on ye, do ye hear?"

Zach nodded, a big smile pasted across his usually sour face.

"I'm beholdin' to ya, Angel," Lightning yelled. "I love ya, I truly do. When I strike it rich, I'm buyin' ya yer own saloon!"

"I'll hold ye to it. Now git back into that cabin," Molly yelled back. "Ye'll catch yer death out here."

Chapter 29

October 1883

> 30 October 1883
>
> Dear Parents,
>   The snows are already deep here in Murray so miners are still flocking in. They're so forlorn when they wander about waiting for spring. Sometimes they fight just to keep from freezing. It's a hard life but they seem to love the danger of it all.
>
> > Your daughter,
> > Maggie

Sam arrived back in Murray dressed in a handsome buckskin suit fringed on the sleeves and pant legs. A loose red kerchief hung around his neck, knotted at the front, while a new cinnamon brown Stetson covered most of his curly-black hair. The horse he rode was a spirited paint that seemed to enjoy prancing like a parade pony. Tied to the saddle was a bedroll, saddlebags, and a heavy fleece overcoat.

Everyone stopped to admire the stranger as he rode toward the White Elephant saloon. "Seen Molly today?" he asked, ordering a sarsaparilla to quench his thirst.

Wyatt was watching him from beneath a dark hat pulled low over his eyes as he pretended to be engrossed in a game of poker.

"Who are you?" Wyatt asked. "And why ya lookin' for Molly?"

"She's a friend," Sam replied light-heartedly. "She's expecting me."

"She don't come around 'til after dark," Wyatt replied. He held no claims on Molly but felt jealous when somebody else looked at her. He wasn't sure he wanted to tell this half-breed anything.

"Okay, guess I'll go by her place," Sam said, tipping his hat to Wyatt as he left the saloon. His spurs clinked lightly on the board-walk as he headed straight toward The House of Pink leading his horse.

The lanterns were dim when he knocked on the door. When no one answered he tried the door which had been left unlocked.

"Girl, you here?" he called out. "Your door was unlocked. You're looking to get yourself robbed. Where are you?"

He found Molly still sleeping. Her around-the-clock care of Lightning had weakened her considerably and she couldn't seem to get enough sleep. Sam's voice startled her awake but before she could sit up, he was at her bed.

"Come here, Sweetheart," he grinned, wrapping her in his arms. "I've missed you." He kissed her long and hard then leaned back and looked at her. "Are you all right?" he asked, concerned.

"Sam," she sputtered, "what if I'd been entertaining? You shouldn't just come in here without knocking." She glared down at Nicky and wondered why he hadn't barked a warning.

"Your door was unlocked. Besides, you said you didn't entertain anymore and I believe you. Are you glad to see me or not?"

Molly smiled. Yes, she was glad to see him.

"I wasn't serious about giving up entertainin'," she lied, hoping to get a rise out of him. "I only said that to get rid of you." She wiped the sleep from her eyes as Sam swept his hat off and sent it sailing across the room into a chair near the door.

"You weren't waiting for me?" he asked, pretending to be hurt. "Well, I'm gonna find the scoundrel that's horning in on my time with you. Is he hiding under the bed?" He raised the blankets off the floor and peered underneath.

"Stop it," she laughed. "You know no one's there. Did you find your father?"

"I did but we didn't get to Utah in time to see Ma before she passed. She did leave us a long letter, though, and forgave Dad. She told him she still loved him but couldn't stand sharing him with another woman. After the funeral, Dad signed everything over to me and my siblings so I'm in charge now. Daniel's my younger brother so he's taking over while I'm here in Idaho looking for my woman." He grabbed Molly and tickled her until she giggled out loud.

"Stop!" she insisted, squirming to get away.

"Dad rode back with me so we had a lot of time to get reacquainted," Sam explained, pulling Molly back against his chest and wrapping his arms around her. "He told me some tall tale about a woman who saved his wife and girls from freezing during a blizzard. Ever hear that story?"

"Nope, never did," she replied, knowing full well he already knew the truth.

Sam just snorted and held her tighter, kissing the top of her head.

After a time, Sam got up and walked over to stoke the fire in the stove. When he returned to Molly, he pulled a blanket up over her shoulders, concern showing on his face.

"You look cold, Girl. Let's warm you up a bit." He lifted her up in his arms and carried her to a couch near the fire. He tucked the blankets tightly in around her but kept her on his lap.

"Dad wants to be a part of my life again so that's a good thing. He's applying to the governor for amnesty from the polygamy charges. If he's pardoned, he can go back to Utah and won't need to sneak into town just to visit us. He says there's a new settlement developing in Spring Creek north of Ogden. Thinks we can both get work there and still do our horse trading business. It would be good to work with him again. I've always admired him, and no one has a better horse-trading reputation than he has."

"You're going back to Utah?" Molly asked, snuggling closer to Sam's chest, her face nuzzled into his neck. She tried to rub the sleep from her eyes but still hovered somewhere between sleep and awareness.

"Don't know yet. Depends on a certain lady I know."

Molly's eyes drifted closed.

"Are you all right?" he repeated, leaning back to study her more closely.

"I'm just tired," she replied softly. "I nursed an old miner who had mountain fever and it tired me out more than I realized."

"Should I be sending for the doc?"

Molly shook her head. "No, I just need rest."

"All right, I'll take yer word for it but if you ain't better by tomorrow, I'm sending for the doc. For now, I'll fix you some hot tea then you can go back to sleep. I'll wait around 'til you wake up."

Molly slept for hours. When she opened her eyes, the shadows of night were already approaching but Sam was still there, his feet propped up on a table while he read one of her books.

"I'm awake," she told him.

Sam set aside the book then walked to her side. "You do look more rested," he admitted.

Molly smiled sweetly, pleased just to see Sam in the same room with her.

"Are you up to some serious talk?"

Molly cringed. "Right now?"

"Right now. Remember what I told you before I left?" he continued. "Well, I'm here for an answer. Will you marry me, Molly?"

"Sam, we already talked about this. You don't know what you're asking."

"I don't care about your past. It seems to disturb you far more than it does me. To me, you're warm and exciting, you make me happy, and I just like being close to you, talking to you, looking at you."

"I don't want to hurt you, Sam." She took hold of his arm, her eyes pleading.

"I'm not David," he replied quietly. "I'm nothing like David. I'll never do anything like David did. I would never harm you, physically or emotionally."

"Is it my money you want?" Molly asked abruptly.

"Ouch, that's harsh, Girl," Sam replied. "If you think that, then I'm out of here."

He stood up abruptly and headed for the door, picking up his hat along the way. "Money means nothing to me, Molly. I'm no drinker, I don't gamble, I don't seek out women to be with, other than you, of course. I'm a simple man with simple dreams. If you don't want me, I'd best be going."

Molly stared at his back as he opened the door.

"My heart hurts when I think of marriage, Sam. Your words sound sincere but I'm afraid." Molly began to tremble, covering her face with her hands as she began to cry.

"Come here, Girl," he consoled her, returning to her side and enfolding her in his arms. "I don't want you to cry. I just want you to believe in me and to love me like I love you. Do you really want me to go?"

Molly couldn't even speak much less look at him.

"All right then," he sighed heavily. "If I don't hear from you by tomorrow, I'll move on." Then he left.

Molly's head was spinning. "Wait!" she cried out, scrambling to the door. She flung it open only to see Sam standing there, a devilish smile on his face.

"Ah, she does love me," was all he said.

"Come back in here and we'll talk," she laughed, swiping at her tears as she led him back inside.

"How about this," he suggested. "Since I've got time on my hands right now, why don't we just spend it together getting to know each other better. Would that help ease your fears?" His gentle hands stroked her rumpled hair.

"Yes, yes, that would be good. You need to know me better. I may be more than you bargained for. Just promise me, if you change your mind you'll say so. You can leave with no questions asked. Agreed?"

"It's a deal," Sam replied. He touched the tip of his hat in a mock salute then headed back to the door. "I'll be back at eight o'clock to take you to dinner."

The days that followed were wonderfully happy. Molly and Sam were together daylight until dark, sometimes riding horses into the snow-covered hills, sometimes walking around town meeting her friends, sometimes just sitting in The House of Pink discussing books or playing faro. They took their meals at different restaurants and saloons or stayed at Molly's where she prepared meals in her spacious kitchen.

One sunny day they took a horseback ride through the snow-covered meadows outside of Murray simply to enjoy sights of wildlife banding together for the winter. They rode farther than they had planned when a sudden squall caught up with them. Frantically, they galloped toward a rugged outcropping where they could see a small cave that would offer shelter from the rain. Once inside, Molly was able to start a small fire using the flint given to her by Sally Winnemucca.

"Is there anything you can't do?" Sam asked, shaking his head.

Molly just grinned. "I can't sew!" she laughed out loud.

They huddled together near the fire and watched as the rain turned to snow then back to rain again. Lightning flashed on the shale mountainside sending balls of fire rolling down the shale in a cosmic display of power and wonderment followed by torrents of ice-cold rain that soon cascaded off the granite overhang directly in front of them like a waterfall. Below they could see Lake Elsie with its pristine waters dancing and shimmering in the deluge of the snow and rain mixtures. Reflections of nearby pine trees rippled in mir-ror-like waters.

"Are you afraid?" Sam asked, his cheek resting against Molly's head as he held her cradled in his arms.

"No, not with you here. Oh Sam, this must be what Creation was like. Wild and powerful yet thrilling and magnificent," she mused. He nodded.

The storm moved on as quickly as it came but they were in no hurry to leave so nibbled on bread and cheese from their saddlebags. They marveled at the beauty of the lake, the rolling white clouds overhead, and the trout leaping from the waters. Several whitetail deer approached to drink from the waters not far from two snowshoe rabbits that were hopping across the snowdrifts, almost invisible to the eye. A Redtail hawk keened overhead he dove toward the rabbits but they disappeared in a snowbank before he got to them. The hawk then swooped down on a blackbird perched in the tall grasses on shore. He caught it then flew away with it. Nicky barked a few times then set off chasing a couple scolding chipmunks. For a while, time seemed to stand still.

"I'm leaving tomorrow," Sam told Molly as they rode back to Murray.

"You're leaving?" Molly asked, reining Willow to a stop. She had assumed he would stay in Murray all winter.

"It's time," was all he said, riding on ahead of her.

That evening they dined at the White Elephant Saloon. Molly was dressed in a wine-red gown enhanced by fur, pearl wristlets and earrings. Her hair was pulled back on her neck. Sam was handsomely dressed in the buckskins he wore when he rode into town days ago.

James Earp met them at the door explaining that Wyatt and Josie were on a trip but he had ordered in a surprise especially for Molly. It was fresh salmon from the Pacific Ocean, brought to town packed in ice on the last mule train. Molly had so often teased the brothers about the lack of variety where fish were concerned that Wyatt had decided to surprise her.

Grinning like a schoolboy, James soon was setting the steaming entrée before them on the table. The salmon was encircled with lemon-flavored steamed rice. He popped the cork on a bottle of imported red wine then brought out two French pastries for dessert.

Molly was giddy with happiness. It was a fitting end to a week of pure pleasure. Neither she nor Sam spoke about tomorrow.

They were nearly finished with their meal when a commotion erupted outside the saloon. Moments later Captain Tonks,[18] the self-professed clown of the Coeur d'Alenes as well as the town derelict, stumbled inside.

[18.] Captain Tonks was, as depicted, the self-proclaimed clown of Murray. He lived there until 1906 when he died at age sixty-one.

Tonks was a slight fellow, barely five-feet tall, who always brandished a smile to anyone willing to let him entertain with a poem or a song. His hair was long and stringy, and he always needed a shave. As was his style, he wore clothes either too large and baggy or too small.

"Who is that?" Sam asked, staring at the derelict.

Molly explained people didn't know much about Captain Tonks or even where he lived. Some believed he stayed with friends. Mostly, he just bummed around town begging coins for drinks or a hot meal, preferably the drink before the food. If a coin was left over, it was always spent on candy for the children who followed him around through most of the daylight hours. For those willing to buy him a drink, an impromptu performance was always given as payment.

Tonks, she explained, loved performing and could tell tales every bit as tall as those of Calamity Jane's. He was warm, spontaneous, witty, and wildly-animated as a performer with his outrageous facial expressions and a mastery of improvisation. For props he used curved sticks, pieces of rope, and odd little hats that were always perched quirkily on top of his head, sometimes two or three deep. If his pants were too large, he held them up with strands of rope. The clothes enhanced the delightful oddity of his performances.

"The world is Captain's stage," Molly beamed, "and he is a dear friend of mine. He once told me he was a friend of Mark Twain, the writer from Missouri whose real name is Samuel Clemens."

What she didn't tell Sam was that Tonks adored her as much as she adored him. She was always kind and he never forgot it for a moment. "Beautiful lady," he had once whispered in her ear as he bent low to kiss her hand, "I would gladly go to my eternal joy if I could pass from life in the glorious light of yer smile shining down upon me."

Those simple words had earned him a special place in her heart so his performances were always well paid for with coins from her own pocket.

They watched as Tonks staggered up to the bar, his voice trembling as he asked for food. He told the barkeep he needed food. He hadn't eaten in days.

"You got gold to pay with?" the barkeep snarled.

Molly's eyes turned dark, her gaze riveted on the drama unfolding at the counter. Sam spoke to her but she heard nothing, only the exchange happening between Tonks and the barkeep.

Tonks smiled lamely, turning his pockets inside out as he teetered against the counter. His eyes begged for compassion. "I got no coins," he muttered.

"Git out of here, you worthless beggar," the bartender snarled, shoving Tonks backward. He fell back against a stool then dropped to the floor with a sickening thud. As he struggled to stand, he licked his parched lips and glanced around the room, embarrassed and pitiful. When he saw Molly, he turned away like a whipped dog and began crawling toward the door.

Molly exploded with rage. She rose so abruptly that she startled Sam. She rushed to Tonks' side, kneeling down to help him up.

"Sam, help me," she yelled.

They got Tonks into a chair where Molly smoothed his hair and spoke quietly to him until he regained his composure. That's when Molly turned on the barkeep. James, just coming out of the back, groaned.

"Oh, no," he gasped, "Molly's mad!" He rushed toward Molly and the barkeep but her anger was already spilling out.

"Ye black-hearted devil," she screamed so loud everyone could hear, even out on the street. "This man's starvin' and ye can't even give him a morsel? Ain't ye got no feelings? Ain't ye ever been hungry, ye blackhearted devil?"

The bartender backed away and James backed up.

"Well, here's how it's gonna be," she snarled, leaning over the counter to shove her finger right into the barkeep's face. "Git him some food—now! And it better be the finest steak ye got, piled on with potatoes and bread and anything else he wants. Give him all the whiskey he wants to wash it down with. Ye'll do it and ye'll do it free of charge, do ye understand, 'cuz Captain Tonks is a friend of mine and friends of mine don't get treated like dumb animals. When he's done eatin', yer're gonna personally serve up dessert then ask him to perform for us."

The bartender tried to ignore her but James Earp rushed to his side, ordering him to do whatever Molly asked. He and Wyatt knew full well what would happen if Molly grew angrier.

"Boss, the man's a drunk," the bartender argued.

"He's a human being," Molly shrieked, sweeping her arm across the bar sending glasses sailing through the air then crashing to the floor. She spun around and began up-ending tables and chairs.

"Molly, whatever you want, we'll do it," James promised, glaring at the bartender.

Molly nodded appreciatively at James.

"Thank ye, James. Hereafter, ye're gonna feed Tonks anytime he wants food, do ye hear? If ye don't, I swear to God Almighty, I'll shut yer place down. Ye know I kin do it, don't ye, James?"

"I do, Miss Molly."

The barkeep's mouth dropped open, his face now as white as snow. He'd never seen Molly when she was angry but James had, and James knew this was but a small demonstration of Molly's angry side.

"Ye're lucky I ain't got m' whip or I'd be paintin' yer face with yer own blood, ye lowly scum," she muttered to the barkeep. "And while ye're at it, give free food and drinks t' everybody in here."

She hiked up her skirt, withdrew her .38 Colt revolver from the leg holster on her boot, and fired three times into the ceiling as she shouted out the words that had become her trademark.

"Belly up to the bar, boys. Drinks are on the house!"

James Earp just laughed. Wyatt's orders were to never, ever rile Molly so they deserved what was happening now. She carried more clout than anyone in town and no one wanted to be the target of her rage.

"James, ye can tell Wyatt what I did. If he wants paid, send him to see me. 'Til then, teach this worthless scoundrel to be more Christian if he wants to keep workin' in Murray. Ye don't want this place to become poison 'cuz nobody will ever again cross through them doors if I tell 'em to stay away. Do ye understand?"

A crooked smile tugged at James' mouth when he nodded.

"Ain't she something?" he whispered when she walked away. "What a woman!"

It took a while for Molly to calm down. She stayed near Captain Tonks, stroking his head while he tried to stop shaking.

"Git Captain a drink, now!" she ordered. "He's got the tremors."

When the whiskey arrived she held it to his lips. "Here, old friend, calm yer nerves," she whispered. "Want me to drink with ye?"

His reddened eyes met hers. "It'd be m' honor," he whispered.

Molly kissed his grizzled cheek. "Ye don't never need to be hungry again, Captain. The White Elephant will always give ye food."

She slipped a gold coin into his pocket. "That's fer candy fer the children," she smiled.

After eating his fill, Captain Tonks was ready to perform, and perform he did. The poetry was directed to Molly, his songs were sung to her, and his skit featured a slap-dance routine honoring an earth-bound angel named Molly.

Sam was so dumbstruck by what had transpired between Molly, Captain Tonks and the owner of the saloon that he didn't know what to say. When she returned to the table, he just sat there stone silent. He never said much even after they returned to her place.

"I warned you about my dark side," she began to explain. "Are you still certain you want to hook up with me?" She offered no apology.

"Does this happen often?" he asked.

"Not often but my anger can surface without warning. I've no tolerance for those who hurt others."

Suddenly Sam began to laugh. "Heaven help the world, Molly, if you ever decide to become a crusader. You are unbelievable!" He reached out and grabbed her around the neck, hugging her affectionately.

"I'll never be a crusader, you can bet on that. The Church wouldn't let me through the door. But then, you probably don't want to know how I feel about that."

"You're not an evil woman," Sam told her. "You've got the biggest heart of anyone I know. That means a lot to the Lord. He ain't gonna punish you for being kind and compassionate."

"The priest promised me a spot in Hell right next to Lucifer himself."

"Then he's wrong. God isn't vengeful. He doesn't hand out endless punishments to people just for spite, especially if people are kind and truly want forgiveness. He's a loving God."

"Do you really believe that?" Molly felt calmer just hearing the words.

"I do. And when I leave here, I'll leave a book for you to read. It might let you see God in a much different light. You might even decide you're not such an evil person."

"I don't blame myself," Molly protested.

"I think you do. That's why you're still angry at the Church. They only confirmed what you already believed about yourself—that you're a lost sinner who deserves punishment."

"I've read the Bible, Sam."

"This book isn't a Bible. It's a companion history called the Book of Mormon."

"People are judged by their actions, are they not?" she asked.

"Yes, they are but life was given to mankind as a time for making choices. No one makes all the right choices all the time but we all learn from our actions. That's the way it's supposed to be."

"Is that what makes you so cock-eyed certain of yourself?" she scowled.

"I've made plenty of mistakes, Girl. I've had to deal with hateful people who don't like half breeds, for instance. When Dad left us, things got pretty bad for my mother. A lot of people hate Indians but she was strong minded and held herself above the scorn. It was she who taught me to believe in myself and to accept who I am. Just imagine having to honor not only a different religion that's still hated by a lot of people but having to honor two entirely different heritages, too. I learned to deal with it and to believe in myself. Now it's your turn."

Chapter 30

November 1883

19 November 1883

Dearest Parents,
   Sam, my friend, is gone again. He wants to marry me but I'm afraid. I could use your advice.

Your loving daughter,
Maggie

Sᴀᴍ ʟᴇꜰᴛ ᴛʜᴇ ɴᴇxᴛ ᴅᴀʏ for a month's exploration of a region supposedly full of new gold discoveries in Montana Territory. The weather was mild at the moment so Sam thought he might check things out in person and give Molly time to make up her mind about him. Phil was more than happy to outfit him with basic equipment so he would leave Molly alone for a while. He didn't dislike Sam but he certainly didn't want him getting too close to Molly.

"If I strike it rich," Sam promised Molly, "I'll buy you a saloon of your own. We'll call it something like the Dublin Emerald. You can even play your fiddle there if you want."

Before she knew it, he was gone.

Molly missed having Sam around. To pass time, she read the book Sam had left with her. It was difficult to understand at first but as the chapters unfolded, she found herself becoming more and more intrigued by its messages. Over and over the message came to her that the people in the book were not unlike the people of today. They, too, had ongoing struggles maintaining their faith in God.

By the end of December, the snows came back with a vengeance. Sam didn't return as expected and that worried both Molly and Phil. The ladies of the line continued keeping Molly up with their new plans and ideas but Molly was concerned. He should have come back by now.

"The White Elephant is up for sale," Broncho Liz told Molly one day. "Them Earp brothers want to go south where it ain't so gol-darned cold."

Molly asked Wyatt about the rumors and learned they were true.

"Ya know it ain't like me to stay in any one place too long. We're going to El Paso then over to New Mexico. I hate this bitter cold. If you want to come along, we'll make room. Josie would enjoy your company." He smiled warmly, half serious and half certain she wouldn't accept the offer.

"I bet Josie would just love having me along," Molly giggled, tweaking Wyatt on the cheek. "Will I ever see you again?"

"You can't get rid of guys like me. We always pop up when nobody's looking. I'd stay 'til spring but the county's takin' my saloon to pay the taxes I owe so there won't be any holdings left to keep me here. I've got some claims but they ain't pannin' out much. We'll come back this way sometime to see if you're still around." Wyatt kissed Molly on the cheek, gave her a lopsided smile, then whispered "Be safe, Angel."

"Do ye think the county would let me buy the White Elephant?" Molly asked Phil. "Murray needs a high-class saloon with fancy chandeliers and them wall-to-wall mirrors. I'd put ye in charge of the makeover—so long as ye cover the walls in Irish-green brocade and put red carpets in all the sleeping rooms. Ye could even hire a French chef out of San Francisco to do the cooking. I think we can afford that."

"Ye think so? Well, let me ask around," Phil replied, excited with the idea. He was getting tired of panning for gold and having little success. "It'd be good to barkeep 'cuz I like being close to m' beer at all times." He nudged her on the arm then chortled aloud.

Two days later, death rode into town and changed everything. It arrived in the form of a stumbling, incoherent stranger with dull, glazed eyes who rode slowly down the entire length of Main Street, looking all around but seeing nothing. His horse found its own way to the livery stable where the man slid unsteadily out of the saddle, dropped to his knees for a moment, then staggered back onto his feet before stumbling down the street to the Gold Strike Saloon. Ordering a pint of whiskey, he drank it down then slowly set the empty bottle back onto the counter. Without another word, he toppled backward off the stool and lay there on the floor staring up at the ceiling. As a crowd gathered around him, he gasped a couple times and died.

Efforts were made to revive the man-with-no-name since he appeared to only have been in a drunken stupor but then someone touched his forehead and recoiled in terror.

"He's burning up with fever!" the man yelled, scrambling backward away from the corpse. "It's smallpox! I seen it in Leadville and Virginia City both. It's that dreadful scourge, smallpox."[19]

The crowd scattered like buckshot. They had all unwittingly exposed themselves to the deadliest disease on the frontier. Smallpox was known to have annihilated an entire nation of five thousand Indians only a year before in the Bitterroot Valley of Montana, and now the people of Murray were exposed to a disease that had no cure.

Mass panic erupted as word spread of the man's death. With desperate urgency, he was bundled up in blankets, dragged up to Boot Hill and hurriedly buried in a shallow, unmarked grave. Though his name would never be known, he would always be remembered as the man who brought the kiss of death into Murray.

The epidemic exploded throughout the region, sweeping through town, into the valleys and up the mountain draws, traveling like an avenging angel. Schools closed, churches bolted their doors, and only the bravest of businesses opened up even for an hour each day. The doctors were inundated with sick people, and no one was

---

[19.] The narrative in this chapter is authentic.

immune. In fear, families became reclusive, hiding behind locked doors with the curtains drawn. Even the ladies of Pleasure Alley shut their doors. Then the dying began.

Molly grew increasingly concerned by the way people were reacting to the disease. People were cowering in fear refusing to help one another, even friends and family, but the disease kept spreading. It was not only killing the citizens but was strangling the town itself.

When she couldn't stand it any longer, Molly bundled herself up and stormed over to the steps of the court house. She ordered Phil to call for a town meeting.

"Everyone has to come!" she barked.

Within the hour, nervous citizens were gathered to see what their beloved angel had to say. They stood apart from one another, kerchiefs tied across their faces to ward off germs.

"Look at yerselves, ye miserable souls," Molly yelled unkindly, her blue eyes blazing. "How can ye act this way, sniveling and whining, and hiding like scared babies? Why ain't ye helpin' each other? We ain't this kind of people, fearful and scared. We're people what care about one another. We sit together in church, we shop in stores, we teach yer children, we sip coffee together and drink whiskey beside one another.

"Do ye think ye kin just close yer doors and curtains and the scourge will go away? Well, it won't. Ye can't escape it but ye kin fight it. Ye kin fight fer yer loved ones by standing up to the black Angel of Death and saying no, ye can't take m' wife, m' children, m' sweetheart. Ye can't take me 'cuz I ain't ready to go.

"I ain't goin' easy 'cuz I intend to fight to m' last breath. If the ladies of the line are willin', we'll fight alone if we have to but we'll save some lives doin' it. If they don't want to stand with me, then I'll fight alone—but I will fight. I ain't ready to give up, not yet!"

The ladies stepped forward, united behind their leader, and she rewarded them with a grateful nod.

"Tell me now, who's gonna stand with us?" she asked, watching the crowd shuffle and look at one another nervously. "Ya gonna join us or die shakin' in yer boots?"

The mood of the town folks slowly began to change. Molly felt encouraged.

"If ye aim to live, then we got work to do."

Her eyes scanned the crowd as though recording the faces of everyone in attendance. Then her arm shot into the air as she began to shout. "Live, live, live!" The chant took on a life of its own as the excitement swelled and more and more voices joined in.

"If ye ain't sick, roll up yer sleeves and git to work. Clean out the hotels and saloons so sick 'uns can be housed there and nursin' will be easier. Phil, git a group of men together to ride to Osburn and Wallace fer all the medical supplies ye kin carry. Ride fast and hard 'cuz we need all the help we kin git. If ye need gold, take mine." She pointed to the banker and told him to give them whatever they needed from her account. "The rest of ye, gather blankets, rags, towels, firewood, pots fer water, and lumber to build cots fer the stricken to lay on. Ladies, set up cookin' stations 'cuz people will be needin' nourishment. Those what can do nursin', help the doctors. Wear kerchiefs across yer faces so ye don't take in anymore germs than need be. Infected peoples' clothes need burned and graves need dug. That's the fact of it. It ain't gonna be pretty but it's gonna be necessary. Everybody needs to choose a task and commit to it 'til the last soul is either dead or cured. We're gonna beat this plaque, I swear to God."

"But Molly, what if we get the pox, too?" somebody yelled.

Molly stood silent for a minute, fully aware that many of those in the crowd would die.

"Some of us are gonna get the pox, that's a certainty. If ye do, ye know we'll be doin' our best t' save ye. If the Lord decides to take ye, then we'll make sure everyone knows ye died heroically helpin' yer friends. The Lord will take note of yer good deeds and will personally be waiting t' welcome ye through the Pearly Gates.

"Now, who's gonna volunteer fer what? If ye don't raise yer hand, I'll shoot ye so ye won't need to worry about the fever." She had meant to lighten the severity of the moment but her face stayed sober.

Phil, fired up by Molly's rousing speech, leaped up beside her and shouted out the words people needed to hear.

"Molly's our Silver Dove and I fer one will stand beside her to the death, same as she would fer me. Now, who's with us?" His voice was high-pitched and frenzied.

People's hands went up as the spirit of survival surged through their veins. Molly took Phil's hand, gratitude glistening in her eyes. "Thank ye, Phil. I'll not fergit," she told him.

"I'll not let ye," he grinned. He had told the truth. He would willingly die for Molly.

The Mayor, standing in the crowd, argued against the direction this meeting was taking. He wasn't ready to expose himself to the pox.

"Why ye standin' there starin'?" she asked, obviously annoyed with his behavior.

"You're inciting these people to willingly expose themselves to the scourge. More people are going to die if they do what you're saying," he blurted out.

"Mayor, I ain't askin' nothin' of nobody that I'm not askin' of m' own self. If ye got a problem with it, say so now, but if ye ain't got no problem then order them hotels cleared out and the sick folks carried in. Fight me on this and I'll call in the vigilantes to run ye clean out of town so ye can never show yer face here again. We won't let ye come back. Ye know I can do it, don't ye? If ye ain't with me, yer against me!"

Defiantly, she stood there waiting for him to answer but her words were so forceful even he dared not defy her. Whirling around, he began barking out orders and making assignments. People would work in shifts but still would make sure to rest after many hours of work. Fatigue could undermine their efforts and make the situation even worse.

Within hours every hotel and saloon had been converted into hospitals with make-shift beds lined up side by side by side. When the beds were full, people were bedded down on the floor. Volunteers lined up to provide nursing, laundry services, and foods for the workers as well as the patients. Huge bonfires in the center of town burned infected clothes and blankets around the clock. Cauldrons of water simmered over open fires to provide warm water for the doctors.

Herbs and natural remedies provided by Indians who had survived the outbreak in Montana were applied as were old-wife remedies brought to town by emigrants from around the world. Nothing was left untried since no one knew what treatments would work. What they did learn was each day patients survived, the greater grew their odds of beating the disease.

For three torturous weeks, day in and day out, Molly helped nurse the suffering souls. She refused to stop even for sleep. When exhaustion overcame her, she could be seen slumped on the floor next to a patient where she would lay without moving for perhaps an hour or more. Then she would open her eyes, look around, accept a bowl of hot gruel and a chunk of crusty bread, choke it down with coffee, then go back to nursing the sick and dying.

Slowly the number of new patients began to dwindle. That's when Molly called the fairy-belles to her side. There was another pressing need. Up in the hills there were infected miners needing help. Taking the lead, she loaded her horse up with supplies and rode off into the hills to seek out sick miners. The other women followed suit. They moved from valley to valley, cabin to cabin, despite the bitter cold. People called them Molly's Ministering Angels.

Weeks later they straggled back into Murray, exhausted but jubilant over their successes. Not one of the women contracted smallpox.

Daily funeral processions took place at two different cemeteries, the Pioneer and the Grand Army of the Republic. Services were held on-site because of the vast numbers. No one knows how many people died that year. Estimates ran into the hundreds, maybe even thousands. In contrast to the many lives lost, even more were saved Murray's people became living testimonies to the power and determination of the human spirit—and to the fire ignited in their hearts by a brash young Irish woman who would forever be known as the Silver Dove of the Coeur d'Alenes.

Chapter 31

January 1884

4 January 1884

Dearest Family,
   Smallpox came to Murray and killed many people. It was terrible. I was not affected so am grateful but I am worn down and tired. Mum, I put red candles in my windows on Christmas and baked up seed cakes and puddings to honor my Irish tradition. It seemed to give heart to the ailing to see traditions practiced even in such trying times. I played the violin for them, too, and people joined in the singing.

Your daughter,
Maggie

"We'll call your saloon the Dublin Emerald," Sam laughed, "and it will have a grand piano, ruby-red carpets and sparkling chandeliers that glisten brighter than diamonds. French chefs will bake magnificent French pastries, the best ever. Just tell me, Girl, where are you? Why aren't you here with me?"

   The dream was so vivid it woke Molly from a shallow, restless sleep. The dream had been recurring ever since the smallpox epidemic. Worry about Sam dominated her waking hours and interrupted her rest. He had promised to return but hadn't so she could only imagine he was either sick, injured or dead. A thought popped into her mind that maybe Sam had contracted smallpox.

"Another bad dream," she told Nicky, rubbing his fur just beneath the collar. Her face felt flushed and warm. "Last night I dreamed of Charlie and Becca, too. What's happening to me, old dog?"

She swung her legs over the side of the bed then reached for a sleeping robe before slipping her feet into rabbit-fur slippers. Even with the heavy rugs, the floors felt unusually cold. The night fire had burned low so she padded to the stove and fed the embers more wood, watching until flames took hold. She paced the floors like a caged tiger, absentmindedly picking items up and setting them down again. Pulling back the draperies, she watched for the approach of dawn. New snow clung to the window glass causing her to shiver. She felt a gust of wind shiver through the boards on the roof before causing the fire to crackle as if a demon spirit had just slipped down the stovepipe.

"Do ye think Sam went on into Yellowstone to trap with his father? He said Joe was plannin' to go there to enjoy the hot pools. Makes m' think of takin' a warm bath right now."

She opened a can and took out a cold biscuit to nibble on after making herself a cup of hot tea laced with whiskey. Ever since knowing Julia, tea had become a traditional morning drink for her. She sat down at the table to re-read a letter from her parents.

> Dearest Maggie,
>
> We will visit America in the summer. Too much time has passed since we have seen you, little girl. The sale of the goldsmith business brought us good profits. We may decide to stay in America with you. Our plan is to visit Charlie, too. Nicholas sends his love. A new baby is on the way.
>
> Lovingly,
> Mum and Da

Molly looked around the room trying to see it with her parents' eyes. It was already one of the largest buildings in town. She knew her parents would be pleased with it, especially since they would have their own rooms on the upper floor. Her hope was to entice them to remain in America forever. The only unsettling concern was how to explain to them the source of her wealth. Would they understand or would they be disappointed in her? They didn't blame her for the failed marriage but they also didn't know of her excommunication.

Nervously, Molly picked up a book and tried to read but her thoughts just wandered. Setting the book aside, she returned to the window, peering out at the raging ground blizzard. A shadowy figure was approaching. It was Phil.

He stepped inside then quickly shoved the door closed behind him to keep out the blowing snow. Without speaking, he brushed past Molly and went straight to the stove to warm himself. He pulled the beaver-fur cap with earflaps off his head then unbuttoned his heavy wool coat.

"What's goin' on, Phil?" Molly asked, confused by his behavior.

"Molly, 'tis time we cleared the air," he said, facing her.

"About what?"

"I love ye, ye must know that, don't ye?"

"Aye, and I love ye back," she answered flatly, sitting in a nearby chair. "Ye're m' dearest friend."

"'Tis only as a friend that ye love me?" he asked. "I need to hear the words once and for final. Is there a place fer me in yer heart, Molly, as more than a friend?" His eyes reflected the depth of his feelings for her.

"Phil, ye're the one I count on most, and that's worth more than gold t' me but if ye're talking about romance, I cannot give ye the answer ye're wantin'."

"Do ye love the half-breed?"

Molly turned away. Why was it so important for men to hear those words? She couldn't answer that question for herself, much less for Phil.

"Fergit I asked, Lassie," he told her. "Yer lack of words tells me the answer. Half the town already knows how ye feel about him but

I been hopin' it wasn't true. I just needed to know fer m'self. He's a lucky scoundrel, that's fer certain."

"The town knows? I don't even know that fer m'self, Phil. How can anyone else know how I feel?"

"It's on yer face, Lassie, every time ye look at him. But that's not important now. I came to tell ye Sam's got hisself into trouble over in Montana."

"What?" she gasped. "Tell me."

"A rider on the mule team coming over from Thompson Falls yesterday says Sam found an abandoned claim near Anaconda and spotted color. Lots of it. The weather was good so he started working the vein and having good success until some hombres passin' by noticed what he was workin' at. They demanded to be made partners. Sam run 'em off all right but they kept comin' back t' harass him. They stole his gear, even his mule, then took pot shots at him from off the hillside just to wear him down. When another miner rode past, Sam sent word to the sheriff to come roust the hombres away from his claim but they wouldn't do it. Since he ain't got no partner to help out, he's stuck all alone at the claim. Can't get to town to even register the claim much less get supplies. All he kin do is sit there until somebody comes to help or the bushwackers shoot him."

"Git m' horse saddled up, Phil. I'm goin' soon as I kin git packed." She was already at the wardrobe pulling out warm clothes.

"Molly, git hold of yerself. 'Tis freezin' out there—and 'tis a long ride even in good weather. Ye can't just hop on yer horse and gallop there in a day!"

"Stop complaining, Irish," she snapped. "I'm a-goin' and ye can join me if ye want or ye can just git m' horse saddled and git out of m' way. Pack up a mule with supplies enough to last me awhile—include some whiskey too. Where on earth is Anaconda?"

"Molly..." Phil tried to interrupt. "'Tis two weeks travel in the best of weather but in the worst, it could take twice that long. There ain't a pack train crossing the mountains fer a week so ye need to wait 'til the weather clears."

"I'm a goin'!" she repeated more forcefully, her eyes darkening.

"Not in this weather, ye ain't!" he insisted. "Try to go now and I'll tie ye to the bed if I have to. I ain't arguin' over this. Ye can't help Sam if ye're dead now kin ye?"

Molly stopped what she was doing and faced Phil once more. He was right. She needed to use common sense.

"Kin ye get clear directions fer me and write 'em down? Soon as the storm passes, I'll need m' horse and supplies ready to travel. Book me onto the mule train and let me know when it's leavin'. I'll be ready. Will ye come with me?" Her eyes were pleading.

"No, I ain't goin' all the way to Anaconda but I kin ride part way once the storm passes. I'm workin' with the Earps on buying that saloon fer ye so I can't just leave. I'll ride with ye to teach ye what ye need to know to camp along the way, then I'll turn back. Fer now, focus on yer clothes. It's gonna be a dangerous trek so ye need to be well prepared or ye kin die."

Five days passed before the storm abated. Phil had everything ready by then and she was booked on a small mule team headed into Montana the following day. Phil traveled with them to Thompson Falls where they learned travel was indefinitely delayed due to avalanches so her only course would be to go it alone from there. Phil rode with her for one more day, teaching her how to pitch a tent, to make a fire, and to find the best protection from the weather. She would ride Willow and lead a pack mule. In Anaconda, she could pick up a second mule and buy more supplies.

"Ye got yer pistol?" Phil asked as she prepared to set out on her own. She nodded and raised her skirts to show where the gun was lashed to her boot. She then patted the rifle poking out of its scabbard on the saddle.

"Keep that pistol close and don't trust no one," he warned. "Ye got no friends once ye leave this place. And make sure ye always set up camp before dark—or if ye see a storm rollin' in. Git into a shelter and stay there. Storms in this country come fast and are unforgivin'. M' thinks they're devil made just to kill people. Don't start out again 'til the skies are clear. Ye got plenty of dried venison fer yerself and the dog and frozen bread dough strips to cook over the fire. The bread alone, with hot tea to keep ye warm, can sustain ye indefinitely. Just don't wear Willow down. She'll need rest if the drifts are deep. When ye camp at night, feed the critters good. There's dried grass and oats on the mule's back. And stay to the trail except when ye camp at night," he reminded her over and over. "When ye reach Missoula, head east."

It was a fast farewell. Molly was more than anxious to get moving. Phil wanted to ride with her but dared not. She was following her heart now and nothing would keep her from reaching Sam. He knew he would only get in the way after that.

"I've got a bad feelin' about this, Molly. I'm afraid I'll not see ye again." His face was dark with concern.

Molly cupped her friend's face in her warm hands, smiled sweetly, then tried to soothe his concerns.

"Phil, no matter what comes of this, ye know I've loved ye like a brother. Ye're one of the few men on earth that I trust. When I return in the spring, I'm gonna be wantin' to see what ye done with that saloon."

She flashed a bright smile then kissed him on the mouth. "I love ye, Phil O'Rourke, and I'm forever grateful to call ye m' friend." She hugged him tightly then climbed into the saddle and resumed her journey, this time alone.

The first couple of days proved to be slow but uneventful. The trail was full of drifts but had been breached by other riders so she was able to keep a steady pace. By late in the days, she was able to shuck the fur robe and ride just in her winter gear. Each evening she set up an off-trail camp where the animals could be tied without passers-by noticing them. Staying out of view was essential to her safety, Phil had warned her. Once the tent was up, she built a small fire, opened a can of beans and baked a few strips of bread for herself and Nicky. A dash of whiskey always warmed up the tea even more. Then, after banking the fire, she crawled into the tent, pulled the buffalo robe up over her and Nicky, and slept. The worry about Sam always invaded her dreams so she was up before dawn and on the move by sun-up.

The muleskinners had suggested she veer off the path to go west to Lolo Hot Springs. It was a major landmark where she could bathe in hot pools and rejuvenate her aching muscles. When she saw the sign, she decided it was too far off the main trail so kept right on going toward Missoula.

At St. Regis, a settlement of less than half-a-dozen shacks, there was a warm-water creek emitting clouds of steam into the air. A sign swinging in the breeze over one dilapidated shack bore the shack's name. Molly tied Willow and the mule to a hitching post then looked around. Attached to the hot pool building was a small saloon and supply store.

The interior of the saloon was dark but moist and smelled heavily of sulfur from the hot pools. A partition separated the bathing room from the saloon where half-a-dozen cowboys were drinking and gambling. A single, scantily-dressed fairy-belle sat perched on one elderly fellow's lap sipping a beer and thoughtfully stroking his beard and sparse white hair.

Molly ordered a whiskey, drank it down, then ordered another, aware that the room had grown silent when she entered and the men were staring at her.

"What's the matter, boys? Ye never seen a woman drink whiskey?" she asked without turning around. "I don't much like bein' stared at so why not git back to yer business?"

"Am I headed right to get to Missoula?" she asked the barkeep.

"You travelin' alone?" he asked.

"I am," she replied. "What's that got to do with anything?"

"It ain't smart for a woman to be riding alone in this here country," he replied.

"Ain't none of yer business whether I'm alone or not. I asked fer directions, not advice."

The bartender, a burly, half-bald fellow with a thick handlebar moustache, just shrugged then told her Missoula was more than three days travel if the weather cooperated.

"Who do I pay fer time in that hot pool?" she asked, dropping a gold coin onto the counter. "And kin I take the whiskey bottle with?"

He nodded then handed her the bottle.

"I kin scrub yer back fer ya," someone said from behind. She felt a man's arm encircle her waist and pull her back against him. He reeked of cigar smoke and too much beer.

"If ye want to see the sun set, ye best take yer hands off me," Molly warned, not even looking at him. Nicky pushed his way between them, growling a warning. The stranger ignored him.

"Lookee here, fellas, a feisty she-cat," he snorted.

Molly's elbow instinctively slammed backward into the startled man's midsection just as her foot stomped down on his instep. Her foot clipped his ankle, giving it a yank that dropped him hard onto the floor. She remained standing by gripping firmly onto the bar. As he hit the floor, Nicky leaped upon him, fangs bared. He sank his teeth into the man's thigh, fiercely shaking his head back and forth as he bit ever deeper.

Screams of pain filled the room as the man fumbled for his pistol. Before he could get it, Molly's booted foot was pressing down on his gun arm.

"Ye don't want to be shootin' m' dog," she advised him, shaking her finger in his face like he was a naughty boy. In her other hand was the pistol, already cocked and ready to fire. "I love m' dog and ain't nobody gonna hurt him—just like nobody ain't gonna touch me unless I say so."

She clicked her tongue, signaling for Nicky to release the man's leg. Whimpering in pain, the cowboy rolled onto his knees and crawled back to the table where his friends were snickering over his run in with a woman.

With her back to the bar, Molly waved her gun in the air for all to see. "Don't bother about us, boys. Just go on with yer fun," she smiled sweetly. She released the pistol's hammer then slid the gun back into her boot. "Now, what about that hot pool? Kin I use it or not?"

The barkeep told her it was open and he'd keep everybody out until she was done.

Suddenly, a man leaped up out of his chair.

"I know you!" he shouted. "Ye're that angel o' mercy from Murraysville. The one what saved all them sick folks from the pox."

He removed his hat and tipped his head respectfully. "Ye're the angel, ain't ya? I heard of ya."

"I ain't no angel," Molly replied.

"Yes ya are. Ye're Molly B'Damn."

Molly looked away but the cowboy kept grinning at his friends. "Don't none of ya be hassling this lady. Treat her respectful 'cuz she's a fine lady," he warned.

Molly slowly turned to look at the cowboy. She smiled sweetly then offered to buy him a drink. "I'm needin' exact directions to Anaconda. Kin ye give 'em t' me?"

"Better than that. I'll take ya part of the way," he offered.

After enjoying a leisurely bath in the hot pools, knowing full well the men were crowded around the knotholes watching, Molly dressed herself for the trail again. The bath had soothed her aching muscles so she was ready to ride.

The fellow offering to ride with her was named Ike Murphy. When she stepped out of the saloon, he helped her mount up then took the lead down the trail. As they rode, he told her how he had grown up in the area and knew a dozen shortcuts that would cut miles off the trip.

They took a well-used trail leading up through the timber, over the saddle, and down through a meadow where the snows weren't so deep. Herds of deer and elk bolted from the trees when they startled a small wolf pack off the ridge. Molly snapped her fingers to Nicky so he would jump into her lap where she could buckle him into the saddlebag before the wolves spotted him. Ike fired his rifle into the air to send the wolves dashing for cover.

Chapter 32

January 1884

26 January 1884

I don't know when this letter will get to you. Things have changed again and I am no longer in Murray. Please delay your trip until I write again.

Your daughter,
Maggie

BRIGHT SUNLIGHT REFLECTED OFF THE snow banks coaxing tiny rivulets of water to puddle up on the trail.

"This type of weather causes avalanches," Ike warned. "Things get mighty unstable when warm spells show up unexpectedly. Keep away from steep hillsides what's got lots of snow." He squinted at the high mountains looming ahead along the Great Divide. When they neared Missoula, he announced it was time for him to turn back.

"The Missus probably thinks a grizzly got me," he laughed. "The trail's plain from here." He pointed toward the landmark called Georgetown Lake fed by the waters of the Rock and Flint Rivers. By heading straight for the lake, she would reach her destination.

"Ike, ye're a kind man and I'm forever beholden to ye fer helping me." Molly reached into her saddlebag and withdrew a small, golden broach with a cultured pearl inset and held it out to him.

"No, no, miss, ain't no need for this. It's been an honor fer me to ride with ya." He pushed her hand away but Molly would have none of it. She slipped the broach into his coat pocket.

"Then give it to yer missus. Tell her an angel done give it to ye." Molly's smile was brilliant.

"I knew you was the angel," he smiled. "I hope we meet again."

"Even if we don't, ye'll always be considered m' friend. Thank ye, Ike Murphy!"

That night, Molly slept in a room in Missoula.

After bathing, Molly donned clean clothes then left the hotel to find food. A saloon offered fresh venison and cheap beer, both of which suited her just fine. After eating, she talked to locals about the best route to Anaconda, particularly Lost Creek where Sam's claim supposedly was located. Everyone she talked to agreed it was an easy ride, especially in mild weather, but Anaconda lay at the base of the Great Divide so if storm clouds blew in, she might want to make camp early or find a town to stay in.

The next morning she was back on the trail. She was still fifteen miles from town when darkness approached. Turning away from the trail, she scouted out a camping site beneath a large, well-protected rock overhang. It wasn't a heavily snow-covered hillside so she didn't worry about a snow slide.

Willow and the pack mule were tied a short distance uphill hidden behind pines in a thick stand of aspens. Clouds were rolling in suggesting a storm before morning so she wanted them as sheltered as possible. After feeding them, she gathered wood for the fire and pine boughs to sleep on. Once the tent was set up and securely tethered, she started a fire. Snow was heated over the fire for her tea and sausages and bread strips were cooked for herself and Nicky. The little dog was licking his chops in anticipation of his share.

By the time she banked the fire, the wind had died down but snow was falling lightly. Inside the tent, she and Nicky crawled beneath the fur blanket and were soon fast asleep.

The crack of a rifle startled Molly from her sleep. It wasn't yet dawn but Nicky was already awake and positioned at the door, a low, warning growl rumbling in his throat. Molly rose up on her elbows, straining to hear more but all she heard was Nicky. She lay back but felt uneasy. Something was wrong. She decided to pack up and head out earlier than planned.

It was still dark when she crawled out of the tent. More than a foot of snow had fallen during the night so she had to push the snow aside to get to the fire. The air was biting cold but there was no wind. Just as she reached for a stick with which to stir the embers, she heard men's voices, distant but distinct. She crawled back into the tent to find her pistol, all the while watching Nicky whose head was cocked to one side trying to sort out the sounds. Abruptly, he rose to his feet, hackles raised. The voices were closer.

"We can't get caught in here, Nicky," she whispered, raising the back of the tent high enough for her and Nicky to crawl under. She dragged out the fur cape and the buffalo blanket, wrapped them both around her, then reached back in for the rifle and ammo. Crawling slowly up the hill, they took refuge behind a large boulder not far from the horse and mule. Motioning for Nicky to be quiet, they waited.

The fire embers still had enough glow to cause shadows from the two fellows creeping toward her tent. One man was limping.

"It's the fellow ye bit," Molly whispered. "What they up to?"

A brand was snatched from the fire and whirled toward the tent where it lay for a minute before beginning to smolder. Suddenly the darkness was broken by flames consuming the tent.

"Come on out, tramp. Come meet the fellow yer worthless mutt bit into!" the cowboy yelled.

"Dutch, what ya doin' that for?" the other man whispered. "Ye're gonna trap 'em in there!"

"That's the idea," Dutch laughed, no longer trying to be stealthy. "Come on out, whore!"

The flames engulfed the tent, lighting up the darkness. The pine boughs crackled and sent sparks flying.

"Dutch, there ain't nobody in there," the second cowboy exclaimed. "Where'd they go?" He stood up and looked around.

"Damn, she heard us comin'. I told ya not to shoot at that darned wolf! Now she's got away," Dutch grumbled. "How we gonna find her?"

"She can't be far. There's no tracks I kin see."

Dutch picked up another firebrand and waved it in the air, trying to light things up so they could see where Molly might be hiding.

"Can't see her horses neither," he reasoned.

Molly and Nicky watched as the men stumbled around in the dark. The sun was beginning to rise above the hilltop.

"There's the horses!" Dutch yelled. "Shoot 'em. Then she'll be as good as dead. We'll leave her out here with no way to get help."

"I ain't wantin' to shoot no horses," his friend argued. "Let's just take 'em. We kin sell what's in the packs, and she kin stay here to freeze." He hadn't been too keen about killing Molly outright but he didn't seem to mind letting her freeze to death.

"Ain't nobody touchin m' mules," Molly called out, cocking the rifle and shooting into the snow bank scant inches from Dutch's feet.

Dutch yelped and stumbled backward looking for cover. The other man bolted uphill toward Willow and the mule so Molly fired again, the acrid smell of gun smoke scenting the air. A third shot hit the pine tree close to him. Stumbling to a stop, the man backed away just as Nicky broke free and sped down the hill, lunging at the intruder. His teeth sank into the man's coat sleeve just above the wrist.

"Git him off me," the man screamed.

Dutch ran toward them, hitting Nicky hard with the butt of his rifle. Nicky yelped in pain as he sailed through the air, landing in a drift of snow. As he lay whimpering, Dutch hobbled up to him, leveled his rifle at the dog just as Molly's bullet hit him in the shoulder. A second shot hit him in the chest, knocking him backward into the snow. He gasped for air.

"Git out of m' camp," she screamed. "If ye killed m' dog, ye're dead men."

She shot again, this time hitting the other cowboy's arm. He yelled then took off running back down the trail, blood dripping down his arm into the snow.

"Wait fer me," Dutch yelled. "I'm dyin' here. Help me!"

His friend struggled onto his horse then rode back to Dutch with the second horse in tow. He extended his good arm to help Dutch into the saddle then turned and galloped back down the trail.

"Ye better follow him, ye devil, 'cuz the next shot will be through yer heart, I swear. If ye come back here, I'll kill ya both," she yelled as Dutch spurred his horse to follow his friend.

Convinced they were gone, Molly hurriedly slid down the hillside to where Nicky lay whimpering.

"Ye put 'em on the run, Nicky. Serves 'm right. Wish I'd a killed 'em both."

Tenderly, she lifted Nicky into her arms and carried him close to the fire where she stoked the embers and melted snow to use for wiping the blood off his shoulder. She dosed him with laudanum from out of her pack then hurriedly went about breaking camp. By the time the drug took effect, he was cradled in her arms and they were headed into Anaconda. Nicky fell asleep in her arms.

Chapter 33

January 1884

IT TOOK ALL DAY TO reach Anaconda. Molly rode straight to the stable, ordered her animals to be well fed, then nestled Nicky down in a straw bed near Willow's feet. He was still sleeping soundly.

The streets of Anaconda were quiet so late in the day. A few buckboards rambled down Main Street past a couple cowboys who had just left a saloon. A mule team destined for Butte City stood in front of the mercantile store loading up for an early morning departure.

Molly desperately needed a drink. Her nerves were stretched and she was worried about Nicky. Besides, she was still seething with anger over being ambushed. After downing a few drinks, she went straight to a restaurant and ordered food before asking directions to Lost Creek.

The men who offered to help had been discussing the wonders of the Yellowstone region where hot pools were abundant and geysers of water routinely exploded from the earth into the skies above. Pools of mud, they insisted, bubbled up like cauldrons of hot melted chocolate alongside rivulets of cinnamon-brown water that reeked of sulfur.

"Bet there's gold there somewhere," one man said. "You can tell the water's full of minerals 'cuz the dirt's stained with such bright colors. Too bad it's such a danger to go there. I heard how a fellow tripped into one of them hot pools and got boiled alive!"

Another fellow, tall and blonde, stood at the bar listening. He didn't say much but his eyes suggested he knew more about Yellowstone than they did.

Molly was fascinated by what she heard. She remembered Sam talking about his father's journeys into the Yellowstone region. Annie said she had been there many times, too.

By the time she left the restaurant, Molly not only had directions to Lost Creek but knew about a cowboy camped there. When she asked why nobody had gone to help him, she was told the bushwackers were part of Plummer's vigilantes so nobody wanted to take them on.

Molly made a bed for herself in the straw next to Nicky. She planned to sleep a few hours then finish the journey to Sam's cabin.

In the morning, she bought a second mule then paid a young fellow to buy the extra supplies she needed. Within the hour, she was back on the trail, Nicky in her lap but now wide awake and hurting.

They rode south through an open valley leading back toward Bozeman then turned down a fork in the trail leading directly east toward the Great Continental Divide. There were dozens of veering trails worn by individuals headed in and out to mining claims in different canyons but she kept her sights on Lost Creek. Five cowboys rode past herding a small band of wild horses. Knowing the free-roaming animals often brought high prices in the sale ring, Molly watched with interest. One of the riders, a pock-faced redhead, tipped his hat to Molly then uttered a coarse comment regarding her good looks. His companions grinned luridly at her.

The trail forked where an artery of mountain water tumbled down the canyon. She knew she had reached Lost Creek. Molly nudged Willow into the ever-narrowing canyon, taking note of the many abandoned sluicing operations where waters had been diverted and hillsides washed away by channeled waters the miners used to extract gold by washing it out of the soil. Perhaps the gold had played out which was why so many sites were abandoned.

Phil's warning about claim jumpers was foremost in her thoughts so she was keenly aware of everything. By midday, she stopped to let the animals rest. The trail had grown much steeper.

Stretching her back and aching legs, Molly groaned at how stiff she felt. She gently laid Nicky onto a sun-warmed boulder then took pieces of jerky from the saddlebag for him to eat. He was so hungry he ate them almost faster than she could tear them off. She sat down beside him on the boulder, her eyes on the trail.

"You're either foolish or incredibly stupid to be up here all alone," a voice called down from up on the mountain Startled, Molly instinctively scrambled to get the pistol out of her boot. The rifle was still in the scabbard on Willow's saddle. Nicky lay still, his eyes alert. He didn't even growl as he looked up the hillside to where the voice originated.

"Put your toy gun down," the man laughed, now visible and slip-sliding down the shale, reaching for scrub brush to slow his descent. "I ain't gonna cause you no trouble."

Warily, Molly waited until she could see his face more clearly. He was the blonde fellow from the restaurant, dressed in worn buckskins. Up the hill, a large stallion stood near a dead tree.

"People don't usually call me stupid," she said quietly "And I don't appreciate being spied upon." Her fingers still gripped the pistol.

The man laughed as he gained solid footing and walked toward her.

"I been behind you long enough to know you're traveling alone. That ain't such a smart idea for a woman, especially in these parts. There's wolves waiting—and they ain't necessary the four-legged ones." He laughed as he walked over to Willow and patted her on the neck, taking note of Molly's rifle. "My stallion's been wantin' to come meet your filly ever since you rode past us a couple miles back. I'm surprised his snickerin' didn't give us away. Damn horse never can pass up a pretty lady."

Molly noticed Nicky was struggling to stand, favoring his injured shoulder but determined to introduce himself to the stranger.

"Nicky," Molly said, puzzled at her dog's behavior, "git over here." He ignored her, choosing instead to hobble up to the stranger, his tail wagging.

"Who are ye and what do ye want?" Molly asked, annoyed at herself for having been so easily blindsided.

"You can put the pistol back in yer boot. If I'd wanted to rob you I'd have done it an hour ago. I'm just curious, I guess, wondering what you're doin' out here all alone?" He walked up to Molly and stood there, his hat shoved back to reveal long, blonde curls and amazingly bright blue eyes.

Molly grinned. "Ye're Joe Maddison, ain't ye?".

"I am," he replied, a puzzled expression on his face. "Now, how did you know that? I ain't that popular around here."

Molly slid off the boulder, brushed past him, and went straight to the white blanket strapped on the mule's pack.

"How did you get that?" he demanded, stomping past her to untie the blanket and let it fall free.

"'Twas a gift, and if ye try to take it back, I'll shoot yer head off. Ye can't take back gifts."

He spun around to look at her.

"You're the angel," he exclaimed, a broad grin lighting up his face. "You saved my Annie and the girls?"

Before she could answer, he grabbed her in his arms and swung her around. Setting her back on her feet, he held her at arm's length and grinned. "I never expected to meet you in person but I'm honored. My life belongs to you. Now, tell me what you are doing here? Annie said you were living in Murray."

"I'm lookin' fer yer son," she explained. "He's in trouble somewhere up this creek. Claim jumpers been harassing him for weeks."

"Sam's here?" he exclaimed. "Where?"

"Don't know fer certain, just that he's on Lost Creek, so that's where I'm a-goin'. Nobody in Anaconda wanted to take on Plummer's vigilantes to help him so I came m'self."

"You're the one my son's in love with, aren't you? I should have known soon as I saw that shock of curls. You're all he talks about."

Molly presented him with one of her dazzling smiles. "I know a fair bit about ye, too, Snow Buffalo."

To her surprise, Joe threw back his head and laughed so hard his hat fell to the ground. "So Sam sent for his lady to save him. He and I need to do some serious talking."

"He doesn't know," Molly smiled, almost embarrassed. She could hardly imagine Sam ever calling for a woman's help.

"How long ago did you hear Sam was in trouble?"

"It's been over three weeks now," she replied.

"He could be dead. We'd best get moving. I was headed for the stinking waters of Yellowstone but if Sam's needing us, we gotta go."

Joe whistled for the stallion and watched as the horse whipped his head back and forth then headed straight down the slope to Joe. He was the biggest horse Molly had ever seen.

"I'm grateful fer the company. Been ridin' alone most of the way. A fellow rode with me from St. Regis to Missoula so that was good," she volunteered.

"St. Regis?" he asked, surprised. "You stopped at that hell hole and walked away unscathed? That's the devil's own lair. Not as bad as Lolo but nearly so. Is that a story I need to hear about sometime?"

"Perhaps, if the mood strikes fer me to tell ye."

Mountain shadows come early so by late afternoon, darkness was already approaching. Joe led the way up the trail with Molly close behind.

They came up a small cabin nestled against a stand of aspens. It was dark and appeared abandoned except for the pole corral holding Sam's pinto.

"This don't look good," Joe muttered. "Don't see any activity. Stay back while I ride closer."

He hadn't even reached the cabin when a rifle shot cracked the air. Joe let out a shout then swung out of the saddle, dropping to his knees as the stallion reared up, his hooves pawing the air.

Nicky broke away from Molly's arms, leaping to the ground to limp painfully up the hillside.

"Nicky, come back!" Molly whispered but the dog kept on, oblivious to his injuries. She slid out of the saddle and dashed behind the cabin.

"Get off my claim!" a voice yelled.

"Don't be killin' your Pa," Joe yelled back. It ain't nice to shoot me. Now get on down here."

"Dad? Is that you?" the man shouted.

"That's what I said, didn't I?"

Joe stood up, braced his hands on his hips and waited until Sam came scrambling off the hill. Before he got to the bottom, Nicky reached him.

"Nicky?" he exclaimed. "What you doing here?" He looked around and saw Willow standing with the pack animals. With a whoop and holler, he hit the clearing, running right past his father.

"Where is she?" he laughed. "Where's Molly? I know that's her horse!"

"Do I get a hello?" his father asked, pretending to be slighted.

"I'm glad to see you, old man," Sam grinned, slapping Joe on the back then looking around. "I've even resorted to praying help would come."

When Molly stepped out from behind the cabin, time stopped for the two of them.

"Molly," he whispered, dropping his rifle and running toward her. She leaped into his arms, laughing as he hugged her tight then kissed her long and hard.

"What are you doing here?" Sam asked moments later. "And how did you find my father?"

"We sorta found each other," Joe explained. "She was dead set on finding you and I just happened to run across her on the trail."

"I told you she was something special, didn't I, Pa?" Sam grinned, hugging Molly again.

The horses were set loose into the corral while the supplies were unloaded off the mules. Sam was thrilled to have fresh supplies since he hadn't eaten much in over a week. He had reached a point of extreme desperation. While the men attended to the animals, Molly set about cooking a meal of bacon and fried bread, bringing out a jar of fruit preserves to top it all off.

"When I got here," Sam explained, "I found an old miner dying of mountain fever. He left me this claim for helping him but said it hadn't been recorded yet. After he died, I did some panning but it didn't show much. Then I shot at a rabbit one morning and the bullet nicked a rock. I spotted a glimmer of gold winking out at me in the sunlight. Pulled out a nugget as big as my finger. I guess the moss and shrubs had kept it hidden. I staked the claim but didn't get to town to register it since snow was getting too deep. I decided to wait for the weather to break. Since the cabin needed fixing, I was pretty busy 'til some hombres rode up wanting my claim. When I said no, they got mad. I ran them off but they kept coming back, harassing me and stealing my belongings. They been pesterin' me for weeks."

"They got names?" Joe asked as he finished wiping gravy off his plate with a piece of fried bread. "Maybe I've heard of them."

"The leader's name is Clark Charlton. He's a big red-haired fellow with a loud mouth. Don't know the names of the others. They're just no-good followers of his, I think."

"Where are they now?" Joe asked.

"Haven't seen 'em in a week. Heard they went rounding up wild horses to sell for grub and whiskey. They'll be back, though. I can feel it." Sam rubbed his hands over his face. He hadn't slept in days and it showed.

"I was pretty much out of supplies when you two showed up. Don't think I could have stuck it out much longer."

"Well, they found the mustangs," she said, looking back over her shoulder. "I saw them riding into Anaconda."

"That means they'll be back," Sam groaned. "It's gonna be a long winter, I'm afraid."

"Tell you what," said Joe. "I'll ride into town tomorrow and file the claim for you. You can stay here and guard the place and get re-acquainted with Angel." He grinned.

"Molly's my name," she reminded him, "and I ain't no angel. Sam can attest to that, can't you?' She glanced back at him then wiped her hands on a strip of flour sack before drizzling bacon grease onto a piece of fried bread for Nicky who was curled up near the fire licking his sore shoulder.

"What?" she asked when she saw the men watching her. "I got flour on m' nose?"

Sam just winked at her. "What did I tell ya, Pa?" he beamed. "Ya ever met a woman like that?"

"Yeah," Joe answered. "And I married them both." Everyone burst out laughing.

Chapter 34

February 1884

14 February 1884

Dear Mum and Da,
The letter will be short and I don't know when I'll be able to post it but I want you to know I am well. I'm with Sam again and life is good. As soon as I can, I'll send for you.

Your daughter,
Maggie

JOE LEFT BEFORE DAYLIGHT. HE wanted to be in Anaconda when the clerk's office opened. He and Sam had agreed to file in both their names with Molly as third owner should anything happen to either of them. The claim would be called the Irish Angel. Joe also intended to file charges of claim jumping against the cowboys.

When Molly woke, she could hear Sam's soft breathing as he lay asleep on the floor near the fire. Wrapping herself in the fur cape, she stepped outside to enjoy the crisp Montana air. The sky was brilliant, clear, and cold. Nicky's cold nose bumped against her leg so she bent down and patted him affectionately. His shoulder was healing nicely. She was glad for that since he was no longer a young, frisky pup. Down at the corral she could see the horses huddled together, sharing their body heat.

How difficult would it be, she wondered, for bushwackers to get to the horses and mules? Across the creek she could see a granite hillside sparsely covered in small shrubs and cedars. Its boulders and crevices could easily hide a shooter. In the other directions a narrow trail hardly wider than a single horse led both ways past the cabin. It would be difficult for anyone to get past without being seen. Behind the building was a dense growth of aspens and timber that led up another hill, another place where a person could hide.

Sam startled her when he came up from behind. He slipped his arm around her as he nuzzled his nose into her soft curls.

"It's cold out here, Girl. Come back inside."

Molly smiled. It felt good to be near him.

"Soon as it warms up a bit more, I'll feed the animals and scout out more grass and willows for them. I need to chop through the ice, too, so they can get water," he promised.

After preparing a hearty breakfast of more bacon, fried bread, and peach preserves, she watched as Sam built up the fire then headed out to take care of the livestock. Molly fed Nicky then sat down by the fire to wait for Sam's return. She enjoyed listening to the fire crackling and the sound of Sam splitting firewood.

By the time he returned, she was already preparing cornbread and stew for dinner. Sliced apples were simmering in a pot over the fire.

"Um, that smells so good," Sam exclaimed, grabbing the coffee pot to fill his cup before peeking in at the bubbling stew. "Where did you learn to cook?"

"Mum taught me, remember? She's legendary as a cook," she smiled, wiping her hands on a cloth before sitting down beside him. Her expression turned serious. "When do you think Joe will be back?"

"It might be a few days, depending on the clerk's office. He took gold samples with to prove the claim. Why? You worried about him?"

"No, it's us I'm worried about." Around Sam, she spoke without her accent.

"If you're worried, maybe we ought to work out a plan. We should keep our rifles loaded and close at hand. Did you bring your pistol?"

Molly nodded, patting her boot where the gun was strapped.

"Good. I don't want those varmints thinking you're an easy mark if they do get to me," he confided.

Molly was taken aback by his words. She didn't want to even consider that Sam might get hurt. Back in Murray, there had always been rowdy skirmishes going on but they seldom resulted in outright killings. Then she remembered Julia. She had been killed while she slept.

"Here's how it will be," Sam continued. "If any of those hombres show up, I'll slip out the back window and find an advantage point on the hill where I can see everything. If you don't see me, don't be scared 'cuz I won't go far."

They talked about things for a while then turned their talk to other things. Dwelling on the idea of being shot was stressful.

Joe didn't return that day so Molly and Sam waited. Sam was aware that Molly's behavior was changing. She didn't say much but seemed more open to the idea that there might be a future for them together. He wondered what had happened to change her mind but all she told him about was the smallpox plague that came to Murray and the hundreds who died as a result. It had given her a different perspective on the sanctity of life.

The following morning, Sam decided to chink more of the cracks in the cabin and to pile in more firewood. Late winter storms were common and usually severe. Willow had taken to pawing at the fence poles as though she intended to make a grand getaway when no one was looking so Sam spent time making certain that didn't happen. Molly had trained her long ago to come at a whistle. Molly's pockets were always harboring treats for her, such as apple slices, so the training had been easy. Willow was always nosing into Molly's pockets looking for a treat.

"She's almost human," Sam decided, brushing the pony's silver mane out of her eyes. "I can't quite figure it out but you two seem to have a bond."

Molly agreed, rubbing behind Willow's ears and crooning softly as she slipped her another slice of apple.

Suddenly Willow raised her head and stopped chewing, her ears straight up and alert as she looked beyond Molly to the trail leading up toward the cabin. Nicky, too, was on alert, growling deep in his throat, the hair on his neck standing straight up.

"Somebody's coming!" Sam exclaimed. "Quick, get inside and remember what we talked about. And be careful!" He grabbed his rifle from inside the door then disappeared into the trees behind the cabin.

Ten minutes passed before a stranger rode up alone to the cabin. It was the red-head Sam had talked about. He sat on his horse awhile just looking around, making note of the curl of smoke floating up out of the chimney and the two horses and two mules now in the corral.

"Anybody home?" he called out.

Getting no answer, he slid out of the saddle and walked slowly up to the cabin door.

"Hey, anybody home?" he called out again. "Maddison, you in there?"

"Who wants to know?" Molly called back. She was positioned off to the side of the door but could see the man through the cracks.

"I'm needin' to talk," he replied. "Kin I come in fer a minute?"

"Who are you?" Molly asked.

"Clark Charlton. I'm a friend of Sam's."

She opened the door far enough for him to see the pistol in her hand aimed right at his chest.

"Sam ain't your friend. You're a bushwacker. What do you want?"

Nicky stood at her feet, snarling at the bearded stranger who stood a full head taller than Molly. He was thick chested, well built, and dressed in a fur hat and a fur-trimmed wool coat with a double scarf wrapped around his neck.

"Ya must be mistaken, Miss. Sam and me's partners. Kin ya spare me a cup of coffee? It's mighty cold out today." He stepped toward the door and was met by Nicky snarling like a wolf. Clark stopped in his tracks.

"Git off our property," Molly warned. "Ain't got enough fixings for m'self much less for every cowpoke who wanders by."

"Ya ain't very friendly, are ya? Last time I saw Sam, he didn't have no woman guarding his place. He hiding behind yer skirts, is he?" He tried looking around her, a lewd grin on his face.

"Git lost," Molly spat. "We got no use for claim jumpers—and I'm pretty sure ye're a claim jumper."

"Now that ain't nice," the man snapped back. "And what makes ya think I care what a woman says anyhow? You got no say in this. 'Course, if ya need a man's company 'til that half-breed gets back, just open up that door." Clark grinned then turned to spit tobacco juice into the snow.

"I ain't alone," Molly replied, stepping back inside. "Now move on."

"Ye're not very friendly," Clark repeated.

"I was born unfriendly, cowboy," Molly replied. She cocked the pistol then raised it toward his face. "When I say I don't want company, I mean it."

"Now don't be that way," he replied, bravely stepping forward, betting Nicky would back away, but he didn't. Instead, the dog bared his fangs and stepped toward Charlton.

"Great guns, there's no need to be so hostile." He backed away from the door then looked over at the corral. "Awful lot of livestock out there fer a woman who's alone."

"Who said I was alone?"

Just then a shot from up the hill pierced the snow bank near Clark's feet sending a shower of snow exploding onto his legs. Before he could react, a second shot hit the snow bank.

"Told you I'm not alone. Now git. Sam don't miss unless he wants to."

"This claims not legal," Clark shouted angrily. "Maddison, it ain't yers 'til it's legal and we know it ain't been recorded yet. Cut us a deal and we'll leave ya alone. Ya know I've got enough backup to take this claim today if I want to but I been nice about it up until now. I ain't gonna be nice much longer. We want part of the claim but we don't want to hurt you or yer lady friend to get it unless we have to."

"Get out my claim," Sam yelled from atop the granite cliff. "The claim got registered yesterday so you're too late."

"Ye're lying!" he yelled back.

"Go into town and see. I ain't lying."

As Molly stepped back, shading her eyes against the light, she dropped her guard and Clark lunged at her, pushing her inside the cabin while kicking Nicky out the door. The door slammed shut before Nicky could get back in so he clawed at the door, barking frantically.

"Now we'll see just how bad yer boyfriend wants to save ya," Clark snorted, shoving Molly across the room. She fell to the floor, dropping the pistol.

"You're asking for trouble," Molly snarled, brushing the hair from her eyes.

"I am trouble," Clark chortled as he picked up the pistol and slid it into his belt. He turned his back to her and peeked out the window to see if he could spot Sam. He was so intent on watching the hillside that he didn't see Molly crawl toward the window and hurl a piece of firewood through it. Nicky scrambled through in an instant as Clark spun around, grabbing Molly by the hair just as her fist plowed into his nose. He bellowed in pain just before her other fist caught him in the throat. Gasping for air, he stumbled backward. When he again lunged toward her, she had taken up a fighting stance, ready to fight like Nicholas had taught her. He grabbed for her as she feigned away, her knee connecting with his groin. He groaned and doubled over just as Nicky's fangs buried themselves in the collar of his coat.

Just then, Sam crashed through the door, his rifle leveled at Clark's chest.

"You wanted to talk to me?" Sam asked hoarsely, his booted foot knocking Clark to the floor where his foot pinned down the intruder's gun arm.

"Time fer talkin's over," Clark growled. "Yer a dead man."

"You don't look like you're in much of a position to make threats right now. It's too late anyhow, I told you that. But I don't take kindly to people messing with my lady."

Sam turned to Molly.

"Did he hurt you, Girl? If he did, I'm killing him right here and now. Any scoundrels that breaks into a man's home deserves to die, and the law will back me up." He motioned for Nicky to back off.

"Just hold on," the man moaned. "I'm goin'."

He reached for his gun but Sam kicked it away. Molly scrambled over to pull her pistol out of his belt.

"If ye want to shoot him, do it," Molly told Sam. "He's a snake. If you don't do it, I will. I hate snakes."

Clark scrambled on hands and knees out the door, pulled himself onto his horse then hightailed it down the hill.

Once things settled down, Sam broke out a bottle of whiskey and poured them each a drink. It was cause for celebration, he insisted, since the claim was probably now legal.

Joe returned that evening. After turning the stallion loose in the corral, he dumped feed onto the ground then hurried into the cabin. The wind was picking up and promised snow before the hour was up. He was stunned by what had happened while he was away but reassured them the claim was now legal.

The storm raged on, howling like a band of demons, for nearly a week. The snow depth rose to nearly five feet and kept both men busy digging paths to the horses. When the storm moved on, Joe began gathering his belongings. It was time for him to head on down to the Yellowstone area. He was hankering for time in one of the hot pools.

"Where you going after that?" Sam asked. "Even the Yellowstone ain't fit fer man nor beast in this type of weather."

"I got an offer to work for Kittie Wilkins down in the Owyhees. She's always needing cowboys. Her herd count is over three-thousand strong now. My hope is to take some of my pay out in palomino stock I can take back to our herds in Utah once I'm pardoned."

Sam was impressed. Palominos always brought top prices.

"Where's Annie and the girls?" Molly asked.

"They like wintering up in the Salmon River country where her people live. I'll collect them when I head back to the Coeur d'Alenes in the spring. I do hate being away from them. If you two go back to Murray, I'll stop by next summer and say hello. Unless you're hell-bent on being a prospector, Sam, you might want to sell this claim. You'll get top price if it's still got color."

Before leaving, Joe hugged Molly tightly.

"Seems us Maddison's are destined to be forever indebted to you, Angel. Annie's people believe if you save a life, that person's soul belongs to you always. Guess you own all our souls."

Joe kissed her cheek then reached for Sam's hand. He pulled his son into his arms, patting him on the back as he whispered into Sam's ear.

"Don't turn your back on those men, Son. They won't be after your gold anymore. They'll be wanting your hide to hang on their wall."

Chapter 35

March 1884

29 March 1884

Dearest Mum and Da,

    So much has happened. I am writing from a cabin in Montana Territory, waiting for spring to arrive. Sam is here with me. I don't know when this letter will be mailed but I want you to know I'm alive and well. We'll leave here when the thaw comes.

Your loving daughter,
Maggie.

THE BITTERNESS OF WINTER HUNG around for weeks before another warm spell set in. The snow kept Sam from panning but he did set up trap lines at the creek and around the beaver pond down the trail. Muskrats were easy to trap and it helped pass time taking off the pelts and treating them. With the help of Nicky's keen nose, fresh rabbits were sometimes caught to add to the stewing pot. The bones made good soup and chewing bones for Nicky. Mourn howls were often heard close by the cabin as wolves searched for food. Usually shots from Sam's gun sent them running. A hungry cougar circled the corral late one night until shots from Sam's rifle sent him running, too.

By lantern light, Molly and Sam spent hours comparing the Bible to the Book of Mormon he had left with her.

"What makes your beliefs so different?" she asked one night.

"First of all, I think it's the belief that anybody can gain forgiveness, and secondly, that families can be bound together throughout eternity. That's pretty important to me. Third, we believe in choices. Sometimes we don't make the right choices but we can repent and try to do better. It's an on-going process. What matters most to me right now is that you accept the fact that you aren't doomed to Hell."

"Do you truly believe that, Sam?"

"I do but every person has to come to that belief on their own. I can't make you believe. I can only tell you there's choices." He didn't know of any other way to explain it.

"Can I trust you never to betray me?"

"Trust is with you or it's not. There's no guarantees. It's just how you feel. If somebody betrays you, trust can be lost forever. The thing is, I'd never betray you on purpose."

"I'll never be a prostitute again either," Molly confided. "Do you believe me?"

"I do," Sam replied. "When you make a decision, you live by it, that much I know about you. That's the kind of woman you are. What matters to me is that you love me as much as I love you. Love is the only true reason for living. When we die, we can enjoy eternal life with our loved ones. What can be better than that?"

He turned to the fire, scraping away at the rabbit hide laying across his knees.

"You are a strange man, Sam Maddison. So is your father. You both act so tough but you're actually sensitive, honorable men. There aren't a lot of honorable men in the world that I know of." Molly was standing behind Sam trimming his long hair with a sharp knife.

Sam turned to face her. Her words had touched him deeply. "I never thought of myself that way. It means a lot to hear you say that."

"Does he know you love me?" she asked.

Sam laughed. "How could he not know? How could anyone not know? It must be stamped on my forehead in bright red letters."

"Does he know I'm a prostitute?" She crossed around to sit on Sam's lap, right on top of the hide he was scraping.

"Does that matter?" he asked, toying with her curls. He loved touching her hair.

"It matters. I'm tired of living that kind of life. I want to be young again, carefree and innocent. I want to forget the bad things and pretend I'm Maggie Hall again."

Sam smiled. How could Molly possibly know that she was, in truth, already reverting back to that spirited Irish girl she once had been. Since arriving at the cabin, he'd become aware of a happier side to her personality.

"Molly, what is it you want from life?" he asked. "Is it a new identity, a new place to live, a new type of life? Whatever you want, we'll go for it. We'll work it out together." He slid his fingers slowly down her cheek.

"Sam, why, in all the time I've known you have you not tried to bed me? You know I'd not turn you away. Instead, you beg me to marry you. Why is that?"

"I believe in the sanctity of marriage. When we marry, things will change, you can be sure of that." He smiled lopsidedly.

The following day dawned clear and warm with the distinct promise of an approaching spring.

"I'm going to run the trap lines," Sam announced. "Nicky wants to come, don't you, pooch? Maybe I can chop a hole in the ice at the beaver pond and snag a couple of fish for supper. When I get back, let's take a ride."

"I'll pack a lunch," Molly promised, excited at the idea of riding into Anaconda. She was anxious to post letters to her parents.

After setting aside some bread and cheese, she changed into a simple cotton dress then, with only a shawl draped over her shoulders, walked down to the corral. She led Willow back to the cabin and tossed the saddle onto her back, cinching it down tightly. Without securing Willow's reins to a post, she headed back to the corral for Sam's paint but before she got there, the crack of a rifle shot broke the morning calm, followed by another. Inside the cabin she saw both rifles still propped against the wall. A chill passed through her. If Sam hadn't taken his rifle, who was shooting?

Dashing outside, she called Sam's name even though she knew he was too far away to hear. She ran down the trail calling to him then saw Nicky running frantically toward her, barking loudly. Seeing her, he turned and ran back toward the pond.

"Sam, where are you?" Molly yelled. Then she saw a horse and rider galloping away down the trail.

Out in the pond a yawning hole in the ice was edged in blood, and Sam was in that hole, thrashing about wildly.

"Sam!" she screamed, watching as his fingers desperately clawed at the ice. The hatchet lay out of reach.

"He shot me, Molly," he cried.

"Hang on, Sam," she yelled. "I'm coming."

A shrill whistle brought Willow running. "Come on, pony, I need you," Molly declared out loud. When the horse came to her, she took the rope from the saddle, quickly wrapped one end around the saddle horn, then scurried to the water's edge with the other end.

"Hurry, Molly," he pleaded. He was growing weaker by the second, freezing in the bitter cold water.

Knowing her clothes would soak up too much water, she ripped her dress off, dropped it to the snow then, dressed only in woolen undergarments and boots, crawled across the ice with the rope looped around her waist. Sam grabbed for her, pulling her partway into the hole. He was desperate and gasping for air.

"Sam," she cried, "put your arms around my neck and hold on tight."

"Molly, honey," he whispered, "I can't. Just save yourself."

"Sam, don't you dare leave me here all alone. You help me do this, ya hear?" She slipped the rope off herself and slid it over his shoulders.

"Willow, home," she yelled. Nicky was barking frantically at the horse's feet.

The little mare was confused, prancing back and forth while resisting being pulled onto the ice. She kept backing away when Molly tugged on the rope so Molly pulled harder.

"Giddyup, Willow," Molly shouted, shivering uncontrollably.

With Herculean effort, the little mare backed away from the water then turned toward the cabin, straining until Sam suddenly popped out of the water. Molly grabbed his waist and held on as Willow pulled them to shore.

"Whoa, baby," she yelled to Willow.

Scrambling to her feet she ran for her dress then wrapped it around Sam. He was shivering violently, his face and hands blue. Checking that the rope was secure around his chest, she climbed into the saddle then let Willow drag him to the cabin. Once there, she slid out of the saddle and dashed to open the cabin's door, urging Willow inside with Sam still secured to the rope. Molly untied Sam then spanked Willow on the rump, sending her back outside.

"Hang on, Sam," Molly kept saying over and over. She was shivering violently but knew Sam was dying. Wrapping herself in the fur coat, she threw logs onto the fire then heated blankets on the stove to heap onto Sam's trembling body. Casting aside the sodden dress, she used a sharp knife to slice through his wet clothes before wrapping him in hot blankets. Then she covered him with the buffalo robe.

Once he was well covered, she replaced her own wet clothes with a heavy nightgown then crawled beneath the covers alongside him, praying out loud that he might live. When the blankets cooled, she climbed out from beneath the fur blanket and heated them again.

After a while, the intense shivering subsided a bit. That's when she assessed his wounds.

Sam had been shot once in the shoulder and once in the leg. The shoulder wound was dark and gaping, clotting blood all around where the bullet had existed. She could tell he had been shot from the back but it appeared no vital organs had been penetrated. For that, she breathed a sigh of relief. Plus, the icy water had mercifully slowed the bleeding.

Using whiskey as a disinfectant, she cleaned the shoulder wound then packed it with pieces torn from her petticoats. She covered his torso with more warm blankets before looking to the leg.

Just above the knee, a bullet had ripped into the bone, exploding it and all the muscle and tissue around it. It was a terrible wound weeping with dark, nearly-black clotted blood. The oozing meant the bullet was still in there, probably lodged in the bone. For the bleeding to stop, and to keep lead poisoning from setting in, it had to be removed.

"Oh," she gasped under her breath, "I don't know if I can do this."

Summoning up her deepest resolve, she hurriedly brought a pan full of boiling water to her side, along with a lantern, then sharpened the blade of the knife she had used to cut off his clothes. Grateful that Sam was still unconscious, she probed with the point of the knife until she felt the bullet. Sam cried out in pain as fresh blood gushed out, covering Molly's hands and clothes. She pressed hard to stop the bleeding then poured water onto the wound to cleanse it, her hands trembling. She tore off more strips of cloth, disinfected the knife, then said a prayer.

"Dear God, help me help Sam."

With a heavy sigh, she straddled Sam backward, pinning his arms with her body weight. She knew he would fight what she was about to do.

Pouring whiskey over the oozing wound, she began to work. When she touched the bullet again, Sam screamed, bucking to push her off his chest. She held him down as best she could until he grew calmer. Then, inching the knife point downward, she carefully hooked it beneath the bullet's edge then thrust upward, expelling it from the wound. Sam's cries were heart wrenching but Molly dared not listen. She had to fight his bucking and rolling while still pressing heavily on the wound. When he was calm, she poured whiskey into the wound, heated the knife over the lantern flame, then pressed the red hot blade onto his flesh to cauterize the profuse bleeding.

Sam screamed again, begging her to stop but Molly, with tears streaming down her face, knew she couldn't stop. She kept working until the bleeding slowed. When it kept oozing, she knew she would have to stitch the wound closed.

Frantically, Molly scoured the cabin looking for a needle and thread. Miners always kept such things on hand, she knew that. Cursing herself for not learning stitchery, she wondered out loud if she could bumble her way through this and somehow get it right. Then, as if in answer to her prayers, an empty coffee can revealed a coil of thread with a needle pushed through it.

With trembling hands, she threaded the needle, raised her eyes toward heaven, and whispered a prayer. "Dear Lord, if you're the kind of God Sam says you are, please, please guide my hands. Please, please help me," she wept.

Once more straddling Sam's chest and pinning his arms, she stitched the wound shut. It came so easily, she knew God was guiding her hands. A sense of peace settled over her shoulders. When she was through, the bleeding stopped, and through it all, Sam had slept.

"Sleep, my love," she crooned, stroking his face and hair. Exhausted, she curled up next to him beneath the warm blankets then called for Nicky.

"Watch over us, Nicky. I'm so tired." Nicky took his place at her feet.

Daylight was streaming in through the window when she awoke. Sam's eyes were open, and he was watching her.

"Molly," he whispered weakly, "what happened?"

"Somebody shot you, Sam. Your shoulder is hurt and so is your leg. I've bandaged you as best I can but you need a doctor."

"Always an angel," he smiled before slipping away into unconsciousness.

While he slept, Molly bathed herself in the cold waters of Lost Creek. It felt good to wash away the blood. She had been pleased to see Willow had stayed close by. After generously feeding the livestock and hauling in more wood for the fire, she turned her thoughts to getting Sam into Anaconda to a doctor. She remembered Sally Winnemucca telling her how to build a travois to drag behind a horse.

Molly decided to make one. She took the ax to the aspen cluster, cut limbs and branches large enough to hold Sam's weight then chopped down two lengthy trees to hold up the smaller limbs. She tied the branches with lengths of rope then propped the travois against the table to see how sturdy it was. Confident it would support him, she covered it with blankets and hides. The trip would be slow so she needed him to be comfortable as well as warm. The most difficult task would be securing the travois to Willow's saddle.

In and out of the house she trekked, measuring and cutting and estimating until she felt confident the travois might work.

It was nearly dark when she finished so she began gathering necessities to take with them into town. Gold, weapons, blankets. She didn't trust that the bushwackers were gone so she prepared for an ambush, too.

Just after daylight, she was up and ready to take Sam to Anaconda. As she hurried to leave, she heard a horse whinny in the distance. Nicky's hackles raised up as he growled then looked back at Molly. At the window, Molly saw Clark Charlton sneaking through the trees.

Molly grabbed the rifle, cocked it then reached for her pistol, making certain it was also cocked. When he crashed through the door, Molly was waiting. She shot him in the chest, first with the pistol, then, after he had fallen backward out of the cabin, she shot him with the rifle. He gasped for air, reaching out for her, but she kicked his hand away. A second man cleared the trees running for the cabin so she shot him, too. He fell lifeless to the ground.

"You should have left us be," she told Clark as his life ebbed away. Without remorse, she turned and walked away with a strange sense of satisfaction for having avenged Sam's shooting. If God sentenced her to Hell for doing so, then she would happily go to Hell. At least Sam would be safe.

With granite resolve coursing through her veins, she led Willow into the house, attached the crude little travois to her saddle, positioned it to where she could ease Sam onto it, then wrapped him in the buffalo robe. Then she lashed him onto the travois. The process took two hours.

With a final look around the cabin, she prepared to leave. The shelves were well stocked, Sam's gold had been hidden in a hole beneath the floor, the fire was banked, and her pack was loaded with clothing in case she stayed awhile in Anaconda. The animals were well fed as well. She closed the cabin door then began the long, slow journey down the mountain.

It was after dark when they arrived in Anaconda. The streets appeared deserted. At the livery stable, Molly yelled for the keeper to open up then paid a sleepy-eyed youth to feed and water the horse well but before he did that he was sent to fetch the doctor.

The boy sprinted away leaving Molly kneeling beside Sam.

"We made it," she whispered. "The doctor's coming. Just stay with me, fight to live 'cuz I need you, cowboy."

Molly spent the night in a chair at the doctor's office, trying to stay awake as he worked feverishly on Sam's leg. Long before he finished, she fell asleep, not even stirring when he covered her with a warm blanket and left the office. She slept until dawn.

Dr. Moellmer was a stocky fellow of medium height, with thick snow-white hair that matched his handlebar moustache. He was standing over Sam when she awoke, toying with a pocket watch. Deep concern was etched on his face.

"This man your husband?" he asked when he heard her stirring.

"No, just a friend," she replied, stretching her neck to remove the kinks from her muscles. "Claim jumpers bushwhacked him up on Lost Creek. His name's Sam Maddison."

"Who patched him up? You do that?"

"I did the best I could," Molly replied. "Didn't have much to work with."

"Well, you pretty much saved his life. If you hadn't got the bullet out, he'd have blood poisoning by now. The shoulder's going to heal just fine but the leg is bad. The bullet shattered the bone and destroyed the muscle and tissue. It's likely he'll lose the leg."

Molly gasped then broke down and cried.

"Miss, what's your name?" he asked.

"Molly," she whispered.

"Molly, I've booked passage for him on a train leaving for Ogden within the hour. There's a new doctor at a hospital there that's doing good things with injured limbs. If this fellow has any chance at all, it's with that doctor. If he leaves on this train, he'll be there by nightfall. I telegraphed them he's coming, if it's all right with you."

Molly dried her eyes. All she could think of was doing whatever was necessary for Sam.

"Do what you can to save his life. If the leg has to go, then take it. I have gold. I'll pay for everything."

She withdrew a pouch of gold from her coat and dropped it on the table.

"I'll call fer help to get him to the train. You better say your good-byes. Maybe he'll hear you," the doctor advised as he hurried to the door.

"Wait, doc, can I ask you to do something?"

He paused and waited while she asked him to accompany Sam to Ogden.

"If that's what you want, then that's what I'll do. How can I get hold of you when I get back?"

She explained she would be staying at Sam's cabin on Lost Creek until she got word back on how Sam was doing. After that, she would probably go to wherever he would be recuperating.

"Time's important, Miss. Is there anything else?" he asked impatiently.

"One more thing," she admitted. "There's two dead bush-wackers outside Sam's cabin. They came at me so I killed them both and left them lay. They're the ones who shot Sam. Will you tell the sheriff what I done?" Her eyes were pleading.

"I'll take care of it. Right now, we have to get this fellow to the train."

Before the men arrived to carry Sam away, Molly bent over the table where he lay and kissed him tenderly on the forehead. He looked as though he was sleeping.

"Sam," she whispered, "you're going to a hospital in Utah. I'll send word to your family so they know then I'll go back to the cabin to wait for you. Please come back for me," she begged.

Strong arms pushed her away then lifted Sam up to place him on a stretcher to carry him to the train. The buffalo robe fell to the floor, replaced by a wool blanket. When Molly lifted up the robe, it was caked with Sam's blood.

Running along behind, she watched as the doctor barked instructions on getting him onto the train. She pushed her way to Sam's side one more time.

"I'll marry you, Sam Maddison. I love you," she cried out, her hands desperately clinging to his. "Do you hear me? You promised me a grand saloon and I'm holding you to that promise. You come back to me!" she shouted as they finished loading him onto the train.

The train whistle blew, announcing its departure.

"Ms. Molly," the doctor called down to her, "this may not work out the way you want but we'll try our best."

"Just don't let him die, Doc," she begged as the train pulled away.

Chapter 36

May 1884

16 May 1884

Dearest Mum and Da.
My heart is broken. Sam was badly injured
so is not with me anymore. Once again, my plans
are in disarray. I'm confused and unsettled. What
should I do? If only you were here.

Your daughter,
Maggie

W INTER MELTED SLOWLY AWAY LEAVING the land awakening
with spring's rebirth. Then spring gave way to summer. Molly waited
faithfully at the cabin, leaving only to buy supplies and to check
with the doctor for messages from Sam, but no messages came. Dr.
Moellmer had ridden to the cabin after his return from Ogden and
assured her Sam arrived there safely but, despite desperate measurers,
the leg was amputated above the knee. Sam would recover but he
had fallen into deep despair at the knowledge he would be a cripple
for the rest of his life. The doctor kept in contact with the hospital,
asking them to give Sam reassurances that Molly was waiting for him
but he was told Sam had no messages for Molly. The doctor even
made a humanitarian trip to the hospital to personally check on Sam
but the news he brought back was disappointing.

"I gave him your messages, Ms. Molly, but he's so distraught over losing the leg that he can't bear to face you. We tried to reason with him but he's inconsolable. Some fellas are like that when their masculinity is compromised. I don't think he'll be coming back."

"He promised," she argued. "Did you tell him I don't care about the leg?"

"I did but it made no difference. He feels like half a man, a cripple that could never be strong enough for you. He may come around but I'm doubtful."

Sadly, Molly kept up her vigil at Lost Creek. She did a lot of soul searching, too. No one in Murray knew of the events that had taken place since she left so they probably were forgetting all about her.

A headline in the Anaconda newspaper told her why no one was worrying about her. It seems a destitute miner named Noah Kellogg had ridden into Eagle City one day, completely broke and down on his luck. He borrowed a feisty little burro from an acquaintance in town then set out for the hills. The burro promptly ran away. When Noah finally caught up to it, it was standing astraddle the richest silver vein ever discovered in North America. It was more than nine feet wide and was located just off the South Fork of the Coeur d'Alene River.

People named the mountain Jackass Peak and within weeks a town had sprung up nearby known as Kellogg's Town. A new ore rush was on and people were abandoning Murray like rats off a sinking ship. Now they were headed for Kellogg's Town.

For a brief moment, Molly considered returning to Murray but changed her mind. Her life there was over and she had no intention of going back.

After waiting a while longer, she came to admit Sam would not be coming back for her. Like those before him, he was letting her down. It seemed to be her lot in life, being betrayed by men. It didn't make her angry, just disappointed.

"Madame Pleasant called it right," she told Nicky. "We've reached a turning point."

The sheriff had long ago declared the shootings of Clark Charlton and his partner as justifiable so she was cleared of prosecution. The mining claim had not been played out so she put it up for sale and received a substantial settlement since her name was on the claim. The money from the sale was put into an account bearing Sam's name.

Molly sold off the mule and horses, all except Willow, then sold the mining equipment. She kept ownership of the cabin, however, in case Sam did return, but stipulated to the bank that after five years, the cabin would be deeded to Dr. Moellmer.

With iron purpose, she made plans to leave Anaconda. All she left at the cabin was the Book of Mormon Sam had given her. Perhaps someone else would find inspiration with it. It had succeeded in giving her a new sense of believing but her disappointment with Sam gave her pause to question other things he had said to her. She accepted the idea of a loving God and a caring Savior rather than a cruel Deity waiting only to condemn people to hell, and she knew her prayers had been answered during the ordeal with Sam's wounds, but in her heart and mind Sam had let her down.

Dr. Moellmer was pleased to see Molly when she rode into town that last time. They had developed a deep friendship with one another.

"Where will you go?" he asked when she told him she was leaving Montana.

"I'll travel south into the Salmon River country, then on to Fort Hall in case Annie Blue is at either place. I need to leave word fer Sam's father as to what happened. After that, I'll go on to Ogden to see if Sam is there. He owes me a face-to-face meeting, don't you think? If he's not there, I don't know where I'll go. Perhaps to Salt Lake City. I've got enough gold saved up to start myself a business."

"I'll miss you, Ms. Molly," the old man said, giving her a father-like hug. "Is there anything I can do for you?" He pulled out a chair for Molly then one for himself.

"Yes, you can help me in a conspiracy," she laughed. "I want to be reborn as someone else." Her grin was infectious. "Will you help me?"

"Of course I'll help," he smiled. "Just tell me what you want me to do."

"Did you ever hear of a prostitute named Molly B'Damn," she asked.

"Everybody's heard of you," he laughed. "You're a living legend, and since I've come to know you, I suspect all the stories I've heard are true."

"Ah, so you do know," she grinned, touching his arm. "Well, since you know who I am, does it surprise you that I was a very high-priced whore?"

"I know you too well, Molly. Whatever you were or what you did changes nothing. I know the real Molly. Is that the past you're leaving behind?"

"It is, but I have to do it by dying."

The doctor's eyebrows raised up in surprise.

"Not really, of course, but in the eyes of the world." She brushed a curl from her face.

"You want to fake your death?"

"I do. If I'm the legend you say I am, then it needs put to rest. I've worked out the details."

When she left the doctor's office, plans were in place and everything was outlined. Dr. Moellmer held power-of-attorney authorizing him to work in her behalf in all matters, including banking transactions and making funeral arrangements. He agreed to falsify her death certificate and purchase an empty coffin to be weighted down, sealed, and sent to Murray for burial in the pine-covered Pioneer Cemetery just outside the city limits. A local craftsman would be hired to build a wooden headstone marking Molly's final resting place with the following words carved so deeply into the wood that they would withstand all the ravishes of time and elements:

Sacred to the memory of Maggie Hall (Molly B'Damn)
who died January 17, 1884 at age of 30 years

An obituary was prepared for Adam Auhlbach to run in the Coeur d'Alene Sun but he was invited as editor to embellish it as he saw fit. Dr. Moellmer requested a copy of the obituary be wired back to him once the burial was accomplished.

The obituary was written as follows:

> Maggie Hall (Molly Burdan), for that was her maiden name, died at 6:00 yesterday morning (January 16, 1884) in Anaconda, Montana. The deceased came to be known as Molly Burdan and as such was she known from the frozen north to the sunny south. She was born in Kingstown County, Dublin, Ireland on December 26, 1853. She came to Boston, migrated west, lived in San Francisco, Portland, Virginia City, and other places. She came as a pioneer to Murray over the frozen drifts of snow to the Coeur d'Alenes. She has been a conspicuous figure in Murray and, for good and evil, has drawn more public attention than any other woman of her class. In the early days when exposure laid many men low, she was a ministering angel to the sick and suffering. Neither wind nor weather kept her from an unfortunate's bedside. These kind acts made her a sparkling diamond of the west. She was once mistress to a millionaire but drifted with the tide of events as such women often do until she finally found herself in a mining town in the Coeur d'Alenes. She sustained a lingering illness during the winter and her final days were spent in isolation and loneliness. Her final resting place is in the Pioneer Cemetery outside of Murray. A city-wide wake shall be held at her request to celebrate her life.

Molly transferred her personal funds to a bank in Salt Lake City but left Sam's gold in a trust at the bank in Anaconda along with a private letter telling of Molly's death and subsequent burial in Murray.

A letter was drafted to the bank in Murray instructing them to distribute funds from her accounts in the following manner:

Phil O'Rourke would inherit enough gold to buy the White Elephant saloon for himself;

The House of Pink would be kept as an entertainment hall owned jointly by the madams of Murray;

Funds would be given to Adam Auhlbach to put together a three-day wake celebrating Molly's life;

Lightning would be given free access to any of the ladies' cabins and credit for whiskey for up to five years, all paid for from her bank account;

Ten thousand dollars in gold would be put in a trust to be allocated to Captain Tonks at the rate of five-hundred dollars a year so as to keep him from spending it all at once on whiskey;

Her gowns and stylish hats were to be sold and the money split equally by all the churches in Murray, excluding the Catholic Church;

Her jewels were to be shipped to Charlie McTavish in Boston with a request they be kept for Becca when she reached maturity;

The remaining funds were to be sent to her parents in Dublin without explanation.

The only things she kept for herself were a few dresses and a single hat covered in purple feathers.

Molly purchased a one-way ticket for herself and Willow to Ogden. Nicky would ride on her lap. In the hem of her dress were sewn enough coins to get her to any destination. After that, she would access her banked funds.

On her last night in Anaconda, she indulged herself in a luxurious room in a hotel, complete with a long, soothing bubble bath. Later, dressed in a modest gown, with many of her golden curls clipped off, she met Dr. Moellmer for dinner. While they ate, she overheard talk that Clark Charlton's other partners had made the mistake of trying to jump Wyatt Earp's claims in Eagle. The Earp brothers had killed all three of them.

"How unfortunate," Molly smiled. "I'd have liked to have been part of that." Her grin was wicked. "Trust Wyatt to tie up my loose ends. Someday I must thank him in person, or maybe not since tomorrow I'll be dead." Her eyes were twinkling.

"If he passes this way, I'll thank him for you," the doctor volunteered, pleased to see how happy Molly was. She certainly was anxious to start her new life.

In the morning, accompanied only by Dr. Moellmer, Molly waited anxiously for the train. She was composed but anxious to move on. Once she set foot on the train, she would be leaving so much behind. Her name, her legend, her friends, and her troubled past. She was starting anew, with no regrets.

"You're a remarkable lady," the doctor told her, his arm around her shoulder as she peered down the tracks, fidgeting nervously. "It's been an honor to know you." His eyes misted over but he coughed a couple times to regain composure.

Puzzled, Molly looked at him then smiled brightly before kissing him sweetly on the cheek.

"You I shall miss," she promised. "Think of me sometime, will you?"

He nodded then hugged her tight.

"I wish you well, Molly B'Damn," he croaked, his voice breaking.

"Molly B'Damn is dead, don't you remember?" she grinned, her brilliant smile lighting up his world. "Before you stands Maggie Hall!" she exclaimed, spreading out her arms and spinning around. "Do you hear that world?" she shouted. "Maggie Hall is back!"

About the Author

A. JAYDEE IS THE PEN name of Jean Davidson, a long-time resident of Pocatello, Idaho. She was born and raised in Rupert, Idaho; attended Stevens Henager College in Salt Lake City; studied commercial art through Art Instructions schools; and attended Idaho State University, majoring in History and Women's Studies. Her work history is unique and varied, including working as a realtor, a home decorator, a commercial artist, manager of several different retail stores, a historian, and an upper-level university administrator before becoming a published author. Jean has published short stories in the *Rocking Chair Reader* and *Chocolate Soup* series as well as for the *Deseret News*. Her late husband Bill Davidson was her life's companion for over fifty years. She is a mother to three grown children, Marjanna (Barry) Hulet, Darryl (Adrien) Davidson, and Darryn Davidson. Jean is also a grandmother to six kids, Cedar, Colter, and Kestrel Hulet; Ella and Maria Davidson; and newcomer Joseph Davidson. Her passions are family, home remodeling, genealogy, and writing interesting and nostalgic stories of the past.

CPSIA information can be obtained
at www.ICGtesting.com
Printed in the USA
BVHW071652100621
609270BV00002B/131